ENGLISH COMPOSITION PROGRAM

TEACHING ESL COMPOSITION:
PRINCIPLES AND TECHNIQUES

Jane B. Hughey

Deanna R. Wormuth

V. Faye Hartfiel

Holly L. Jacobs

Newbury House Publishers, Inc.
Rowley, Massachusetts 01969
ROWLEY • LONDON • TOKYO
1 9 8 3

Library of Congress Cataloging in Publication Data
Main entry under title:

Teaching ESL composition.

  (English composition program)
  Bibliography: p.
  1. English language--Study and teaching--
Foreign students.   2. English language--Rhetoric.
I. Hughey, Jane B., 1935-   II. Title:
Teaching E. S. L. composition.   III. Series.
PE1128.A2T4426   1983   808'.042'07   82-8255
ISBN 0-88377-256-6

Cover and interior book design by Kenneth Wilson

NEWBURY HOUSE PUBLISHERS, INC.

Language Science
Language Teaching
Language Learning

ROWLEY, MASSACHUSETTS 01969
ROWLEY • LONDON • TOKYO

Printed in the U.S.A.

First printing: October 1983
5   4   3   2   1

Foreword
by John W. Oller, Jr.

What began as a program for *testing* writing skills in users of English as a second language inevitably grew into a much larger project. Over the years the project came to deal with English composition from three different but interrelated viewpoints: *testing, teaching*, and *acquisition*. Thus, the present book, which is concerned with principles and techniques of teaching English writing skills, is the second installment in a series of three volumes. The first, which dealt with testing, has already appeared, and the third, which will address the acquirer's perspective, is now in progress.

The whole series, and especially this volume, affords just the sort of guidance in the teaching of composition skills that I believe second and foreign language teachers have been seeking for many years.

The present volume has passed through many drafts and, because of a genuine spirit of teamwork, through a major shift in the roles of contributing authors. Nevertheless, it is to be expected that the theory and practical techniques suggested here will continue to be adapted and refined as they find expression in the classrooms of many different language teachers in diverse contexts. With respect to the need for constant revision and updating, perhaps the teaching of writing skills is analogous to the process of writing itself. Aren't both of them a good deal more like cutting a path through a jungle than like breezing along on a superhighway? Part of the problem is that battles fought and seemingly won often have to be fought again. Errors that were diligently expunged reappear and have to be chopped away again and again.

The authors of this book, it seems to me, have understood this dynamic and challenging aspect of the teaching of writing. They view writing as a temporally progressive means for the discovery, actualization, and sharing of experience itself. Although they appreciate the fact that writing skills are integrated with reading, speaking, and listening, they also realize that writing has its unique aspects that are not common to other skills.

Perhaps the best recommendation for the ideas contained in this book is that they are the result of years of thoughtful development spawned and nourished by firsthand classroom experience. Is there any other kind of experimentation that teachers can confidently rely on as a basis for developing their own classroom theory and practice?

Therefore, it is an honor for me to be able to endorse this second volume along with the first. It is a pleasure to be able to join with the authors and with Newbury House Publishers in recommending it to the many dedicated teachers of our profession who will, I am confident, forge it into a significant part of the theory and practice for the teaching of writing in the coming years.

PREFACE

The English Composition Program (ECP) series has been written in answer to the need for an improved teaching, learning, and testing program in writing English as a second language. Nowadays, in most secondary schools, in universities, and in the world outside the classroom, there is a need—even a demand—for ESL students to write clearly, concisely, and creatively. As a result, we offer in this text a number of ideas which have worked for us and which we hope will help you in your teaching endeavors, convince you that writing can be taught, and stimulate you in teaching your students to meet the goals of good writing.

Teaching ESL Composition: Principles and Techniques serves two purposes:

Part I sets forth a philosophy of writing as a creative process.

Part II presents practical methods which can be used throughout this creative process to develop an understanding of the principles of writing. The methods focus attention on strengthening a writer's awareness of invention, purpose, audience, shaping, and evaluation in writing.

Part I approaches writing as a creative, ongoing, cyclical process through which beginning as well as experienced writers can and do find meaningful things to say and effective ways to say them. This philosophy, based on our own experience and the research of others, reflects a view of writing which addresses the idea that writing—

1. Remains a lifetime skill
2. Is a creative process of discovering, generating, and shaping propositions

3. Involves a system of analysis, feedback, and revision
4. Uses processes different from those of spoken discourse
5. Requires, for ESL learners, mastery of specific language skills

Further, our philosophy suggests the traits which aid teachers and learners to work successfully and cooperatively through the writing process.

Part II offers practical methods and exercises which reflect the principles of writing as set forth in the philosophy. Many of these methods and exercises revolve around heuristics for discovering subject, purpose, and audience. Methods and exercises for shaping writing are rooted in the ESL PROFILE, an objective, holistic, analytical means of teaching writing principles. It is also an instrument for providing feedback, evaluation, and revision for student writing efforts.

While *Teaching ESL Composition: Principles and Techniques* is designed primarily for university students working at intermediate to advanced ESL levels, it can easily be adapted to meet the needs of students in secondary programs as well.

Our ultimate goal in designing this program is to encourage students to write independently, confident that they will be able to use their English language skills effectively. It is our hope that the information contained in the text will encourage all teachers and student-writers to believe (1) that writing can be taught, (2) that students do have something to say and can learn to communicate their thoughts successfully, and (3) that writing is an exciting, rewarding, and worthwhile endeavor.

ACKNOWLEDGMENTS

Teaching ESL Composition, like the writing process itself, is the result of input from many different sources. It is with this input from friends, colleagues, and mentors that the ideas here have blossomed and grown. All have played an important part in the development of this writing project: some in the discovery, some in the generation, and others in the shaping of this book. First among those, we are especially grateful to Rupert Ingram for his confidence in our project from its inception. He has steadfastly encouraged us to further discover, expand, and develop this series and to strive for excellence. Our editor, Mark Lowe, deserves our thanks for persisting in his demands that the series present a complete view of the writing process. He showed us that what we thought was a finished product was really only the beginning. His patience and attention to detail helped us generate a comprehensive final text. Many others on the Newbury House staff have also assisted us in shaping the final text.

We further acknowledge the vast contributions of our professional colleagues. To John W. Oller, Jr., at the University of New Mexico, goes our special appreciation for opening our eyes to new possibilities, for inspiration, for patient consultation, and for constructive criticism. Our sincere thanks to the faculty of the English Language Institute at Texas A&M University who offered consistent support and valuable suggestions. Among these, we especially thank James Denney and Betty Youngkin for their contributions of classroom assignments, Katherine Wood for her artwork, and Amy Mann for her patience and feedback. Further, we thank Kathryn Smith, Past President of the Oklahoma Reading Association, for her contributions and encouragement.

Most important is our debt to the students, from all parts of the world, who contributed their writing samples, their support, and their enthusiasm to this project. We have truly learned together in this endeavor. We are grateful for special contributions from Mohammed Chihati, Federico Drews, Madelaine Fischer, Nishura Fumitaka, Sheng-Chen Ho, Hann-Jin Huang, Maria Silveira de Jasa, Henry Kuok, Julio Luna, Andrew Mao, Nilüfer Nasif, Sami Shaker, Milton Somarriba, Kuo-Yen Tung, and Palitha Wickramasinghe.

We owe a great debt to Betty Brumbaugh, Sandra Berdar, and Debbie Teguns for tirelessly typing and retyping the manuscript. Indeed, they were creative shapers.

Finally, we express our deep appreciation to our families, particularly John R., Travis, Jay and Melissa; John H., Christine and Jennifer, for their continued patience, understanding, and encouragement over the years this manuscript has been in progress.

Jane B. Hughey
Deanna R. Wormuth
College Station   V. Faye Hartfiel
1982   Holly L. Jacobs

CONTENTS

PART I

TOWARD A
PHILOSOPHY OF WRITING

CHAPTER ONE

WRITING IS A COMPLEX PROCESS

---

*Writing is far more than a way of recording language
by means of visible marks.*

E. D. Hirsch

Speech and writing are similar in many respects. Both spoken and written discourse are "man's use of language symbols to express feelings and needs."[1] Both depend on thought for something to say. Rules of semantics and syntax govern the processing of spoken and written discourse.[2] For a speaker or writer to achieve a communicative purpose, a degree of understanding, common knowledge, and shared expectations must exist between speaker and listener, between writer and reader.

Speaking and writing are communicative acts which depend upon an awareness of social relationships and social expectations. From these understandings, the speaker or writer then proceeds to select ways of speaking or writing which are appropriate and specific to particular situations. In speech we monitor what we say by listening to our statements in order to revise, correct, or backtrack as we are speaking. In writing, this same monitoring occurs as we read and reread what we are writing. The speaker or writer needs to determine how simple or complex, formal or informal statements should be. Further, the attitudes, feelings, and knowledge of the audience about a subject must be considered as statements are developed. Accomplishing these tasks is frequently very difficult for the English as a second language (ESL) student who does not possess a clear sense of the cultural and rhetorical expectations of English. What is appropriate, even expected, in one cultural setting may not be so in another. Unawareness of these cultural expectations and perceptions may cause a listener or reader to misunderstand the speaker or writer's intent, resulting in a miscommunication of the intended message.

Despite these similarities between speaking and writing, writing differs from speech in several important ways. According to Vygotsky, composing written discourse is a "separate linguistic function, differing from oral speech in both structure and mode of functioning. Even its minimal development requires a high level of abstraction."[3]

1.1 Writing differs significantly from speech

Certain psychological, linguistic, and cognitive factors make writing a more complex and difficult discourse medium for most people, in both native and second language.

Psychological factors Speaking, the first manifestation of language we master, as well as the most frequently occurring medium of discourse, is a social act. Because an audience or respondent is present, it elicits some form of action, interaction, or reaction between individuals. Thus speech has a "situational context."[4] A speaker can see the audience and receives immediate feedback in the form of verbal and nonverbal cues. Likewise, the listener or audience usually has the speaker in view and can respond to the speaker's verbal and nonverbal cues.

As a result, both the speaker and the audience have some immediate control over the direction the communication takes, and the two-way bond created provides a means for response from the audience. The speaker's mode of dress, physical demeanor, and use of hand gestures are all nonverbal signals to the audience. Tone, speed, inflection, and loudness, that is, the manner of speaking, serve as verbal signals for the audience. Therefore, before a speaker has finished making the first point, some degree of rapport has been established with the audience.

Furthermore, the audience acts as a teacher for the speaker. The speaker learns quickly from the immediate feedback of the audience by means of its verbal and nonverbal cues. Restless body movements, nodding heads, and angry expressions alert speakers that it is time to alter a sentence, delete a phrase, or completely change the direction of their remarks. Because speech is linear in form, it cannot be retracted, but it *can* be amended. Therefore, speaking can be improvisational, and the whole body speaks.[5]

On the other hand, writing is largely a solitary act. It is communication formed in isolation. The audience is rarely if ever present. Without audience feedback to assist in shaping the discourse and giving it meaning, the written work "must normally secure its meaning in some future time."[6] Writing therefore lacks the clear situational context usually present in oral discourse, and to compensate, the writer has to create an audience in the mind's eye and attempt to predict its responses. Writing requires a sustained act of imagination; the writer needs to "fictionalize" an audience. Writers may cast their readers into roles in which the *readers* must adjust because writers lack the immediate feedback provided by the audience which usually subtly or not so subtly pressures speakers to adjust their statements.

Writers' tasks are further complicated by the fact that as they write they also assume the roles of readers. As readers, they bring their own perceptions and views to the reading task, and assume, therefore, that intended readers will possess those same perceptions, views, and expectations. However, those shared assumptions may only be in the minds of writers' "fictionalized" audiences, not in the minds of their real audiences. Witness the numerous situations throughout history in which a writer's audience did not respond as intended: The heroic but futile charge of the Light Brigade at Balaklavia in the Crimean War is an example of the disasters which can occur when perceptions of reader and writer are not the same. The man giving the order to "charge the guns" was on a hilltop when he gave the order to "charge." He saw a small battery of soldiers not visible to the soldiers in the valley. The soldiers in the valley, to whom the order was given, saw *only* the guns of the main Russian battery at the far end of the valley. They assumed the "guns" meant the main battery that they saw. Hence, they marched into a suicidal situation as the result of a perceptual miscommunication.

Though writers can employ such nonverbal cues as tables, diagrams, charts, graphs, paragraphs, punctuation, and capital letters, writing depends primarily on the words writers choose and the form they give to their ideas. Rapport with readers is established in a far more subtle, complex way than through dress, body movement, or tone of voice. Each idea, word, structure—indeed each mark on the page—must be chosen carefully. Once the writing is in the reader's hand, the writer usually has neither the luxury of immediate feedback nor the opportunity to rephrase, start over, back up, or clarify statements. What is on the page must stand on its own.

Linguistic factors Speech allows use of informal and abbreviated forms and constructions which are uttered almost spontaneously, often tumbling out without careful editing or forethought. In speaking, we are not always concerned with precision in expression. We can make a statement, repeat it, expand it, and refine it according to the reactions and interjections of our listeners. Speech can also be telegraphic, with one word signaling an entire chain of impressions, or we can string numerous sentences or complex phrases together nonstop to clarify or obstruct meaning—whichever is to our advantage.

Furthermore, speech has a higher tolerance for repetition of a phrase or sentence than writing. We can repeat ourselves more frequently to emphasize our point when we speak because the word is ephemeral—we hear it and it is gone.

However, how we develop our sentences and the ways we organize them to carry the reader from one idea to another are our primary means to convey our intended message. Without immediate audience feedback, we do not usually refine or elaborate our statements as we go. As a result, written statements must be constructed more carefully, concisely, and coherently to ensure that our meaning is clear. Writers must be certain that statements are cohesive; they cannot repeat points for emphasis indefinitely without being redundant, thereby losing their audience. Writing employs longer structures which serve to elaborate meaning more fully because meaning can be lost if abbreviated structures are written without careful thought. The word "water" written in isolation on a page conjures up many

4

meanings: "to drink?" "an ocean?" On the other hand, when a child walks into the kitchen with a cup in hand and says "water," the mother responds by filling the cup. The meaning is clear. Writing, then, takes on a much more channeled and controlled direction than does speaking.[7]

Cognitive factors Speech develops naturally and early in our first language. We acquire oral skills seemingly without effort. Two-year-olds communicate their needs quite clearly. We understand completely when, at dinner, they point to their ice cream dishes and shout, "More!"

Speech is acquired rapidly and is also produced rapidly. Words tumble forth at high rates of speed as speakers become more proficient. Furthermore, acquisition of speech is an "ego-building" activity. In first language acquisition, positive reinforcement is given in the form of smiles, hugs, repetition of the child's words, and exclamations of delight. As a result, children continue to try to speak and rapidly develop and expand their repertoire of words and phrases. Once they acquire vocabularies suitable to meet their speaking needs and to create mental pictures which enable them to think symbolically, the act of translating "inner speech" (thought that precedes expression) to external speech is a relatively simple procedure.[8] Full attention can be focused on the meaning of utterances, and their production is fluent and automatic.

Writing, on the other hand, is usually learned through formal instruction rather than through the natural acquisition processes. Writing requires extensive previous learning. A writer must know and use orthographic forms, lexis, syntax, and morphemes. Furthermore, through reading, a writer learns contextual and organizational constraints. Thus writing requires much more complex mental effort. Writers are forced to concentrate on both the *meaning* of ideas, that is, ensuring that what they write conveys their intended message, and on the *production* of ideas, that is, producing the linear form in which ideas actually take shape on the page. Production is rarely rapid or fluent nor is meaning always clear.

In contrast to speech, competence in writing usually develops much more slowly in first language acquisition. One usually learns to write after having essentially completed the acquisition of the "speaking" grammar. The relationship of speaking to writing is very much like the relationship of a first to a second language.[9] Witness the widespread concern among American educators (and the public)

about the inability of both our high school and college graduates to express themselves effectively in writing. A similar level of concern is rarely voiced regarding the ability of native English speakers to *speak* English effectively.

Not only does writing competency develop more slowly, but during the act of writing, ideas take shape on the page much more slowly than during speaking. The mind serves as a monitor for the writer. As writers mentally formulate sentences, they may alter them as their acquired and learned experiences about language appropriateness and structure monitor their statements. There may be "false starts" before an utterance appears in written form. Thus writers must deal with the additional frustration of the slowness with which their thoughts appear on the page.

Furthermore, for many students, learning to write is "ego-destructive." The words produced are part of the self; when we write, we must reveal and record in a more permanent form our "being" on the page. As a result, when a student-writer sees a red-penciled "redundant" on a page, the student frequently assumes the term means the ideas are redundant, not the words on the page. For ESL students the "ego-destructive" nature of writing is compounded not only by the concern of revealing one's "being" on the page but also by the realization that ideas so evident to the self and clearly articulated in a first language may not be so clearly articulated in the second language.

And because many ESL students are thinking in their first languages and translating *sentence* for *sentence* as they write in their second language, rather than translating *ideas* from first to second language, they often experience enormous frustrations as they learn to write in their second language.

WRITING SERVES DIFFERENT PURPOSES

Though writing is infinitely more complicated in its production psychologically, linguistically, and cognitively than speech, it can serve purposes that speech cannot. Because writers are not under the instantaneous time pressures of speakers to articulate statements, writers have time to select more precise words and suitable sentence structures to convey their intended meanings. Writing allows for retrospective thinking; writers commit ideas to paper and then may look back at their words and sentence structures to ensure their appropriateness. Furthermore, writing allows for higher levels of abstraction; more complex ideas can be presented in written form because writing can be read over and over again. Unlike the speaker who utters a statement and moves on to other statements hoping the audience moves along too, the writer composes a statement, expands it, illustrates and explains it knowing that the reader can stop, reread, and reflect upon that statement. The words remain on the page in the form the writer intended. However, the spoken word is transient; what remains with the listener is a remembered interpretation of the speaker's words. They are not evident in black and white.

Writing is also a means of reinforcing other language skills. Writers gather information by reading, observing, talking with others, synthesizing and evaluating data. In pursuing these activities, student writers' abilities to think logically and solve problems are strengthened as they conceptualize and state ideas.

For ESL students particularly, whose individual needs and goals are highly variable, writing is an efficient tool to facilitate and reinforce other language skills. Reading, vocabulary, and grammar skills are employed in the act of writing. As ESL students become actively engaged in the writing process, they read for additional information—perhaps to clarify positions concerning particular topics. As ESL writers read material in English, they acquire an awareness of English prose styles as well as new information presented through the medium of new vocabulary. Reading skills are being reinforced because they are reading for a specific purpose—to gain information. In acquiring new information they are interpreting a text. They scan some sections of a text and scrutinize others and, in so doing, select and reject information to be used in written discourse.

Writing fosters and reinforces vocabulary skills as ESL writers endeavor to make suitable word choices for their writing. In addition, the spelling system of English demands that writers master a wealth of morphological information not required in the speech system.[10] Recognition of these morphological structures enables learners to build their vocabularies more quickly as they visualize (picture in their minds) word development.

Grammar skills are enhanced as ESL writers make decisions about the form in which to present ideas. They must apply their knowledge of sentence patterns, frequently visualized as isolated rules, to shape their ideas into acceptable and effective sentences. They actively use knowledge of coordinating and subordinating structures, for example, to emphasize or deemphasize ideas. In so doing, ESL writers put into practice the theoretical information they have been given.

For ESL students, who are frequently uncomfortable speaking a second language and for whom second language acquisition is necessary to function in a complex society, writing is an essential language-reinforcing skill. Since writing becomes a means to learn, to discover, to develop, to refine, the ability to write is crucial. Because writing differs significantly from speech, students cannot just "write as they speak." They should understand that writing requires more complex levels of physical and mental activity. Writing is clearly more than speech written down.

1.2 Writing requires active involvement

The composing process involves several levels of activities all working at once, either in conjunction with or against one another.

W. Ross Winterowd

There is no question—writing is active. Writing does not just happen. It involves our intense participation, engagement, even immersion in the process. This immersion is usually

1. Both solitary and collaborative

2. Both conscious and subconscious

3. Both physical and mental

These levels of activity are based in our experience, our memories of our experience, and our knowledge of the language. Writing engages us in a *"solitary, personal, self-rhythmed process,"* but it is also "a way of engaging the *world* by becoming aware of how our minds perceive it."[11] The activity that occurs in making connections between the self and the world is both multiple and simultaneous, much like the workings of a computer when a signal is

FIGURE 1.1 LEVELS OF ACTIVITY

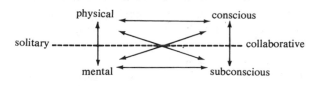

given to retrieve or process specific information. A flurry of activity ensues at all levels as the "computer-like" brain filters and selects to bring the needed data forward. Further, these multiple levels of activity allow us to collect our thoughts and write them down, view them, review them, revise them, and shape them for ourselves or for a given audience.

Unfortunately what we know of the composing process is "at best primitive."[12] But we can learn much about these physical and mental, conscious and subconscious activities by observing writers at work and by asking them about their perceptions of the process as they write. We do know that there are observable levels of *physical* activity and also underlying *mental* activities that we cannot easily observe. Sometimes the activity stems from the writing process itself. At other times the activity gets the writing process started and even stimulates its development. Furthermore, these levels of activity appear to be interdependent, and often all seem to be working at once, as suggested by Figure 1.1.

When writers engage the world, they have contact with someone or are affected by some event; the external image or experience triggers a response within the writer, at either the *conscious* or *subconscious* level or both. The personal response—internalized reaction—based on the writer's language and experience is monitored and filtered as it moves into the writer's conscious level and finally takes form in the written word. In fact, the very act of writing words may trigger the cycle of activity anew. Researchers such as Britton, Stallard, Perl, and Emig have described the active processes that occur during writing.

SOME PHYSICAL ACTIVITY IS SOLITARY

When Britton and his colleagues observed physical activity in a group of writers during an actual writing session, they noted that writers questioned, moved about, chatted, complained, and then, in some instances, suddenly started writing. Often student-writers stopped, began again, paused, scanned, altered, corrected their writing, gazed into

space, and so on (1975:25). Like Britton, we have observed in our student-writers other activities such as wadding paper, sharpening pencils, doodling, drawing, wiggling, shifting positions, stretching, and sighing. While this movement is easily observable, it is "the most difficult to study" because "the writer is essentially alone with his thoughts, his pen, and his paper."[13] We can *see* the outward manifestations of what is happening in writers, but we cannot peer into their minds. Whether these actions are conscious or subconscious during the writing process we cannot be sure. However, we might hypothesize that all this activity is a necessary part of the writing process. Some may stem from the fear our student-writers—indeed most writers, ourselves included—have of the writing process. Such seemingly nonproductive activity may simply constitute avoidance tactics, putting off recording those first words on paper. On the other hand, for some, physical activity seems to stimulate the process. It gets more of the brain working, initiates more rushes of thought so that more connections are made. Much of the solitary physical activity we observe in struggling writers is an outward sign of the internal writing processes at work—the incubation of thoughts and the discovery or invention of ideas and form.

Stallard, based on his observations of 12th grade writers, arrived at the conclusion that this kind of activity usually is characteristic of good writers who "spend more time at prewriting activities than at actual writing" and who "tend to be slower, do more revision (particularly as they read what they have just written), and do stop more often to do this reading."[14] Thus we conclude that good writers appear to be active writers.

SOME PHYSICAL ACTIVITY IS COLLABORATIVE

A very different but crucial level of physical and mental activity occurs when writers collaborate or interact with their peers and their teachers. When writers talk with each other, read, talk about writing, and actively write together, new thoughts and ideas as well as new perceptions of old information are stimulated.

When writers are actively receptive to each other, interaction helps them expand their ideas. Active participation in class projects, debates, discussions, interviews, roleplays, and brainstorming activities helps writers understand and appreciate views which are different from or opposite to their own.

By reading, analyzing, and discussing pieces of writing, student-writers gain an understanding of reader expectations, develop the critical reading skills they need for their own writing, and begin to understand why a piece of writing succeeds or fails. They have the opportunity to question: What did the piece of writing say? What form did it take? Was it easy to understand? What response did it evoke in the readers? Was it what the writer intended?

Collaborative writing (when the whole class, a small group, or even two people jointly write something) and peer evaluation (student appraisal of fellow classmates' writing) allow students to experience reader expectations as well. On-the-spot teacher or peer feedback about a piece of writing gives the writer the rare opportunity of knowing, immediately, the audience's response to the writing, thus allowing the writer to determine whether the intended message has been communicated successfully. Such feedback helps writers in the same way that a listener's response helps a speaker. By giving students opportunities to talk, read, write, and evaluate together, teachers can create, in the classroom, settings in which the two-way process of active communication can occur and develop.

Most of the activity at this level of writing, then, gives writers feedback about the "nature"—the validity, the relevance, the specificity—of their ideas. In addition, each interaction triggers images, which in turn trigger more images, which require further analysis. Thus, writers' general awareness is heightened and their acquisition of language occurs more frequently and more naturally in this situation than it does in a rigid, formalized, one-way, "rule" learning situation. As Elsasser asserts, "active, engaged learners" are more likely to "understand the nature of the written word, the possibilities for its effective communication, and the difficulties in its production" (1977:368).

MENTAL ACTIVITY OCCURS CONSCIOUSLY AND SUBCONSCIOUSLY

Although we can *see* many physical manifestations of the writing process, research has shown that much of what happens during writing is unobservable mental activity. Recent research in cognitive psychology has contributed vital information about the functions of the brain's hemispheres and how they affect the mental activity involved in writing.

Beaugrande likens accumulated knowledge—the "data bank" for the writing process—to a network in which everything is patterned and organized (1979:262). When a stimulus enters the process, successive images in the pattern are flashed across the screen of the mind. Buzan further points out that "the brain is certainly *not* dealing with words in simple lists and lines" (1976:86). Although a single line of words is emerging either in speech or on paper, a continuing and enormously complex process of sorting and selecting is taking place in the mind. Whole networks of words and ideas are being juggled and interlinked in order to communicate. The writer engages in a highly sophisticated, *unobservable* level of mental activity: a "computer search" of his mind, to find or link or create ideas, the programs for which are filed away in its recesses. Without the writer's active involvement, however, those ideas often remain beyond reach. Thus, writing simplifies as the writer reaches the subconsious level of writing and "disappears into the act itself."[15]

Constant interaction occurs between the conscious and subconscious. Mental activity in the writing process seems to begin with the intake or awareness of a reason for writing. This reason is relayed to the subconscious, where writers sense their reactions to it, and then it works its way back to the conscious for production and analysis.

In any situation where a writer chooses or is given a topic or a problem to solve, the topic itself evokes what Gendlin, cited by Perl, calls the "felt sense"—vague fuzzy feelings within the body—created by the "images, words, ideas. . .evoked by the topic."[16] There is, in effect, a subconscious stirring within the writer which begins the process of developing thoughts and formulating ideas. This mental activity is not readily apparent to the observer, or necessarily to the writer either. Often writers are unaware of what is happening within themselves during this composing cycle until they begin to verbalize and record their thoughts.

Perl's study, based on writers' self-monitoring of their actions and reactions during composing, sheds some light on how a writer's "felt sense" works at this level. Anne, a New York City teacher, taped what was happening to her as she thought and wrote:

I'm searching for a beginning, a pattern of organization, I'm watching myself, trying to understand my behavior. As I sit here in silence, I can see lots of things happening. . . .My mind leaps from the task at hand to what I need at the vegetable stand for tonight's soup to the threatening rain outside to ideas voiced in my writing group this morning, but in between "distractions" I hear myself trying to point to the more steady attention I'm giving to composing. This is all to point out that the process is more

8

complex than I am aware of, but I think my tapes reveal certain basic patterns that I tend to follow (1980:364).

Notice that Anne talks about the activity of her mind, the way it leaps from one task to another, and about the distractions she senses. In effect, she is in what we might call a state of daydreaming, or "wool gathering," or perhaps even general inattentiveness to the world around her or to the subject at hand. This state, which is often mistaken for boredom or disinterest by a teacher or casual observer, is actually the outward sign of mental activity—the incubation process at work. We can see from Anne's introspective report that, in fact, Anne-the-writer is at work: her ideas are gestating and forming; she is searching for related ideas and connections. She may even be imagining an audience. Anne, like most writers, has become engaged and involved with the information and experience that are internally available to her.

Anne also tells us that her mind travels far and wide. Addressing this point, Beaugrande cautions that "since the mind can stray far afield. . .effective use of knowledge in such an activity in writing demands the imposition of special controls upon the formulation of associations" (1979:263). In other words, writers need to focus on ultimate goals as they allow their minds freedom to explore. They need both to produce and to analyze their thoughts.

Britton's view of the writer in the dual role of participant/producer and spectator/critic-analyst suggests that writers do indeed exercise these special controls. As *participants,* writers search their minds, question, speculate, and theorize about problems. As *spectators,* they view their writing from a detached position to discover gaps in their information or flaws in their perceptions. In this role writers constantly "monitor" what they produce based on the life experiences they have had as well as on the language experiences they have acquired or learned. Writers move back and forth between these two roles in order to analyze their thoughts and then to continue the search for further facts or connections. This extensive mental activity probably stimulates a large part of the physical activity we can often observe in writers.

Whatever Anne's random thoughts, and no matter how far removed they seemed from her subject, it is likely that somewhere in her daydreaming state the participant-spectator was causing synapse to occur by coordinating and subordinating the thoughts she would eventually produce on paper.

Usually, when timing is left to the writer, the decision to write comes after the awareness that something has "clicked." Ideas have begun to form and take on meaning in light of the subject to be addressed. The mind has made relevant connections among and between ideas. At this point, activity increases to include other levels of both mental and physical processes—pencil chewing, shuffling, doodling, and finally writing.

MENTAL AND PHYSICAL ACTIVITY COORDINATE TO PRODUCE WRITING

Emig, in *Research on Composing,* addresses yet another aspect of writing activity—the complex interactions and responses between the mind and the body. She shows the important connections among the hand, the eye, and the brain during the actual act of writing (1978:61). The writer's hand plays a crucial role in the writing process because it may be a helpful agent in the process, or it may be a source of frustration and difficulty. For instance,

1. Physically, the very act of writing—putting words on paper—is "activating and mobilizing." It thrusts the writer from a state of conscious or subconscious mental activity into physical engagement with the process and the writing task. The writer has actually, physically, independently begun to do something.

2. For some, however, the physical formation of a letter may be difficult, especially for ESL writers accustomed to other orthographic or ideographic systems.

3. Aesthetically, the literal act of writing may produce in the writer a sense of sculpting or carving statements—an aesthetic sense of the process. Recent research reported in *Science* suggests that brain patterns elicited by scribbling are not significantly different from those elicited by writing. "When writing is treated as a natural outgrowth of scribbling, [one] . . . learns to enjoy using a pencil and paper for communication."[17]

4. Psychologically, the act of writing, moreover, with the linear organization evidenced in most Western systems, may reinforce the work of the left hemisphere of the brain. This act focuses writers' attention on analytic activity, thereby putting them into the role of the spectator.

9

5. Lastly, the very act of writing words keeps the process slowed down. This has both a positive and a negative effect. Since writers think much faster than they can write, new ideas can pop up and present themselves for consideration. On the other hand, unless quickly recorded, some of those ideas may be lost to the writer because the mind cannot retain or recall all it has to process.

In addition to the hand, Emig and others also stress the role of the eye in writing. Some of the more prevalent theories suggest that

1. The eye acts as a sense modality for presenting experiences to the brain during invention: discovery and generating ideas. Not only does the eye snap pictures of its surroundings, but it also calls up experiences for the mind to view. We have all at some time had the experience of "picturing" events in our minds.

2. The eye coordinates the hand and the brain during the physical act of writing. In the act of writing, the eye follows the hand doing the writing; and, therefore, reading and writing are practiced simultaneously—an added bonus since both skills improve together.

3. During revising or reading to explore further, the eye is the instrument we use to review what we have written. Murray says of re-

writing that the writer "can't stop" until he knows what he wants to say and has it in focus. "It is a physical process almost as much as a mental process involving dictation, use of pens, pencils, markers" (1968: 10). Britton relates an experiment in which writers wrote on pads with carbons, using pens which contained no ink. In other words, they had a record of the words they produced but were unable to review or scan what they had written. The result—the writer's efforts were largely unsuccessful (1975:35).

Perhaps then, as Irmscher says, "most important of all, writing permits us not just to say, but to *see* what we have to say. Thus, we have a new concern for the *how* as well as the *what*, the manner as well as the substance" (1979a:20).

To sum up our discussion of levels of activity in writing, we borrow from Burke, who says that "writing is an actualization or dramatization of the thought process through transcription. Writers become agents acting on an audience that is part of the complex scene. . .they are people acting through and with words and symbols. Writing. . .is then a dramatic attempt to complete an action that begins with a linguistic struggle with the world out there and closes with a re-creation of that struggle for readers."[18]

Let us now examine the multifaceted creative thought process we follow in acting on our audiences with words and symbols.

1.3 Writing involves creative processes

Writing is exploration—discovery of meaning,
discovery of form—and the writer works back
and forth, concentrating on one of the . . .
basic skills at a time so that he can discover
what he has to say and how to say it more efficiently.

Donald Murray

A writer creates. A writer causes a message to come into existence through a linguistic struggle with experience by searching out ideas and uniquely combining, developing, and shaping them into new perceptions. In this process of searching, discovering, generating, and shaping, the creative elements of writing overlap and frequently recur. They do not

necessarily occur in stages (though they may), since the writer can initiate writing at any point in the process and work into and out of any part of the process at any time.

As teachers, the greatest assistance we can offer our students is, first, to understand the writing process ourselves and in so doing to help them understand it as well. What, then, is the creative process of writing? Is it prewriting, writing, rewriting? Is it the use of heuristics in preparation for writing? Is it inspiration? Is is preconditioning, incubation, production? Our answer is YES. It is *all* of these and more.

THE CREATIVE PROCESS MODEL FOR WRITING

Even though writing is complicated, according to Murray there seems to be "a consistent pattern of work" (1968:1). There also seem to be some specific actions that most successful writers perform in varying degrees, in various combinations, and at various times throughout the composing process. From writers themselves and from many who have observed the actions of writers, we know that there is usually some kind of stimulus for writing, either internal or external, which *initiates* the process and provides the reason or purpose for writing.

With purpose in mind, writers' *knowledge and experience* are brought into play. A period of preparation, of incubation, of mental and physical activity ensues—a searching out or sifting through knowledge, experience, intuition, and emotions to find (or create) the subject or the problem the writer wants or needs to address. Next, or in concert with this preparatory period, is the time for *discovering* (1) what bits and pieces of information are available to writers, (2) what information is missing, and (3) how the topic is to be limited. As writers begin to find out what is in their experiential bases—or data banks—and what language they have available for expressing their experiences, they begin the synapse, the process of linking and relating words, phrases, and ideas to form thoughts appropriate to the advancement of their purposes.

Where gaps exist in their information, they *generate* material to fill them; they gather specific support for their ideas from both internal and external sources. All along they are steadily *shaping* the content they are creating to fit their purposes, their audiences, and their situations. They add, delete, order, correct, change, find their voices, choose specific words and structures which best carry the intention and meaning of their messages. Finally, the piece of writing moves beyond the process. . .to an audience. We do not say that the piece is finished; we say that it moves beyond the process. Sommers suggests that a piece of writing "is never finished, just abandoned" (1980:384). It may be abandoned in the sense that the writer ceases to revise it and sends it on for the perusal of an

audience, or it may be abandoned because it does not suit the intended purpose of the writer at the time. At another time, in another situation, or for a different audience, the piece may prove suitable. Therefore, we reemphasize the concept that all writing can be worthwhile, since it is possible for the writer to bring any product back into the process for revision and reworking at any point. . .even after it has been abandoned (just as John Fowles did when he rewrote *The Magus* for its second publication).

The writing process itself is an unending cycle, the core of which is the writer's data bank: the ever-expanding storehouse of knowledge, experience, intuition, emotion, and expectation from which a writer may draw and/or create thoughts.

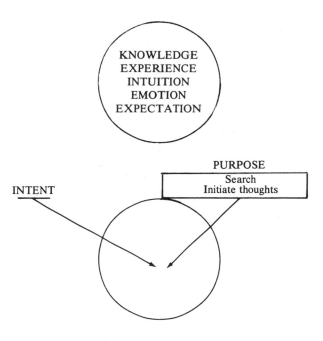

Purpose or intent stimulates the search for, initiation of, or incubation of thought or of a subject. As a result, purpose or intent constitutes the point of entry into the cycle; but entry (or exit) may occur at any point in the cycle. For example, a writer may enter the cycle because of a specific assignment: "Discuss the existing land use conditions in your country." This writer begins by tapping the knowledge and experience available and moves forward from that point. Another writer may have made a discovery through laboratory or field experimentation which needs to be explained to others. Yet another writer may need to generate new material to update an old report. And still another writer may enter the cycle at the point of shaping, that is, at the point of using a body of information already

11

compiled and recorded and putting it into acceptable form for a specific purpose.

The writing process embodies as well the elements of discovery, generation, and shaping which continuously interconnect so as to lead a writer from one to another element.

New perceptions may also occur at any point in the cycle to create a spin-off for a completely new or different idea from what the writer originally intended. Thus a new process may be initiated *or* the new perception may feed back into the original process.

The product is the finished form the writing takes; in other words, it is the piece of writing released from the cycle. The product is represented

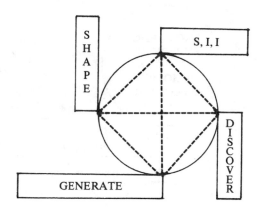

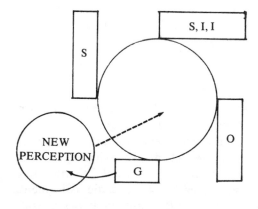

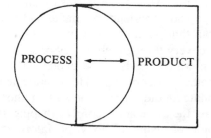

as overlapping the process because it usually can be and sometimes is returned to the writing cycle.

The creative processes are all related and interrelated, but because we are limited by one-dimensional, linear means of recording our conception of the process on paper, we have illustrated a model of the process in Figure 1.2.

- Central to the process is the **data bank**: knowledge, experience, intuition, emotion, expectations.

- **Purpose** or **intent** trigger entry to the process of exploring the data.

- Entry level to the process is usually the **search** or **initiation** of a topic and **incubation.**

INVENTION

- **Discovery**—"Eureka! Now I see it!"—is illumination of purpose or intent, of what we want to say, of what we need to say, of form, of organization.

- **Generation**—"Aha! It fits!"—occurs through (1) linking or synapse of stored ideas, opinions, feelings, and facts with each other and with new information; (2) filling gaps by actively seeking new experience and information; and (3) forming new perceptions.

- **Shaping** is molding opinions, feelings, experiences, knowledge, and language (1) to project what we personally want to communicate, and (2) to meet the needs and expectations of an imagined or thoroughly analyzed audience. It is choosing words, phrases, structures, and patterns which best convey the intended message.

- **The product**. . . is effective communication of a message to a reader.

Why is this process so important? All of us are called upon, or have the need, at one time or another to write. All too often, though, we seem to lack, or believe we lack, the creative powers necessary to bring thoughts forth on the page. We face the blank page. It remains blank, even after many minutes or

FIGURE 1.2 CREATIVE PROCESS MODEL FOR WRITING

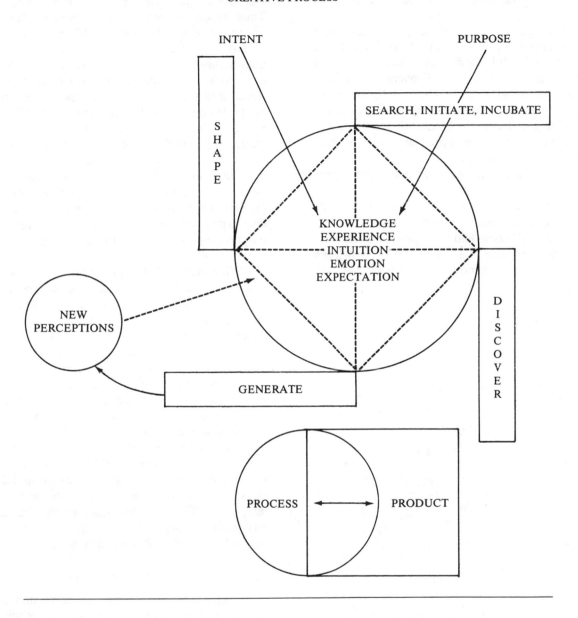

CREATIVE PROCESS

hours. Sometimes we give up, deciding the task is too difficult. Other times, we perform the task without fully understanding what we want to say and ultimately are frustrated and dissatisfied with our efforts. As teachers we are confronted daily with students who see the act of writing as beyond their capabilities. How often we have heard, "I don't know what to say." "I know what I want to say, but I don't know how to say it," or "I have lots of ideas, but I haven't the vaguest notion of where to start."

GETTING STARTED

For years now, many of us have taught writing, and have ourselves written, on command: We have been told, or have told our students, "Write," and only after the fact have we given attention to what was produced. Michelangelo did not sculpt the David "on command." He spent many years learning and practicing his art before he could create such a masterpiece. We should not then expect ourselves or our students to be comfortable writing and to produce effective writing when we have spent little or no time in learning/teaching the process of writing. It is time for us to question what happens when we write.

"Writing is not just a question of inspiration: it also generally involves a lot of hard work and organization."[19] It is hard to get started. And since "getting started," according to Irmscher, "is a major barrier—a mental block—" (1979a:10), how do we teachers help our students overcome frustration with writing and eventually experience the act of writing as a rewarding, important, and positive experience? First, we help our students learn how to examine and use their own knowledge and experience.

A better understanding of the creative processes involved in writing can facilitate the teaching and learning of ESL composition. Helping our students learn how to explore and use their own knowledge and experience will remove a major barrier to their success in writing.

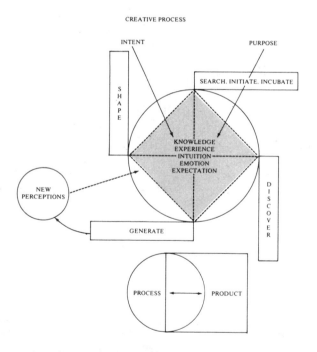

CREATIVE PROCESS

KNOWLEDGE AND EXPERIENCE

All invention, whatever its end products, rests firmly upon a common repository of knowledge and experience shared by writers and readers.—de Beaugrande

A shared body of knowledge and experience is essential to the writer's successful communication, and to the reader's understanding, of a message. Commonly shared life experiences and commonly accepted and understood codes of language further the aims and purposes of both writers and readers. Thus, before writing can occur writers must call upon their personal resources. When writers claim, "I have nothing to say," they are reflecting an unawareness of the vast resources that exist within them, as well as an inability to make these resources work for them. Smith points out that "research has never demonstrated that children have nothing to say. Quite the contrary. . .it is the easiest thing in the world to persuade a child to write another sentence. . .Teachers can always ask another leading question, and children can be trained to ask themselves questions to elicit yet another sentence" (1981b:11). Adult writers, too, simply need to learn *how* to draw on their repository of raw materials, to question themselves, and to develop their experiences.

What then is the basis of our shared knowledge and experience? The knowledge, experience, intuition, and emotion we bring to the act of writing are an accumulation of our reactions to what has happened to us throughout our lifetimes. Even the words we use to express experience are "socio-historically determined and therefore shaped, limited, or expanded through individual or collective experience."[20] However, Ben Shahn indicates that artists should not be satisfied with the experiences that they already possess. For artists to strengthen their creative powers, they should experience the real things—they should look, feel, listen, read, know, talk, draw, paint, travel—and look and listen some more—in other words, they should "try all things."[21] Writers, no less than artists, should be aware of the importance of adding to their experiential and knowledge base in such ways.

There is a universal core of experience

The brain has more interconnections than there are atoms in the universe, thus providing us with an almost infinite number of experiences to call upon, if only we allow them to surface.[22] Not one of us is without some of the experience portrayed by the brain pattern in Figure 1.3.

There exists in each of us a universal core of knowledge based in our individual and collective human experiences. We know that fire is hot, the sun rises in the east, seasons follow general patterns, our bodies function in certain ways, we live and die, etc. Because of these natural and human universals, we share common knowledge and thus common understandings in these realms.

FIGURE 1.3 EXAMPLE OF A BRAIN PATTERN which allows writers to begin with a central idea and expand it as ideas pop into mind.

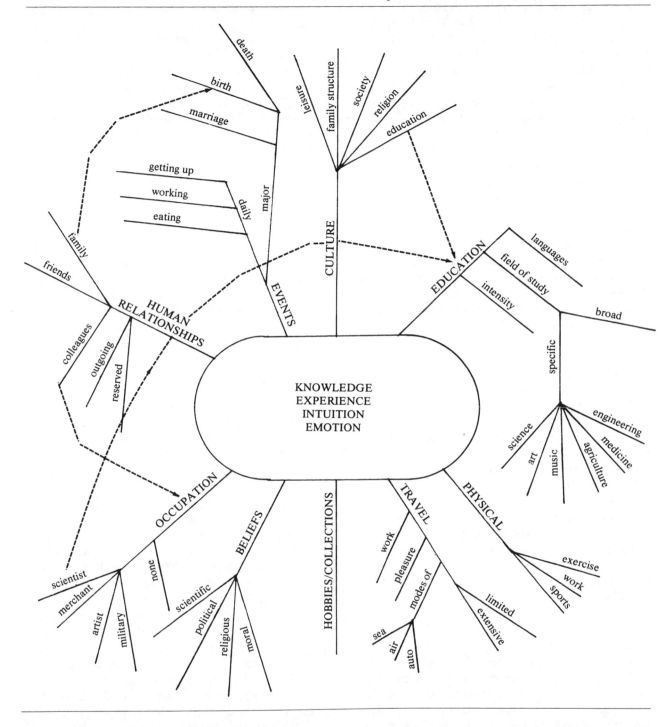

Adult ESL writers share this universal core of knowledge, but most often it has been acquired, learned, and stored in a language other than English. One of the major tasks then for ESL writers is to discover the "English way" to express these universals and to find the English words and structures which will give the writer a base of knowledge in common with the reader and will allow the writer to meet the reader's expectations on the printed page.

There are variations in experience

We must also be keenly aware of the variations in experience. Most ESL writers are rich in experience and knowledge, some through extensive education and travel, some through practical experiences. In most cases their cultures—beliefs, customs, and traditions—may be quite different from our own as well as from each other's. Consequently, each one does have something valuable and worthwhile to communicate. But these student-writers need to be able to dip into their inner reserves to discover what they do know or do not know *in English*. By effecting this discovery, they can often bring fresh perspectives to their writing and different methods to the solutions of problems.

Suppose that a group of ESL writers were asked to discuss "Modern Technology and Its Effect on My Country." A Botswanian and a Japanese would probably perceive the subject from completely different vantage points, since their experiences with technology are different. Furthermore, the subjects of "Women's Rights" or "The Role of Old People in Today's Society" would trigger vastly different responses from writers of various cultures. Thus, when writers take an idea or a thought from their minds and attempt to make it clear to someone else, they must be careful to clarify it and exemplify it so that readers can identify with it, believe it, understand it, respond to it, and/or be persuaded by it. Most importantly, in searching out their own experiences, writers must also attempt to perceive or imagine the knowledge, experience, emotions, and expectations of their readers.

Sometimes, however writers have limited experience reading and writing in their native language as well as in English. Further, they may have had limited exposure to the world outside their own cultures. When this is the situation, writers need the benefits of new and shared experiences. They need help and encouragement in generating and creating both ideas and forms in English as well.

The ESL writer's task is further complicated by the fact that he or she lacks an intuitive sense of the English language conventions and rules more available to native English speakers and writers. ESL writers often do not have the second language maturity to express the knowledge they may have in their own languages. They may be frustrated with writing as a result of vocabulary and grammatical structures too limited to convey adequately what they know and want to say. On many occasions, student-writers have said to us, "If only I could tell you what I am thinking in my own language." They obviously have experience and knowledge of their subjects which they want to relate, but they do not yet have the means to express that knowledge in English. That is when we, as teachers, can take the role of collaborators with our students and help them

find means to clear expression. Further, when ESL writers are hindered by a lack of experience in understanding reader expectation, they need the opportunity to participate in a combined program of reading and writing which can build their knowledge as to how writers express concepts in English and, consequently, what readers expect.

"The challenge," then for us as educators, "is to develop teaching methodology that expands experience (that allows people previously excluded to master the written word)."[23]

How do we gain access to experience?

How is our knowledge and experience stored, and how do we gain access to it? In order to use our experience or our data more efficiently, we should know as much as possible about how it is stored in our minds. In recent years there has been considerable research and speculation about the brain's functions. We do not attempt here an in-depth discussion of how the brain works because too little is known to make definitive statements. However, some of the current speculation appears to hold importance for the composing process.

In describing the composing process, Richard Young in *Research on Composing,* tells us that the psychological processes of invention are too unpredictable to be controlled by formal procedures (p. 32); Buzan adds that the brain patterns are not only nonlinear but so complex and interlaced as to defy description (p. 17). However, he does suggest ways of tapping them which are discussed in Chapter 4 of this text. Beaugrande further suggests that the "processes are more accessible and orderly than widely supposed (1979:262). Indeed, based on recent biochemical, physiological, and psychological research, both Buzan and Beaugrande believe that the brain patterns are a network of key concepts arranged in an interlocked and integrated manner. For writers, this is an important theory; because if we can learn how to use these connections effectively, when we tap one concept, others are automatically made available to us. Buzan suggests that the network functions in such a way that rather than starting with a subject at the top, as we usually do, and working down in sentences and lists, one should start from the center or main idea and branch out as dictated by the individual's ideas and the general form of the central theme. From the illustration of the brain pattern about knowledge and experience in Figure 1.3, we can see that this method allows space for the expansion of the main idea, easy access to linking related concepts, and

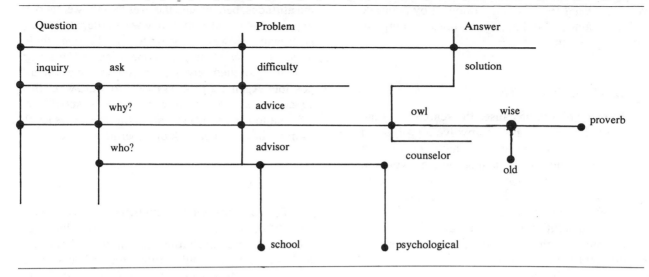

FIGURE 1.4 COMPUTER PSYCHOLOGY REPRESENTATION of the network of associations (at the word level) brought about by elements such as tropes, metaphors, synonyms, antonyms, examples, characteristics. Adapted from Beaugrande (p. 263).

quick recording of the concept. Further, such a diagram does not preclude an order of importance.

Beaugrande, on the other hand, describes the network as being made up of a series of links between words and concepts similiar to the network one might see in the representation of computer psychology given in Figure 1.4 (p. 262). "The links are stated in the form of propositions because . . . the mind stores knowledge precisely in that form."[24] The writer's task then is to find meaningful and unique relationships among those propositions. Free association exercises based on a key concept can help call up information from this kind of network for the writer.

We also have evidence that there is constant interplay between the conscious and subconscious mind. The subconscious mind usually provides the *design* for the process, the conscious mind the *development* (although the reverse is possible).[25] By active brain patterning or by proposition linking, writers are able consciously to develop ideas and thoughts from the subconscious network of the mind. Thus, writers should initially prepare their minds through thinking, reading, analyzing, talk- ing. . .so that the subconscious can take over the process of designing, that is, finding the writing subject or problem and showing what writers feel and know about it in preparation for further development in the writing process.

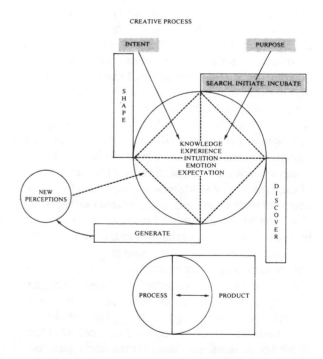

PURPOSE/INTENT

Why do writers want to gain access to their data banks? First of all, writers recognize or identify a purpose or intent for writing. . .or even, the need *to create* a purpose or intent. "Writing often begins with an intent not a finished thought;"[26] this intent may be either tentative or definite; and depending upon what writers discover in the process, it may be

17

subject to change. Lloyd Bitzer identifies three things that stimulate discourse or writing in the "real world": a *need* to discourse, followed by audience and constraints.[27] But first, need—reason—purpose: the *why* of writing.

SEARCH/INITIATE

The *why* of writing causes the search for or the initiation of a subject: it may involve a problem in need of a solution, an event which results in a specific outcome, or a feeling which evokes a reaction. Among the "whys" or stimuli which may impel writers to write are—Why? Because—

I feel strongly about. . .

I need a solution to the problem of. . .

I want to tell someone about this new or different idea I have. . .

I wonder what if. . .

I want to explain how to. . .

I require some assistance with a project. . .

I want to!

Through questioning, examining, and. . .waiting. . .the writer finds a subject or a problem to solve: art, energy, law, "to be or not to be." . . . Whether the writing problem is chosen or assigned, whether it is intended only for self-expression or for an audience other than the self will influence both the manner and the extent of the writer's search. The writer who poetically describes a terrible storm—because of a quarrel with his sweetheart—taps far different experiences and develops an idea in a vastly different form from a writer who is asked by a superior for a recommendation on the advantages of expanding sales to a new market. The first topic becomes elaborated only to the extent that the writer is willing to search out and discover his innermost feelings about his sweetheart and their quarrel. His purpose may be satisfied by jottings that make sense only to him. The other writing problem necessitates use of the full creative process of generating and shaping material, in addition to discovery of what writers know about their assigned task. Writers in this situation will discover, for instance, what they know about sales, the new market, their superior's attitude toward the expansion, and so on. Where they find their knowledge of the subject limited, they will research it and add new information to their data bank. Finally, they will consider the subject matter and the audience in determining the further shaping of their recommendations.

The search for answers to both these writing problems involves writers in processes of self-discovery. Through self-discovery, writers explore the attitudes, beliefs, and theories that they consider important—and also that they wish others to see as significant. However, for writers to discover their topics, they must prepare their minds by making available to themselves as much information as possible. Again the process moves forward when the subconscious begins to work on this supply of information and sends signals to the conscious level from its internal network of experience.

INCUBATION

To reach the subconscious, or intuitive level, writers often need "down time" for thinking, collecting, and incubating information about the topic—both before and during the physical writing process. As Murray puts it, "The writer gets ideas by spending time in open susceptibility." The writer is "particularly aware and uniquely receptive to impressions and ideas," whether they come from within or without. The good writer has a "tough sensitivity"—like that of high-speed film—able to record both the horror and the beauty of life. However, in this cycle the writer is not necessarily looking for new ideas but is "trying to handle the ones he has."[28]

Inner reflection

To develop a sensitivity to one's available ideas requires inner reflection. As described by Perl, this process begins "with paying attention" (1980:366). If we are given a topic, it begins with taking the topic in and attending to what it evokes in us. This "attending" is a basic step in composing that skilled writers rely on, and a step that developing writers can be taught.

Even without a predetermined topic, the process remains the same. We can help ourselves discover, define, and understand our writing purpose by asking ourselves, "What's on my mind?". . . or "Of all the things I know about, what would I most like to write about now?". . .and wait and see what comes. This is the "felt sense" or "inner voice." As Perl says, "it begins with what is already there. . .and brings it forward by using language in structured form" (p. 367). Not only does the process require reflection but "it requires concentration, focus, and discipline usually in a silent and solitary setting" if we are to "determine what we know and what we don't know."[29]

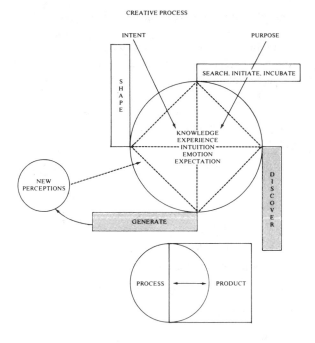

CREATIVE PROCESS

DISCOVERY

Invention is the discovery of meaning, the generation of ideas, and the linking of those ideas into coherent thoughts. Some would limit the discovery of ideas to only that phase which occurs *before* the final form of the writing takes shape, that is, during what is often referred to as the prewriting stage of the process. But as Irmscher has noted, "we discover as we write" (1979a:20). Therefore, discovery continues throughout the creative process. Furthermore, Winterowd says prewriting "is only that fraction of a second between the generation of a specific idea and the putting down of that idea on paper" (1975:33). Since those fractions of seconds also occur continually throughout the process as well, we prefer to think of discovery and prewriting as the stimulation of both thinking and writing that occurs off and on during the entire composing process rather than as a stage that begins and ends before serious writing occurs.

Further, discovery is often referred to as the process of searching the mind to *find* whatever meaning is already present there. However, the act of searching the mind to find meaning has its limitations. According to Flower, this searching is a complicated intellectual process which also involves *creating* ideas. It is a problem-solving, cognitive process—the most crucial point of which is finding or defining the problem to be solved (1980:21).

Thus, we **discover** in order to define—

1. *Why* we have decided to write something to someone
2. *What* we want to write about; what aspect of the subject we want to examine
3. *What* we know about the subject; what we don't know
4. *How* we will write about it; what form we need for communication of the problem/ subject
5. *Who* we will write for

Discovery helps us define the dimensions of all these considerations.

Discovery as a cognitive process requires conscious stimulation

Such conscious stimulation is physical writing itself. Physical writing, as a discovery process, begins the moment writers begin to scribble, doodle, or draw symbols leading to the synthesis of ideas and thoughts. Such activity does not necessarily follow, or come after, the extensive mental energy expended in inner reflection but rather is or becomes a part of that process. Since "Invention is the modification of existing knowledge," to modify effectively, "beginning writers must record every thought that comes into their heads during the thinking, prewriting, and invention stages."[30] Buzan further suggests that this kind of recording is beneficial for any writer, not just the novice—and we agree. Since the brain works more rapidly and efficiently than the hand can record, capturing the key concepts and propositions for later recall is vital in discovery. Whatever the writer puts on paper at this point is exclusively for self-discovery; and, therefore, it can be recorded in any form the writer chooses. It can be notes jotted on scraps of paper, a formal outline, a diagram. *It can even be messy.* The important consideration is to get the ideas down on paper. If they are not all usable, as is almost always the case, they can be discarded; but rarely can they be recaptured. Therefore, writing itself becomes the agent of prewriting and discovery.

A number of discovery techniques, or heuristics, for quick recording such as brain patterning, listing, outlining, questioning, and associational or free writing—that is, writing whatever comes into one's mind (these are discussed in detail in Part II of this book) are essential discovery tools for the writer. In any writing task, writers are able to get at more of their reserves of experience, knowledge, intuition, and emotion if they give that information a chance to enter conscious levels of activity. Students accustomed to keeping daily journals, drawing brain patterns, or doing wet-ink writing (writing for a set amount of time without stopping) often have a much easier time finding and defining subjects—and—they also have a repository of ideas to draw upon later. "Wet-ink writing," says Mandel, "will help students discover a point of view more truly and penetratingly than one who is expected to organize first, follow [formal] heuristics, provide reasons, enumerate details—all of these may only serve to inhibit illumination." "Free writing (prewriting, associational writing, journals, etc.)," he further states, "is...*actual* writing. [These forms of writing] rehabilitate a student's ability to tap the right hemisphere of the brain" (1980:376). At the same time, the linear act of recording is exercising the left brain—so that the writer has brought all mental resources into full operation for discovery.

For some ESL students these free-form activities may be so totally alien to their previous educational experience that the more formal heuristics, such as Aristotle's *topoi*,* can better help them find a point of view, a thesis, a form...These heuristics are equally valuable in helping writers generate new information, substantive details, and the organizational form needed to expand the piece of writing. Discovery techniques, indeed, need not be exclusively "free" or "controlled," but since some writers, native or ESL, have greater success with one method than with another, writers should be introduced to as many discovery methods as possible so that they have the maximum opportunity to develop their thoughts.

Whatever method is used, eventually illumination of the problem or subject does occur and writers may have the feeling of "Eureka! I've got it!" With this initial inspiration, they continue the process by further defining the subject, generating specific ideas, and reexamining and refining the message so that it is an inspiration to the reader as well as to themselves.

Let us examine how one writer selected, defined, and discovered a subject. The writer chose to discuss *art*. The whole subject of *art*, however, was far too general; and besides, there was no apparent purpose or intent for the writing. After 5 minutes of free writing, "art forms in architecture" emerged

as the writer's prevailing interest. Yet, how could he more clearly discover and define his subject? He found his real purpose only when a thesis, or a controlling idea for what he had to say, was formed. To accomplish this, he tied the most important propositions and the purpose together into a succinct statement. By doing this, he was beginning to bring order to chaos and was developing a "vague idea into a well-aimed thought."[31]

ART

He questioned:

What kind of art? art forms in architecture—symbolic and functional

When? in ancient times, before Christ

Where? in Egypt

Which ones? Pharaoh's cities and workers' villages

Why? influence on the development of modern cities
    Such as ... (example) Paris, Washington, D.C.
    Because of ... (reason) symmetry, control of boundaries
    Although ... (contradiction) time differentiation

He concluded:

"Because of their methodical design, their accuracy, and their organization, ancient Egyptian architectural forms have influenced the development of cities all over the world for thousands of years."

By working through the methods of discovery such as these, writers can begin to relate concepts and connect what they know with what they want to say (see Shaker's paper in Chapter 7).

Whatever set of questions or techniques is used, there are two conditions which Irmscher says are important for any scheme (1979a:90). First, keep it simple: A series of questions should number about five to seven, and no more than nine, because the mind does not easily retain more. Second, the questions or terms should be blanket terms which can apply to any subject. These considerations are especially important to ESL students, who often

---

*See Appendix A for further information.

need just as much help as native speakers, if not more, in finding something to write about. Furthermore, they need devices which are clear and easy to use. In fact, invention for ESL students performs an additional function to what it does for native speakers by also allowing them to discover what they know (or do not know) about a given subject in *English*.

When writers find out at this point what they need, but do not have in their data banks, they can generate further information in whatever way is appropriate to the subject matter. Through discovery, writers generate material; and through generating material, they discover—often finding totally new and unexpected perceptions.

GENERATION

Generation and discovery seem to overlap, and indeed they do, as do all elements of the writing cycle. However, while discovery is basically the flow of thoughts that already exist in the data bank, generation is more often the calculated design of finding needed data, facts, and examples to expand the discovered ideas. By filling in details, writers may also further discover the subject or their perception of it. Thus generating ideas effectively and appropriately in relation to a topic often requires more systematic processes than does discovery.

"It is not enough that in the process of composing the writer *see* his subject whole. . .the process of composing begins with a general idea, but the main process is one of filling in the details."[32] When the rational or conscious level takes over, it proceeds in a logical and analytical manner. In the process of filling in the details, Murray suggests that the writer *show* rather than *tell* readers about the subject (1968:13). In this way, readers are more likely to accept the conclusion and be convinced. Readers thus become actively involved in the process itself through the writer's technique.

Where do writers go for the details they will need to authenticate their subjects? If subjects are familiar ones, writers may have all or almost all of the needed information in their own internal data banks. If subjects are new or unfamiliar, a wealth of information is usually available, and appropriate external sources become obvious. Books, journals, magazines, reports, government publications, experiments, computer calculations, films, tapes, interviews, music, art, and observations are only a few of the resources writers can tap. In either case, writers will want to think through or even write out series of questions which will lead them and keep them from tracking away from their purposes or intentions. Occasionally, critical questioning and analyzing will tell writers that they need to change the focus of their subjects. In other words, as writers generate material, they may also rediscover—or—discover the topic anew. Writers will see that they didn't want to say A but really wanted to say B after all. By questioning the topic—What is A? What is it like? What is it unlike? Where does it exist? When did it begin? What effect does it have now? Why? On whom? Why is this important? To whom is it important—writers have looked at many aspects of the topic and have a better idea of what kind of specifics are needed for expanding and filling in. Obviously, "invention is no miracle or sleight-of-hand where things suddenly appear out of nowhere."[33] It is a complex process by which writers must look *within* themselves as well as *out* upon the world.

In looking out upon the world, "Writers develop ideas," as Smith says, from "interaction and dialogue with other people" (1981b:10). "Reading, writing, talking about writing, and talking in order to write must be continual possibilities; they overlap and interlock" (1981b:5). Group invention, in the more unstructured forms of brainstorming and discussion, can give writers insights into other's experiences, beliefs, and opinions and help stimulate further inquiry into their topics, often resulting in the acquisition of new information. More highly structured group invention activities such as creating a thesis and actually developing a paper as a class activity, debating a current issue, or role-playing a problem-solution situation are all valuable not only in stimulating and generating ideas but also in demonstrating appropriate patterns and forms for the content generated. Thus, heuristics are valuable aids not only in identifying sources of information for individuals but also in facilitating searches through group interaction. After a group has worked through a heuristic pattern, individual writers can more often and more easily analyze subjects according to that pattern. That is, the heuristic eventually becomes internalized or "acquired" for future learning and writing.

Neman recommends brief exposure to background theory and definition and *intensive practical experience* with the strategies themselves (1980:55). She cautions, however (and we do too), that writers should not, for a moment, think the purpose of any writing (assignment) is to demonstrate the heuristic or technique. The technique should be determined only by the purpose for writing and the content.[34]

Nevertheless, again writers are in the situation of "the chicken and the egg"—because content determines technique and form, and yet technique and form can lead to further development and refinement of content; both are essential elements.

A number of heuristics for external discovery have been developed in the past decade, many of them patterned on the classical topics: Burke's Pentad, the Tagmemic approach, question series, and problem-solving techniques, to name a few. Although the topics (topoi) were originally designed for orators, not writers, for the purpose of advancing agrument in support of controversial positions, they and other heuristics still work in helping writers create writing both for personal purposes and for finding factual material. Each of the techniques works best for developing specific kinds of writing. Therefore, writers need to select carefully what will best help them accomplish their aims.

Internal discovery techniques stem from more personal kinds of writing development—those of self-discovery and self-expression. Among the internal techniques are brain patterning, looping, free association, wet-ink writing, journal keeping, and autobiography. There is not, of course, a sharp dividing line between the external and the internal types of invention devices in terms of their use, since many of those classified as "external" techniques will also be used for self-discovery and expression. (An extensive listing of various types of invention devices and their sources is found in Appendix B.)

Since ESL students come to the act of writing without the knowledge or intuitions of English that native speakers possess, heuristics of all kinds are all the more important in helping them identify subject, purpose, audience, or structure, words, and ideas. One word of caution about the heuristics, however, especially in the ESL classroom. Neither writers nor teachers should feel compelled to use these techniques in their original forms. They should be modified in whatever way will most appropriately fit the level and the needs of the individual writers or the class that will be using them. Further, the combination of techniques they use will affect the outcome of these efforts.

As Irmscher states, "The act of invention is situated within a broad range between ungoverned associating (e.g., daydreaming) and mechanical reproduction of conventional knowledge (e.g., dictionary entries). The writer produces a text by arranging elements into a combination which is held together partly by conventional associations and partly by newly created associations. The merits of the text depend upon whether the combination

provides enriching insights into the nature of the object or events covered by the topic."[35]

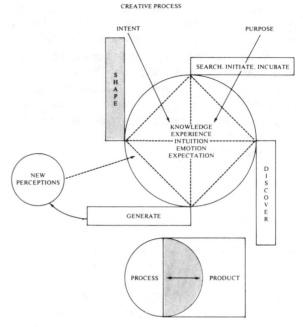

SHAPING

Form! I kept on saying the word to myself, striking the table as I worked; this chaos of life must be reduced, somehow, to form!—Murray

The first principle of composition, therefore, is to foresee or determine the shape of what is to come and pursue that shape.
—Strunk

Through invention, writers create series of propositions about a subject, and as we know, "Language use has to do with propositions and the acts they are used to perform. But these do not occur in isolation: they combine to form discourse," says Widdowson (1978:52). Combining then means giving considered shape or form to writing for meaningful communication of the propositions to others; the combining becomes a vital part of the process.

When the elements of writing are thoughtfully shaped, enriching insights are more likely to occur for both writer and reader. In the creative processes of writing all facets of the process interact and overlap. Writers move back and forth among the parts of the process with emphasis now on discovery and now on generating. Writers need to be aware that shaping, like the other facets of the creative process, is also continuous throughout the process.

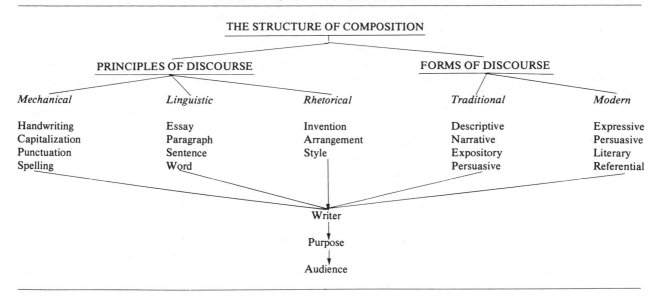

FIGURE 1.5 D'ANGELO'S STRUCTURE OF COMPOSITION shows the many considerations that must be given to shaping a piece of writing.

It begins with finding a message and ends when that message is presented in the most succinct and unified form possible. Most beginning writers think the first draft is equivalent to the finished product and that surface-level editing of that draft constitutes all the shaping that is necessary. Mature writers know, however, that the first draft is just the beginning, and at this point they have completed only a part of the shaping process. Shaping consists of formulating and reformulating a message.

Formulation of the message involves several cycles. In the initial cycles, writers find meaning and compose content; that is, they invent the message to be sent. Through shaping their thoughts—selecting, linking, deleting, adding, and changing—writers (1) facilitate search and initiation, (2) stimulate discovery, and (3) obviate the need to generate further development of the piece of writing. Ideas are formulated, propositions are linked, and content is developed as the writer creates the "deep structure" or the meaning of the message. In the next cycles, writers give outward *rhetorical form* to the meaning. They shape the content by determining which form of discourse is most appropriate and most effective for the message, in other words, just how the particular propositions should be combined, considering the specific or nonspecific audience, the writer's purpose, and the context in which the writing will occur. In the remaining series of cycles, writers continue to apply the *linguistic and mechanical principles,* or the "surface structures,"

to the piece. Writers concentrate on clarifying the theme and on the logical order of ideas and thoughts. They tighten the unity and coherence of the piece through the use of certain linguistic devices and structural elements from theme to internal paragraph organization. They pay attention as well to the fine tuning of sentence structure, word choice, punctuation, and spelling.

Thus, when writers shape their discourse, they are making choices by applying certain expected sets of criteria—rules, conventions, and guidelines—rhetorically, linguistically, and mechanically to their writing (see the criteria in Part II). In sum, shaping is the *production*, invention, and formulation of material both for writers themselves and for their readers. It is also the *analysis* and reformulation of that material to ensure maximum effectiveness in communicating the message to the reader. As such, the reformulation cycles are divided into *revising,* reexamining and rearranging ideas or chunks of discourse, and *editing,* reviewing finally with a keen eye the correctness and maximum effectiveness of other surface elements. Thus, while all writers produce, invent, and formulate their ideas in their own unique manner, still the common denominator—surface structure—basic sentence structures and word meanings—is shared by all writers and helps deliver their meanings.

D'Angelo's structure of composition (Figure 1.5) illustrates most of the elements involved in the shaping cycles in both the formulation and reformulation of material (1976:144).

Rhetorical shaping is a vital part of the overall process in which writers formulate concepts, propositions, and themes in finding meaning for themselves and then, perhaps, for a reading audience. Originating ideas, says Stallard, is "the primary cognitive task for the writer." At this point in the writing process, "Communication is not the writer's initial concern" (1976:182). Before writers can impose order and form, they must first shape, or conceptualize, main ideas and thoughts for their discourse. Furthermore, at the time they are inspired to write, they may not know what form or content they will ultimately communicate. Writers' choices in determining what to write arise partly from (1) the writing context and (2) the writer's purpose, and partly from (3) the writer's resources or experience, that is, knowledge of the language, of the subject, and of the audience.[36] Thus shaping begins with modifying, forming, molding, and sculpting experience and information.

Writers begin to set limits or parameters to their writing by consciously or subconsciously selecting a subject and determining purposes or intents. Then writers gather as much material as possible about the subjects. Out of this inventive shaping often comes chaos, yet while shaping in this cycle can be chaotic and even messy, it is not important to anyone else. *This formulation is for the writer alone.* From the moment the subject or problem is conceived, writers build concepts and connect propositions. From their data banks they select, delete, add, and change material until they have amassed content sufficient for their intentions. In this sense, shaping is a part of discovery and generation.

Shaping takes on new dimensions, however, when the writer clearly defines an audience, a purpose in terms of that audience, and a context for the message. Now, explain the Cowans, *the writing has to matter to someone else* (1980:63). The writer must consider not only what will be communicated, but also why, how, and to whom it will be communicated. Writers are faced with decisions about both principles and forms of discourse and which ones will best convey the message to a "given" audience. Thus, when writers shape their discourse for an audience, they make choices by applying accepted criteria to the text.

When writers begin to arrange the material they have created and gathered, they make a thousand strategic decisions with each outline, brain pattern, loop or wet-ink writing, set of questions, or whatever invention device they use to clarify their thoughts

(Murray, 1968:7). Again the kinds of designs writers use are important only to the writers themselves. The major purpose is to help them see beginnings, endings, and where they are going in general with their thoughts. Meaning and form are still in the process of being born; therefore, whatever works for the individual writer, of course, is the best means of early formulation and shaping of ideas.

Britton observes that planning, whatever form it takes, succeeds best when it becomes intuitive (1975:27). Thus, ESL student-writers need continuous and frequent exposure to actual practice with and various methods of rhetorical shaping in order to find their own best technique for planning.

How writers will further arrange material for an audience involves not only finding beginnings and endings but also determining what they want to accomplish by writing. Writers make choices about their treatment of content in terms of form. They decide whether to use a descriptive, narrative, expository, or persuasive/expressive, persuasive, literary, or referential form. A lawyer's purpose for writing a trial brief would probably demand a persuasive form while an engineer's purpose for writing a project report would call instead for an expository or a referential form. What writers want to accomplish with their audiences will also determine what information will be presented first and last and how much support detail will be included. Consequently, while writers are finding "voice," they may design or arrange the content in several ways before and during the writing process.

In this cycle shaping becomes the part of writing that readies a piece of discourse for someone else. "Where invention is solitary, expression is social. It involves other people."[37] Since the message must now take on importance or significance for a reading audience, it must include "all the conventions and presuppositions accepted in the society in which the participants live [and write]."[38] It must meet the standards of social communication. These standards are those particular uses of the language, rather than forms, which have developed and persisted, and which readers expect to help them along when they attempt to understand a piece of writing. Winterowd describes the process whereby the mind *intuitively* chooses devices, structure. . . that it finds significant (1975:20). But cultural and linguistic differences again often prevent the ESL writer from being able to make these choices in the intuitive manner that a native writer does. These standards—or rules, conventions, and guidelines—are "not predictable to someone who does not already know them. Without knowing the particular language or the history of its derivation, it is impossible to predict or work out what its conventions will be."[39] Since these conventions are the expected ways of expressing particular messages or views, ESL writers have a double learning need, learning to create and arrange content and learning to apply conventional forms and principles to that content. Therefore, it is essential that ESL writers have opportunities to learn, and perhaps acquire, these criteria through study and analysis of various texts, language laboratory practice, and actual practice in writing accompanied by immediate feedback from readers so that they can gain a sense of audience and reader expectation.

What writers create in the rhetorical shaping cycles—invention and arrangement of content—is best described by Winterowd as the "deep structure" (p. 166) of writing, that is, what writers derive from their experiences with life and with language and their ability to put what they want to say (or have to say) into coherent and cohesive form for readers. This involves a melding of *meaning* with *form and structure* which can be accomplished only with linguistic as well as rhetorical shaping of material. In other words, in shaping or forming the message, the writer as well as the reader is operating on a two-dimensional level. Distinctly different are the meaning within the message which, like a chameleon, changes with the different perspectives each reader brings to the piece and the syntactical or surface qualities—the "well-formedness" of the piece.[40]

Linguistic shaping involves the "well-formedness" of the piece—the unity, coherence, and cohesion of the piece of writing. It is the formulation of the surface structures which carry the deep structure of meaning forward. It deals with the mechanisms of the language that make the writing work. As such, it involves writers' "ability to compose correct sentences" as well as their "understanding of which sentences and parts of sentences are appropriate in particular contexts," states Widdowson (1978:3). The linguistic criteria the developing writer should be able to use in shaping range from clearly stating the thesis or controlling ideas of the essay, report, poem. . .to knowledge of grammatical rules, to knowing how to increase the "relative readability" of the text with a clear division of material into paragraph units, with sentence structures that emphasize meaning, and with effective word choices (concrete nouns and strong verbs)

to carry the theme forward to the readers. How then do writers achieve facile use of these criteria?

Coherence in writing is developed by logically relating the writer's series of propositions into larger units or chunks of discourse and by attention to the semantics of the written piece. Coherence of the larger units of discourse, according to Corbett, results from "cultivating the habit of thinking in an orderly, logical fashion" (1971:445). Writers shape material logically by assuring that it has one controlling idea, that all paragraphs support and relate to that one idea, that the ideas flow smoothly from beginning to end of the piece, and that each paragraph is developed cohesively. To assist the coherent display of their thoughts, practiced writers use a number of linguistic devices such as demonstrative and personal pronouns and adjectives, transitional (cause-effect, comparison-contrast, addition. . .) and connecting words, subordinate and coordinate structures, repetition of key words and phrases, and parallel use of words and other structures. (See a detailed discussion of these devices in Part II.) These devices cause the parts of sentences to "stick together" and provide logical consistency between sentences and paragraphs as well.

Cohesion, on the other hand, is achieved by relating nonstructural elements, by tying textual elements together to smooth and clarify meaning. In general, "cohesion refers to the range of possibilities that exist for linking something with what has gone before." Cohesion within the text has to do with the relationships between two or more elements in a text that are independent of the structure.[41] These relationships or ties between elements may be set up either within a sentence or between sentences; nevertheless, they serve to make the piece of writing a unified whole. The ties are directional in that they may point forward (anaphoric) or backward (cataphoric) in reference to other parts of the text. They may even refer to elements not found in the text at all (exophoric). The different kinds of ties writers need to be able to apply for maximum cohesion in a text are (1) grammatical—such as reference, substitution, and ellipsis, which convey general meaning; and (2) lexical or vocabulary—such as general nouns and reiteration with synonyms, antonyms, superordinates, and complementary terms which convey specific meaning. The differences between these two forms of cohesion are largely a matter of degree, according to Halliday. See pages 122 to 125 for an annotated example of how cohesive and coherence devices contribute to the "well-formedness" of a piece.

Further, linguistic shaping has to do with sculpting words to carry the meaning. "Every word omitted keeps another reader with you," says Elbow. Those omitted strengthen those that are left. It is something like "pulling off layers of stone...to reveal a figure beneath" (1973:41). The writer must read and reread to decide—have I used the best word or phrase to express my meaning? Are verbs strong? Active? Are nouns concrete? Are words precise? Is the vocabulary to be formal or informal? To quote Vygotsky, "The relationship between thought and word is a living process; the thought is born through words. A word devoid of thought is a dead thing, and a thought unembodied in words remains a shadow" (1962:242). Without precisely the right word(s) writers' messages too often remain shadows.

Thus, writers must focus on various elements important to the linguistic shaping of their messages. Writers must examine—

1. The overall structure of the discourse in accordance with the theme

2. The coherence of the piece which evolves from logical connections within and between sentences and paragraphs

3. The emphasis brought about by sentence structure; the organization of each sentence and its parts

4. The cohesion within and between sentences by means of ties

5. The effective and accurate choice of words

"Perception of meaning comes about through the interoperation of [the] two concepts: deep structure and grammatical transformations that bring about surface structure . . . the form is . . . the result of the interplay between (1) the invariable deep structure, (2) the surface structure the author has chosen, and (3) the other alternatives made available by the finite system of 'organizing' that the 'proposition' itself makes possible."[42]

With all the rhetorical and linguistic shaping discussed to this point, the piece of writing may be grammatically correct, but if the emphasis is misplaced, the combinations don't work, or for some other reason the message is not clearly communicated, the form is incomplete and the writer must reformulate the material. To borrow again from Ben Shahn's remarks concerning art, "the form is only the manifestation, the shape of the content" (1957:53). Thus if form is a problem, the writer needs to reexamine the content of his text.

Reformulation then becomes a conscious and sometimes even ruthless activity involving the writer as spectator and "monitor." It involves reexamining the whole composition, taking the elements the writer has decided to use and ordering, reordering, connecting, and even changing them. Only after the message is evident and fully developed can the writer proceed with giving communicable form to it.

When are writers ready to reformulate? Writers cannot revise until they have something with which to work. And as Elbow says, "Premature editing makes writing dead" (1973:6). And further, applying these critical skills too soon can cause writers to get stuck.[43] This is especially true for ESL writers whose critical language skills are mostly learned rather than acquired. An ESL writer whose "monitor" is working can consciously inspect and alter the output,[44] but reformulation for these writers is more difficult, even impossible at times, when the monitor is not in operation. Consequently, aids in monitoring are important for them until they further internalize the language conventions. In light of this knowledge, revision should occur only when the writer feels confident that the message is fully formed and worthwhile. Then and only then should the writer begin to rework the piece. However, once the first or even the second draft is complete and the writer is confident of his or her message, reformulation of the material can and should take place.

Reformulation involves two distinct activities:
1. Revision—reexamining concepts and ideas and their arrangement and emphasis in light of purpose, audience, and context

2. Editing— correcting parts of writing which are affected by sentence completeness, phrase and word choice, punctuation, spelling, paragraphing, and neatness

Revision begins when content has been developed and the piece of writing reaches the first-draft form. Most inexperienced writers see the need for revision as a signal that they have failed, and further they view revision only as the need to correct surface errors such as punctuation and spelling. After the first draft, Murray reminds us, the "amateur thinks the job is finished, and the professional knows the job has just begun" (1968:11). All effective writers know that writing is reformulating, revising, and rewriting: (1) by testing the validity of the ideas, thoughts, concepts, and perceptions they have included in the text; (2) by testing the fullness and completeness of the development of those ideas; (3) by testing the ordering of those ideas; (4) by testing the manner in which they are presented and connected; and so on. In this cycle writers must be ready and willing to view the work with a critical eye: to *rethink* the written piece in terms of the established purpose, audience, and context; to tear it apart; and even to throw it away and start again if it does not accomplish what is intended. To do this writers must take on the role of spectator and critical reader. They must imagine themselves as their own reading audience and question the clarity, understandability, and persuasiveness of the message. As spectators, writers are able to pay attention to form in a way they cannot as participants, for example, they may question: Does the writing accomplish what the writers intend or must they rediscover subject and audience? Is there a controlling idea? Is there sufficient concrete support for a thesis, or must writers further research their subjects? What forms of the language have been used? What patterns have been used to establish the intended order?

Outlining or reoutlining the piece may help the writer sift out problem areas in giving shape to the writing now; in other words, the writer may need to do some problem solving on paper before rewriting. And as writers reexamine, they must be willing to perform perhaps the hardest task of all: that of throwing out material that does not fit into the writer's controlling theme. The writer may find in this process the need to reorder ideas or perhaps even the need to change direction completely.

Mechanical shaping is the final cycle in reformulation. As such, this final shaping is what we call editing. "Almost everybody interposes a massive series of editings between the time words start to be born into consciousness and when they finally come off the end of the pencil or typewriter onto the page."[45] Editing, however, should be the last step in rewriting and should be performed only when the writer has a final draft. Since editing tends to cause writers to worry over small details, it also stifles the flow of creative ideas if attempted too soon. It is nevertheless an important function in the writing process, since neglect of mechanical rules and conventions can also impede communication. In this cycle writers check for accuracy of spelling, punctuation, paragraphing, word form and usage, and the neatness of handwriting or the accuracy of typewriting requirements. For example, they check such elements as the difference between the spelling of words like *expend* and *expand* which mistakenly used could result in the gross misunderstanding of a message. Since a misplaced comma or period or a misused exclamation point or question mark can change a reader's entire understanding of a sentence, writers read for accuracy of these mechanical devices and to ensure that all statements in each paragraph relate to the topic sentence or controlling idea. They also look for the accuracy of word forms: for instance, have writers used the form *liking* or *likeness* as they intended to use it?

Shaping is a continuous process from the beginning to the end of writing. It, like discovery and generation, is a creative part of writing, for it is the sculpting of the meaning into a pleasing form for the reader. It is inextricably related to the other functions in the writing process and stops only with the last dot of the pen on the paper.

1.4 Writing occurs through a recursive process

Writing is rewriting.

Now that he has completed that piece of writing, he can begin to write.

Donald Murray

My goal in everything I write is simplicity. I'm a demon on the subject of revision. I revise, revise, revise, until every word is what I want.

Ben Lucian Burman

As we examine the complexities of the writing process, we see that in addition to being active and creative, the writing process is also recursive. Because writers work to compose and present ideas which build upon one another, we can define writing as being linear in terms of product. However, writing is both linear and recursive in the *process* of creating that product. To transform ideas successfully from the mind to the page involves an ongoing, cyclical process during which writers move back and forth on a continuum discovering, analyzing, and synthesizing ideas which they then shape and reshape, define and redefine, evaluate and reevaluate as they write and rewrite them on the page.

The writing process involves continual shifting of the writer's focus from meaning to form and structure—from form and structure to meaning. This "shifting" occurs on two levels: (1) as writers move from the role of writer into the role of reader, and (2) as writers move from the role of writer into the role of editor. The primary focus of writers as they shift from writer to reader is on meaning. As reader, the writer tries to determine if ideas are presented with sufficient development and cohesive organization to convey the intended meaning. The primary focus of writers as they shift from writer to editor is on form and structure. Because shades of meaning and degree of emphasis of ideas are developed, in part, through form and structure, writers try to determine if sentence structure, word choices, paragraphing, and punctuation adequately shape the content to convey writers' ideas successfully from their minds to the page.

However, writers often compose papers which do not successfully transform ideas from the mind to the page. Beaugrande suggests three factors which limit the development of meaningful discourse:

(1) divergence between short-term and long-term planning, (2) the transition from the mental mode to the linear written mode, and (3) differences between forms successfully and appropriately used in composing speech and those used in composing written discourse (1978:139). The ways in which writers address these factors and create meaningful discourse illustrate the recursive properties inherent in the writing process.

1. Divergence between short-term and long-term planning. Writers often develop papers in which their ideas are incompletely explored or inadequately developed or illogically presented. This often occurs because they believe the ideas and concepts for final drafts must be fully formulated in their minds *before* any writing takes place. However, few ideas are ever fully conceived or composed without alteration. The recursive aspect of writing, then, becomes readily apparent as the writer begins to "discover" a subject. Most writers begin with some tentative plan—a vague kernel of an idea. Faced with the task of developing a vaguely formed idea, many writers simply begin writing what immediately comes to mind, "making it up as they go along."[46]

As writers select, connect, and evaluate pieces of information, they call upon personal experience and what they know about a subject and write it down. Then they reread what they have written and try to decide how to develop the idea further, express the idea in another way, or use the idea for some other purpose. Thus, during the writing process, they keep "adapting those [tentative] plans to what is discovered on the page."[47]

As writers are discovering—writing what they

know and perceive—they make systematic connections among data, ideas, and concepts. In so doing, they learn more about their subjects and apply what they have just learned to what they have already experienced. Writing, then, takes on a cyclical pattern, and a process of "developmental chaining" emerges. That is, a kernel idea may be expanded and refined, and/or a new idea may emerge as pieces of information strengthen and lengthen the kernel idea of the chain.

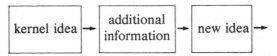

Such "developmental chaining" acts as a clarifier, enabling writers to limit, shape, and revise a subject toward which they then develop a particular point of view. The act of writing, then, makes "discovery possible by creating the possibilities for discovery."[48] The results of this process of discovery through writing may mean that the short-term idea (the writer's initial plan) is drastically altered. Conclusions formulated as the writer works through the writing process may not reflect the initial thesis and the paper may appear illogical, ill conceived, or inadequately developed.

Often writers see their papers as vague discussions of ideas that were clear and fully formulated in their minds. It is important then that they learn to look upon their initial writings, not as final drafts but as "discovery drafts." Writers need to view their first writing as means through which they develop their sense of what needs to be said. When writers are able to move comfortably on the continuum between writer and reader and analyze their work through a process defined by Perl as "retrospective structuring," they are able to develop a sharper, clearer focus for their writing. It is upon completion of this "discovery draft" that students can really begin to write.

2. The transition from the mental mode to the linear written mode. In the process of formulating or "discovering" ideas for a paper, both in the mind and in an initial draft, students often discover that another factor interferes with their ability to compose a successful paper, in one sitting, from beginning to end. They may have difficulty choosing suitable means to express and arrange ideas once the mind begins to formulate them.

The mind does not work in a linear fashion, with ideas arranged in an orderly way like building blocks, each existing as a separate entity. Because of this, writers are often unable to commit words to paper as quickly as the mind produces the sentences and phrases. As Emig's work suggests (see Section 1.3 for an extensive discussion), the hand and eye work to slow down the writing process. As writers put their words on paper, they pause and reread their sentences. As they physically write, their minds do not stop thinking. New insights may come to them or their train of thought may be interrupted and an idea forgotten or confused. As a result of this recursiveness between the mental and linear modes, students become frustrated in their writing attempts, commenting "I know it in my head, but I just can't express it on paper," or "I had it all mapped out in my head, but I forgot how I wanted to put it in words when I started to write it."

We hear these statements because, again, writers shift their focus. They move from the role of writer to reader and focus less on conceptual meaning and more on the form and structure necessary to convey meaning. Here, writers must ask themselves what forms of discourse are most appropriate to convey meaning. Do they want to describe? Explain? Narrate? Or persuade? The decision will determine what structures will most effectively develop the form. They must make decisions about the arrangement of material and style of presentation. Perl suggests that writers, during this cycle, have engaged in "projective structuring" (1980:368), that is, shaping one's sense of what one wants to say so it is intelligible to others. There is constant interaction or overlapping of planning and writing as writers continually evaluate their work by asking, "Is this saying what I am trying to say? Is the main idea evident?"

During this cycle of the writing process, an order for the paper begins to emerge and the writer is able to move back into the writer role and add or delete information to strengthen and clarify meaning. Thus, the writer engages in a process of revision described by Emig as "the outcome of dialogue between ourselves as writer and ourselves as audience, an exchange in which our needs as readers become paramount."[49]

Revision, then, is further writing. Yet the term revising or rewriting has for many writers (particularly student-writers) an "aura of failure about it." Students conceptualize rewriting to mean "I am a failure." "I must be quite stupid or else I wouldn't need to rewrite this." For ESL students, particularly, there is a high degree of frustration coupled with that sense of failure. They see writing inadequacies as a direct result of their limited vocabularies, incomplete mastery of grammatical structures, or incorrect use of mechanical devices. They do not think of revision or rewriting in terms of meaning and form but only in terms of structure. Therefore, they are further frustrated when they correct a paper in the editorial sense and their reader still says, "I don't understand what you mean. What idea are you trying to develop?"

As teachers we need to help our students see that rewriting is an integral part of the composing process, not something done *after* the process is complete. As Sommers says, "I rewrite as I write" (1980:383). Therefore, rewriting should be, as Murray believes, "the most exciting, satisfying and significant part of the writing process" (1978a:86). In order to come to this view of writing, we need to help our students understand what is happening as they are composing. Schor suggests that the "recursive acts of the writing process should be isolated and understood by students as constituent acts in every episode of writing" (1979:78). This is particularly important for ESL students so that they move beyond revising only to satisfy rules (grammar, word usage/form, punctuation, and spelling) and revise also to improve content meaning. We need to encourage our students to think of rewriting as an opportunity to think about, respond to, and restructure ideas.[50] If students recognize that departures from and expansions of ideas are natural to the composing process, then the transition from the mental mode to the linear written mode can be viewed as a factor which does not impede the writing process but instead enhances it.

3. Differences between forms used in composing speech and those used in composing written discourse. Student-writers need to recognize that they cannot simply "write-as-they-talk." Sentence structures and patterns must be more carefully formulated, word choices more precise, and ideas organized in a manner readily coherent to the reader. These factors all contribute to the readability of the text.

Students need to recognize that—

> writing is a highly stylized, conventional system for transcription, rather than a graphic "tape-recorder" of oral language that operates just like an acoustic tape recorder. The written symbols are related to the sound symbols of oral language, but the relationships are stylized, conventionalized arrangements that are socially agreed upon.[51]

Our ESL writers need to learn the linguistic and mechanical conventions of writing because it is only by employing accepted devices that they will be able to communicate effectively to their readers. Thus we need to familiarize our students with conventions of syntax, spelling, and punctuation. For ESL students this often means learning a grammar system vastly different from that of their first language. However, it requires utilizing understandings of first language grammar and applying this knowledge to learning in the second language grammar.

Equally significant are the rhetorical conventions which student-writers must understand. They need to learn that readers do not want to be misled, confused, bored, or lied to, that readers want to understand clearly, easily, and quickly. Readers want to be treated honestly. If the anticipated rapport fails to develop between themselves and the printed page, they will stop reading.

In order to meet these reader expectations, writers must imagine or create reading audiences because they cannot rely on immediate feedback from an audience in face-to-face contact with the speaker. Having formulated audiences in their minds, writers must then work to (1) present ideas that the reader easily understands, (2) develop those ideas completely, in full detail, and (3) arrange them in a meaningful order.

Students will be more effective writers when they arrive at the understanding that writing is a process—a process whose stages can be identified and whose elements can be learned. As teachers, then, we need to provide our students with the methods and materials to understand the stages of the writing process, and opportunities to engage actively in the process.

DEEP STRUCTURE

Sit very quietly and stare at your words
And they will not move or change into anything.
It will be a while till the ideas fall away
Or you fall away from them and begin to see
The linked shapes and the lines where the pieces join.
But do not stop there, listen until you hear
A quiet humming and clicking deep below,
And as you sit looking at your sentence
You will realize it hangs on the edge of a gulf
That drips down, down, beyond belief.
And down there in the darkness you are working
Sorting, shifting, comparing, accepting, rejecting
Cutting a rough thing so it may rise

Taking on color and sex and time and number
And coming into clear as it molds itself
To the precise shape of your ideas.
And when you have seen it, you will begin to know
That where you started is the end, and you must go
Down through the lovely chain of movement and
    change
Down to the bottom of the dark pool
Where furiously sleep ideas, green, colorless.

Robert C. Rainsbury[52]

Notes

[1]Daniel John Fogarty, *Roots for a New Rhetoric* (New York: Teacher's College, Columbia University, 1959), 33.

[2]Loren S. Barrett and Barry M. Kroll, "Some Implications of Cognitive-Developmental Psychology for Research in Composing," in *Research on Composing: Points of Departure,* ed. Charles R. Cooper and Lee Odell (Urbana, Ill.: National Council of Teachers of English, 1978), 51.

[3]L. S. Vygotsky, *Thought and Language,* ed. and trans. by Eugenia Hanfmann and Gertrude Vakar (Boston and New York: The M.I.T. Press and John Wiley & Sons, Inc.), 98.

[4]E. D. Hirsch, Jr., *The Philosophy of Composition* (Chicago-London: The University of Chicago Press, 1977), 21.

[5]Phillip Lopate, "Helping Young Children Start to Write," in *Research on Composing: Points of Departure,* ed. Charles R. Cooper and Lee Odell (Urbana, Ill.: National Council of Teachers of English, 1978), 140.

[6]Hirsch, p. 21.

[7]Lopate, p. 140.

[8]Barrett and Kroll, p. 52.

[9]Barrett and Kroll, p. 53.

[10]Donn Byrne, *Teaching Writing Skills* (London: Longmans Group, Ltd., 1979), 97.

[11]William F. Irmscher, *Teaching Expository Writing* (New York: Holt, Rinehart and Winston, 1979), 243.

[12]W. Ross Winterowd, *Contemporary Rhetoric, A Conceptual Background with Readings* (New York: Harcourt Brace Jovanovich, Inc., 1975), 16.

[13]James Britton, Tony Burgess, Nancy Martin, Alex McLeod, and Harold Rosen, *The Development of*

Writing Abilities (Hong Kong: Schools Council Publications, 1975), 32.

[14]Walter T. Petty, "The Writing of Young Children," in *Research on Composing: Points of Departure,* ed. Charles R. Cooper and Lee Odell (Urbana, Ill.: National Council of Teachers of English, 1978), 78–79.

[15]Barret J. Mandel, "The Writer Writing Is Not at Home," *College Composition and Communication,* 31 (December 1980), 373.

[16]Sondra Perl, "Understanding Composition," *College Composition and Communication,* 31 (December 1980), 365.

[17]Eva S. Weiner and Larry E. Smith, "Language Development through Writing," *Cross Currents,* ed. Gerry Ryan, Howard Sietou, and Nobuhito Seto, 7, no. 2 (1980), 11.

[18]Joseph Comprone, "Kenneth Burke and the Teaching of Writing," *College Composition and Communication,* 29, no. 4 (December 1978), 336–340.

[19]Byrne, p. 120.

[20]Nan Elsasser and Vera P. John-Steiner, "An Interactionist Approach to Advancing Literacy," *Harvard Educational Review,* 68, no. 3 (1977), 359.

[21]Donald M. Murray, *A Writer Teaches Writing* (Boston: Houghton Mifflin Company, 1968), 30.

[22]Tony Buzan, *Use Both Sides of Your Brain* (New York: E. P. Dutton, 1976), 17.

[23]Elsasser and John-Steiner, p. 360.

[24]Robert de Beaugrande, "The Processes of Invention: Association and Recombination," *College Composition and Communication,* 30 (October 1979), 260–267.

[25]Frank J. D'Angelo, "The Search for Intelligible Structure in the Teaching of Composition," *College Composition and Communication*, 27 (May 1976), 53.

[26]Irmscher, p. 20.

[27]Winterowd, p. 21.

[28]Murray, p. 2.

[29]Irmscher, p. 20.

[30]Carol Feiser Laque and Phyllis A. Sherwood, *A Laboratory Approach to Writing* (Urbana, Ill.: National Council of Teachers of English, 1977).

[31]Murray, p. 3.

[32]D'Angelo, p. 53.

[33]Beaugrande, p. 261.

[34]Caroline D. Eckhardt and David H. Stewart, "Towards a Functional Taxonomy of Composition," *College Composition and Communication*, 30, no. 4 (1979), 338.

[35]Beaugrande, p. 260.

[36]Britton, p. 9.

[37]Sharon Crowley and George Redman, "Why Teach Writing?" *College Composition and Communication* (October 1975), 280.

[38]Britton, p. 9.

[39]Frank Smith, "Demonstrations, Engagement and Sensitivity: A Revised Approach to Language Learning," *Language Arts* (January 1981), 2.

[40]Douglas R. Hofsteadter, *Gödel Escher Bach: An Eternal Golden Braid* (New York: Vintage Books—Division of Random House, 1980), 582.

[41]M. A. Halliday and Ruquaiya Hasan, *Cohesion in English* (London: Longmans Group, Ltd., 1979), 29.

[42]Winterowd, p. 166.

[43]H. G. Widdowson, *Teaching Language as Communication* (Oxford: Oxford University Press, 1978), 45.

[44]Stephen D. Krashen, "The Monitor Model for Adult Second Language Performance," *Readings in English as a Second Language,* ed. Kenneth Croft (Cambridge: Winthrop Publishing, 1980), 215.

[45]Peter Elbow, *Writing without Teachers* (New York: Oxford University Press, 1973), 5.

[46]Sondra Perl and Arthur Egendorf, "The Process of Creative Discovery: Theory, Research, and Implications for Teaching," in *Linguistics, Stylistics, and the Teaching of Composition,* ed. Donald McQuade (Ohio: University of Akron, 1979), 118.

[47]Donald M. Murray, "Internal Revision: A Process of Discovery," in *Research on Composing: Points of Departure,* ed. Charles R. Cooper and Lee Odell (Urbana, Ill.: National Council of Teachers of English, 1978), 89.

[48]Perl, p. 120.

[49]Janet A. Emig, "Hand, Eye, Brain: Some Basics of the Writing Process," in *Research on Composing: Points of Departure,* ed. Charles R. Cooper and Lee Odell (Urbana, Ill.: National Council of Teachers of English, 1978), 66.

[50]Nancy I. Sommers, "Revision Strategies of Student Writers and Experienced Adult Writers," *College Composition and Communication,* 31 (December 1980), 383.

[51]Thomas J. Farrell, "Differentiating Writing from Talking," *College Composition and Communication,* 29 (December 1979), 346.

[52]*Journal of English as a Second Language,* 3, no. 2 (Fall 1968), A.

CHAPTER TWO

WHY WRITE? WRITING IS A LIFETIME SKILL

Writing, like life itself, is a voyage of discovery.

Henry Miller

Writing can and should be a stimulating, challenging activity central to all learning and development because, as Irmscher says, "Once we move students beyond those basic levels of proficiency [grammatical structure and basic punctuation], we then see new dimensions of expressiveness, imaginativeness, and intellectual growth that are accessible only to someone engaged in composing, whether that performance is acting, dancing, painting, or writing."[1]

Every sentence uttered is a composition. Each time a series of sentences is successful in gratifying some need, an effective composition has been created. Composing is thus inherent in using language, and every individual has the capability to compose.[2] Naturally, the degree to which each of us uses this capability is highly variable. It is our responsibility as teachers to help learners discover that composing written discourse is a natural act, that it is a means to learn about themselves and the world around them, as well as an important means to express themselves.

Many learners see writing only as a classroom exercise, something done to satisfy the English teacher and then to be tossed aside. They view it as a series of "themes" or essay responses to teacher-created questions. Thus, for most student-writers, writing becomes an isolated act, for an audience of one, with the sole purpose of being graded, returned, and then forgotten. Indeed, much of the writing produced as a result of this attitude *is* tossed aside and forgotten because, all too often, it expresses not the author's view but the teacher's views as perceived by the student-writer. The writing that results is artificial, projecting a "supposed" point of view rather than one developed by exploration of the self—of the writer's own ideas, values, and perceptions.

How much more rewarding writing will be if learners come to view writing as an essential lifetime skill—a skill which, because of its multiple uses and functions, will enable them to continually expand their personal horizons. Student-writers need to recognize that mastering the complexities of the writing process not only will help them attain their immediate goals—well-written essays, reports, and research papers—but will also serve them far beyond the confines of the English classroom.

One of our most critical responsibilities as writing teachers is to communicate to our students this broader view of the functions and benefits of writing. As a lifetime skill, writing serves four crucial, enduring purposes for the learner: communication, critical thinking and problem solving, self-actualization, and control of personal environment.

2.1 Writing is an essential form of communication

Almost all that we are is related to our use of words.

Bergen Evans

Through writing we express our feelings—our hopes, dreams, and joys as well as our fears, angers, and frustrations. Writing, then, is a letter to the family recounting the delights of discovering new friends or the loneliness of days spent in a new environment without the supportive bonds of family

33

love. Writing is a letter to a manufacturer detailing the weaknesses of a recently purchased product. Writing is a daily journal recounting the delights of a vacation abroad. It is a letter to Santa Claus, a memo to the plumber, or a thank you note to a thoughtful friend.

Through writing we express our ideas—our plans, our recommendations, our values, and our commitments. We explain to others who we are, what we believe and understand, and why we believe and understand as we do. For students, writing is a primary medium through which they demonstrate their understanding and interpretation of concepts and theories studied for many weeks or months. For the city council representative, writing is a position statement drafted to detail why increased property taxes will be detrimental to the community. For the engineer, writing is explaining a new design for a piece of equipment. For the lawyer, writing is the briefs and position papers prepared for clients. For the agronomist, writing is a proposal advocating more efficient harvest procedures and controlled use of fertilizers. Almost all these tasks, though disparate in purpose, invariably require use of the multiparagraph composing skills learned in the composition class.

In every composing task, the writer's success depends to a great extent on how well information, ideas, beliefs, and impressions are conveyed "across barriers of time and distance."[3] The person receiving information (the reader) not only must recognize and comprehend the points that the writer is trying to make but must also "assign to them the same relative importance and internal coherence" as the writer.[4] Thus written words are "the fragile bridges upon which our thoughts must travel."[5]

2.2 Writing is for critical thinking and problem solving

How do I know what I think until I see what I say?

E. M. Forster

Written words serve not only as bridges for our thoughts but also as barometers for our thoughts. Words are the vehicle to express our thoughts, which we then measure against our experience and that of others. Used as such, writing helps us think critically, a crucial ability in our complex, media-oriented society which constantly bombards us with information. Some of this barrage is entertaining, some depressing, some useful, some useless, some significant, some insignificant, some inspiring, some frightening. Some information evokes response or action; some does not. The mind is forced to sift through a kaleidoscope of perceptions and thoughts to establish a pattern of what is meaningful and to help us make some sense of our lives and the world around us.

Writing helps us sort through this kaleidoscope of thoughts, as Irmscher notes, to bring "thought into consciousness, making it available both for us and for others to see" (1979b:243). Through writing we can explore our deepest thoughts and feelings, discover and explore our biases, and confront our values. Writing can help us discover gaps in our understanding and flaws in our thinking. It can tell us when we need to gather additional information or insights, when we need to rethink a question, or when we need to discard a belief or idea. Writing becomes then a way of defining ourselves and our problems, of clarifying our knowledge and our ideas, of understanding and solving our problems.

Writing, then, is a means to sift and refine our perceptions of the world around us. It requires us to measure our thoughts on a continuum outside of the self. Once we have written an idea down, we become the reader, the evaluator of that idea, moving outside ourselves and putting distance between the idea and ourselves. From this vantage point we are able to look at and examine the thought, concept, or experience from a new perspective, within a larger framework than existed within us before the idea took shape on paper. We call upon what we have read, what we have observed, and what we have experienced to verify, modify, or crystallize our thoughts. By arranging and sorting perceptions and knowledge "under a relevant and more inclusive conceptual system,"[6] we gain new insights, discover different perspectives, and in the process, are led to the discovery of meaning.

2.3 Writing is for self-actualization

Language is the mother, not the handmaiden, of thought;
words tell you things you never thought or felt before.

W. H. Auden

Edward Albee is quoted by Murray (1968) as saying, "Writing has got to be an act of discovery. I write to discover what I am thinking about." Writing, as a way of discovering and developing ourselves, is a means for self-actualization. What we learn about ourselves and develop within ourselves through writing can help us to realize our individual potential and to achieve personal goals. Therefore, besides being an external activity through which we communicate with others, writing also serves our innerselves. As an inner-directed activity, writing is, as Irmscher notes, "a way of connecting with ourselves, an internal communication. In writing, this externalizing and internalizing occur at one and the same time. Putting out is putting in" (p. 242). Thus, when we write we are also discovering something about who we are and what we believe. Through writing we learn by becoming aware of ourselves.

As we continuously select, reject, codify, and modify the numerous bits of data and sensory impressions constantly impinging on our consciousness, our own understanding and perspective begin to take shape. Writing helps us make the connections, "fashioning a network of associations and increasing our potential for learning."[7] Writing is a contemplative, ever-developing skill which allows us to draw upon our inner resources to explore many different aspects of ourselves as unique individuals. This ability to realign, clarify, and reshape information makes possible the never-ending discovery of new ideas, ideas which themselves trigger whole *new* cycles of sifting, searching, and discovering. Writing thus enables us to continually grow and develop: We can willfully project goals for ourselves. We can more clearly define our own expectations. Pathways are opened and avenues are created, showing us the way for further exploration.

As part of the basic human quest for self-actualization, one immediate goal frequently held by student-writers is success in the academic world. They need to demonstrate their knowledge, their understanding of subject matter, and their ability to communicate that knowledge and understanding intelligently to another person. They are required to write reports, research papers, and essay examinations to show that they know and understand the thoughts of others and can synthesize the new knowledge into their own thinking. Their success is determined, at least in part, by how efficiently meaning is conveyed. The ability to produce well-written papers will enhance students' academic success because of what Hirsch calls the principle of "relative readability":

> Increased communicative efficiency is a universal tendency in the history of all languages. This trend is to achieve the same effects with less and less reader effort. . . . The tendency to greater linguistic efficiency is a universal because for mankind it is a human universal to minimize time and effort in order to produce the same effect (1977:54).

Thus, student-writers need to have writing skills which enable them to address problems explicitly, accurately, and concisely.

Research data from second language learning suggest that writing also serves to foster development in the other modes of language.[8] For second language students, writing becomes a means to improve other language skills. As learners seek to present and explain their ideas in writing, they search for precise word choices and suitable structures in which to frame their ideas. Writing enables them to expand these other areas as they work to develop fluency in the language. As they search for evidence to support a point of view or position on an issue, their reading skills are enhanced. Through reading, their writing skills are reinforced. They begin to acquire a feel for the readers' expectations which in turn influence each student's composing process.

2.4 Writing helps us control our personal environment

Rhetoric is the use of language to promote
human cooperation in the human jungle.

Kenneth Burke

In our complex society, the world has shrunk immeasurably in the last 50 years. Communication is almost instantaneous. Those who are proficient in English are able to compete more successfully in English-speaking societies as well as to engage in social and professional discourse with those in other societies who do not share a common first language but do share English as their second language.

ESL students often see speaking the language—being able to communicate with others in face-to-face encounters—as the only worthwhile goal of the language class. But they also need to recognize that writing in a second language serves them beyond the moments when they are with friends, teachers, other students, and colleagues in a classroom-related setting. Through writing they can continue communication from afar once they have returned to their countries or taken jobs at great distances from familiar academic settings. Therefore, student-writers need to recognize that writing is a tool for survival in the "real world," that is, the world beyond the classroom. Writing is a tool upon which we continually rely.

ESL students frequently view writing in English as nonessential to meeting their urgent and daily needs. Yet writing is closely tied to daily communication in the "real world," and students need to be encouraged to believe that they will never attain full literacy in their second language until they have achieved competence in writing. Writing competence reflects overall achievement in language, and learners who have developed the ability to communicate effectively in the written medium of a language have indeed made the langauge their own.

With increasing numbers of nonnative speakers entering English-speaking countries each year, writing is a crucial component of the language these learners will need to acquire. Many come to acquire skills or technology in a given area and then return to their native countries. Though these students often argue that writing in a second language is not essential, we know that it is essential to their academic success while studying and that when they return to their countries and take up positions of leadership, their facility with the writing process will be critical to their success whether they are in business, industry, government, or social services.

Many other nonnative speakers become permanent residents or citizens of an English-speaking country. To be productive members of their adopted society, they must be able to use English, their adopted language, effectively. This means being able to manipulate the language to meet their daily needs. Nonnative speakers must be able to complete a job application, look up numbers in a phone book, write a note to a child's teacher, fill out a loan application, and read a daily newspaper. It means being able to participate fully in the democratic process by furthering an education and being able to evaluate stated positions in order to make wise decisions at the ballot box. Developing writing skill can foster these abilities, since writing enables writers to look within themselves to clarify ideas, attitudes, and beliefs. Writing, then, is a means to know the self, a means to control the personal environment.

36

Notes

[1]William F. Irmscher, "Writing as a Way of Learning and Developing," *College Composition and Communication,* 79 (October 1979), 241.

[2]Walter Petty, "Writing of Young Children," in *Research on Composing: Points of Departure,* ed. Charles R. Cooper and Lee Odell (Urbana, Ill.: National Council of Teachers of English, 1978), 75.

[3]Donald M. Murray, *A Writer Teaches Writing* (Boston: Houghton Mifflin Company, 1968), 1.

[4]Robert de Beaugrande, "Linguistic Theory and Composition," *College Composition and Communication,* 29 (May 1978), 138.

[5]Nan El Sasser and Vera P. John-Steiner, "An Interactionist Approach to Advancing Literacy," *Harvard Educational Review,* 27 (August 1977), 359.

[6]David P. Ausubel, "Cognitive Structure and the Facilitation of Meaningful Verbal Learning," in *Reading in the Psychology of Cognition,* ed. Richard C. Anderson and David P. Ausubel (New York: Holt, Rinehart and Winston, 1965), 105.

[7]Irmscher, p. 244.

[8]John W. Oller, Jr., *Language Tests at School* (London: Longmans Group, Ltd.), 382.

CHAPTER THREE

WRITING CAN BE TAUGHT

3.1 Perspectives on teaching writing

Language is the tool that makes human beings uniquely different from other animals, and writing is certainly essential in language use. Writing, as a significant part of language, is mysterious and exciting. It is the sum of our abilities to link words and thoughts in order to express ourselves in the most complex of mediums. It is a holistic process we engage in to understand ourselves and to make ourselves understood to others through barriers of time and distance. It is a lifetime coping skill which expands and enriches our lives as it develops, giving us fresh insights and greater power to describe, explain, instruct, persuade, and emote. Writing is also difficult, often the most difficult of all language skills in both first and second language development.

No wonder that so many of us are concerned with the complex mysteries of so important a process and that we continue to question just how it works. Just as in any other complex process, if we are to understand the writing process and use it more effectively, we must divide the whole of writing into parts we can describe, define, analyze, and finally put back together. What writing is and how it is developed has been a subject for discussion and debate for centuries—from its roots in the theories of Aristotle, Cicero, and Quintilian to the current philosophies of Winterowd, D'Angelo, Kinneavy, and many others. As Winterowd so aptly states, "Anyone who has been in the business of composition . . . knows the winds of fashion waft theory and practice from one pole to another and back again" (1975:8). Today, we sense the winds of change in the teaching of writing as debates go on among teachers and researchers.

A look at some of the seemingly dichotomous theories or positions of writing points up critical questions about the nature of writing and reveals insights and guideposts for us as teachers of writing.

IS WRITING PRODUCT OR PROCESS?

The tendency of current traditional rhetoric [is] to become a critical study of the products of composing and an art of editing.
—Donald G. Stewart

The bulk of instruction . . . devoted to writing was instruction after the fact . . . after papers had been written.—Squire, Applebee

If we use textbooks as a guide, we can say . . . that the emphasis in teaching writing . . . was primarily on the product—the final written essay.—Irmscher

The product is not behavior, nor does it represent what has gone on in the individual's mind. It is only a product; process is what people do.—Petty

Writing is a process of problem-solving—a way of processing information to attain goals.
—Flower

When we are successful at this process, we end up with a product that teaches us something, that clarifies what we know . . . and that lifts out or explicates or enlarges our experience.—Perl

Writing is a transcription of the process of composing ideas: it is not the product of thought but its actualization and dramatization.
—Comprone

Most frequently, the writing produced for classes is viewed as product; discussion centers around the produced essay (or poem or whatever). Equal emphasis should be placed on the process. How did the piece of discourse get produced? How did the writer generate his ideas?—Winterowd

To develop . . . strategies we must direct our attention not only to written products but to the cognitive underpinnings of those products.
—Elsasser, John-Steiner

We assert that writing instruction requires an emphasis on *both* product and process. As demonstrated in our discussion in Chapter 1, we see as critical the change of emphasis from focus on the *product* and its analysis to *process* as the means to achieve the desired product. Process and product must go hand in hand, since one is the creative activity leading to the other. But how do we help writers arrive at desired "end" products?

SHOULD WRITING BE APPROACHED THROUGH TECHNIQUE OR PURPOSE?

Present textbooks are technique oriented and taught as if method was the achievement. —Eckhardt, Stewart

The most important techniques to be taught are the integrative, middle range . . . [which] bridge the gap between readable single sentences and readable discourse. —Hirsch

Texts teach writing by showing the abstract form of "prose"; they assume that if the student knows organization and form . . . he can organize and form a paper. —Judy

Good writers are more concerned with the purpose of writing than poor writers. —Stallard

Purpose is catalyst to schema. —Winterowd

*Writing will not emerge without an underlying intention.
A reader constitutes a purpose . . .* —Smith

The aim of discourse determines everything else in the process of discourse. —Kinneavy

It may be convenient, but it is abnormal, to concentrate on the comparison-contrast method of structuring a paper without knowing why one is engaged in that activity at all. . . . An approach through [purpose] may more nearly correspond to the natural way in which the mind assimilates information. The purpose . . . becomes paramount; the writer selects whatever tools, instruments, and tactics seem most functional to that purpose. —Eckhardt, Stewart

Writing instruction must emphasize that both purpose and technique are essential to the creative process of writing. Writers must have intent or purpose before meaningful communication can

occur; purpose, in turn, determines the most *appropriate* techniques to carry it forward. Purpose and technique are inseparable, but as is true with process and product, one must precede the other to achieve the desired "end." Then how do we help ESL writers achieve success in developing the proper techniques and content necessary to create the "end" product?

SHOULD WRITING BE CONTROLLED OR FREE?

When you are sure you understand the model, perfectly . . . make a copy of the model composition. This will help you learn how to write correctly in English. —Baskoff

The most important justification for using controlled composition in the ESL classroom lies in the realm of motivation. —Root

We have to master written forms of the language and learn certain structures. —Byrne

Writing according to formula is hack writing. . . . I think the writing class should be a happy anarchy giving students rich opportunities for any kind of composition they need, either for "real" uses or for self-expression. —Winterowd

Goal . . . to become independent of the controls of both the text and the teacher . . . [to] be able to self-monitor and self-correct. —Buckingham

The emphasis has been on various kinds of controlled and guided exercises, designed to lead the learners gradually and systematically towards free expression. —Byrne

It is possible to structure the development of writing skills in the foreign language situation. [A] teacher who has had to try to assess the "free" writing of inexperienced foreign learners of English will appreciate the need for some kind of controlled or guided writing, at least in the early stages. —Broughton

Free writing (pre-writing, associational writing, unstructured writing, journal keeping) is . . . actual writing. . . . [These forms] rehabilitate the student's ability to tap the right hemispheric functions of the brain. —Mandel

Free association has already been used with moderate success ... as a heuristic procedure for invention.—D'Angelo

Since ESL writers do not bring English writer intuitions of language use and structure to the act of writing, both "controlled" and "free" writing instruction are essential to their development of communicative competence. Controlled writing shows beginning ESL writers what the expected forms and structures are while "free" writing provides them an early opportunity to find their own "voices" and to become independent writers. However, frequent "free" writing activity is more desirable at the middle to upper levels of writing. Thus we are led to ask: Do ESL writers need to practice creative writing, in the traditional sense, as well as to learn functional writing skills?

SHOULD WRITING BE TAUGHT AS CREATIVE OR FUNCTIONAL?

Our three principal categories of writing functions [are] ...
transactional ↔ expressive ↔ poetic.—Britton

It is time for writing teachers to take seriously those who create.—Mandel

Except for private or highly personal expression students write for an audience and need audience response.—Lamberg

Writing is a problem-solving cognitive process.—Flower

I believe the only real "use" of writing ... is self-expression (which I take to be concomitant with self-discovery).—Winterowd

Writing activities should be in the form of realistic tasks such as report and letter writing. ... Mastery of specific forms of writing, such as essays...needs to be taken into account.—Byrne

Most people learn foreign languages for functional reasons.—Broughton

We believe that *all* writing must be taught as creative because of the creative processes that make any and all writing possible. While ESL writers are less likely to need or use literary (or poetic) forms of writing frequently as a lifetime skill, this genre can

help them discover themselves and what they have to say. These discoveries assist writers in "getting something done" in the more frequently used functional forms (exposition and argument) that the real world requires. Therefore, we believe writing instruction is both creative and functional in its approach: creative in its development and functional in its purpose.

SHOULD WRITING BE TAUGHT IN LINEAR STAGES OR RECURSIVE CYCLES?

Rhetorical models are linear because they were created to serve oratory.—Sommers

Our study of the process led us to consider three stages: preparation, incubation, and articulation.—Britton

I rewrite as I write.... Writing is like a seed not a line; it confuses beginning and end, conception and production.—Sommers

Writing is recursive.... If the process is working, we begin to move along, sometimes quickly. Other times, we need to see if we captured what we meant to say. Sometimes after rereading we move on again, picking up speed. Other times we realize we have gone off the track...and we need to reassess.—Perl

We are not concerned with "recipes" or "formulas" for writing ... but with procedures such as outlining, drafting, and improving drafts.—Byrne

Rewriting or reformulation of early drafts enables writers to discover and shape their meanings.—Cooper-Odell

The composing process is neither linear, nor recursive, but must be by its very nature both linear and recursive.—Sommers

The writing path leads to the end product. Writers begin with a purpose and end with the accomplishment of a goal; however, along the way there are many diversions, side lanes, and circular walks writers must take before they arrive at their destinations. From our discussions in Chapter 1, it is obvious that we believe writing must be taught in recursive cycles rather than in the more traditional linear stages of prewriting, writing, and revising. We believe it is crucial for students to perceive the cyclical integrated nature of the various creative processes in writing. Because of the numerous diversions, we are forced to examine—

SHOULD WRITING INSTRUCTION EMPHASIZE QUANTITY OR QUALITY?

The quantity before quality approach, advocated by Briere . . . held that it was better to get students to write as much as possible, even if they made large numbers of mistakes.
—Byrne

If you put all of a student's writing under the gun of quality evaluation, you can only hope to produce correct *or* acceptable *writing, not good writing.*—Elbow

ESL texts should provide fewer exercises and more generating discussion and models to show what good writing is.—Root

A happy combination is the best of both worlds. An emphasis on quantity in daily writing exercises, in journal keeping, in discovery exercises, can help writers overcome their fears, boost their confidence, and develop the writing habit. It can also create a repository of ideas upon which students can draw. Emphasizing quality production in class assignments is also necessary to help writers develop an understanding of the critical role of shaping in the writing process, a sense of responsibility to an audience and pride in a finished product.

SHOULD WRITING INSTRUCTION BE DIRECTED OR FACILITATED?

The primary process of writing instruction consists of having students write compositions followed by teacher "correction" and the subsequent return of compositions.
—Squire, Applebee

For educators the challenge, then, is to develop a teaching methodology . . . that allows people previously excluded to master the written word.—Elsasser, John-Steiner

Good writers do not have to be taught; they can be completely self-taught . . . they have . . . developed . . . a respect for language, a taste for phrase, and a sense of proportion . . . through their own reading. Reading is ultimately the best teacher of environment.—Irmscher

In the actual classroom the teacher speaks and the students listen. . . . the writing teacher who teaches least usually teaches most if his students work in an environment which allows them to teach themselves.—Murray

Writing is learned by writing, by reading —and by perceiving oneself as a writer. . . . None of this can be taught . . . Writing is fostered rather than taught, and what teachers require is . . . an understanding of the task a (child) faces in learning to write. . . . The teacher must provide an environment in which a child will want to write and in which a child can learn about writing.—Smith

A balance of instruction and independent work helps writers mature more quickly in their development. Since ESL students are unaware of many of the structures and modes of the language, and the expectations of readers, these elements must be taught. But the best means of teaching independence is in facilitating writing—that is, fostering or becoming a part of the peer group dynamics in which everyone writes and everyone reacts to the writing.

WHICH SHOULD ESL STUDENTS LEARN FIRST, SPEAKING OR WRITING?

He (Smith) finds that fluent writers normally draw very little on the relationship between the sound of a word and its representation on paper. They relate orthography to meaning.—Britton

Because speaking before writing is the natural order in first language learning, it is not necessarily the only, or the most advantageous order in second language learning.
—Allen

Writing is important . . . paradoxically, we can only improve our spoken language by writing.—Smith

Since these two language modes reinforce and strengthen each other, since ESL student-writers frequently function in an English academic setting where ability to comprehend and express complex ideas with oral and written language is a requisite, and since more abstract ideas and complex concepts can be presented in written forms, writing and oral skills should be learned and/or acquired simultaneously. Indeed, all language modes are highly interrelated and draw on many of the same creative processes. Thus, it is not possible or even advisable to teach one skill in isolation from the others.

Product or process, technique or purpose, controlled or free, creative or functional, linear or recursive, quantity or quality, directed or facilitated, oral or written, cognition or insight. . .we believe these different notions are complementary rather than opposing concepts and thus we have incorporated many aspects of them into our own philosophy of teaching writing.

3.2 The role of the teacher

And gladly wolde he learn and gladly teche.

Geoffrey Chaucer

"Can we teach composition and what evidence is there that we can? And if we can, how?" questions Winterowd. Many writing teachers reach the conclusion that "writing is far too difficult a skill to be taught and yet, we do teach it" (1975:20). We readily acknowledge that writing is complex, difficult, frustrating, and even exhausting. But we believe that writing can also be challenging, rewarding, and exciting for both teacher and learner.

Though writing approaches vary and methods are subject to ongoing controversies and change, we believe writing can and must be taught. And indeed we *do* teach it. Armed with an understanding of the various approaches to the creative processes of writing, let us examine the characteristics and expectations that contribute to the success, the reward, and the challenge experienced by teachers and learners of writing.

We are going to discuss the teaching of ESL writing from the "hypothetical mode"—defined by Jerome Bruner as the position in which the teacher and the student work together. In the hypothetical mode the teacher and student "are on a more or less equal level of participation and collaboration."[1] In such a setting, the role of the teacher is that of a catalyst. The teacher not only disseminates answers but also explores questions with the students. The teacher raises issues which are explored and analyzed by both students *and* teachers. In such a setting, the student assumes a very active role. Students not only are involved in solutions to problems but they also become involved in the formulations and evaluation of questions and answers. Issues are fully explored, questions are frequently raised, strategies are hypothesized; sometimes strategies are discarded and questions are left unanswered. Expectations of both students and teachers are high, progress is recognized, and regressions are treated as opportunities upon which to build rather than as failures.

In such a setting, the lines between teacher and learner are not arbitrarily defined. Both participants take responsibility for their endeavors, and such a setting leads to increased creativity. Learning becomes, as described by Estacio, "a kind of discovery—a method of problem solving, generating the kind of learning which is not mere yielding to insensitive and repetitive pressure from without, but learning through controlled thought—a kind of learning characterized by growth from within" (1969:193).

To ensure that we give our students every opportunity to grow from within, to reach their potential as responsible, productive citizens in a complex world, let's look first at the qualities of the teacher, whose role is paramount in creating a successful writing environment. For many who have observed the productive writing environment, "there can be no doubt that the single most important factor in the instructional process—the most important variable—is the teacher."[2]

What, then, must the ESL teacher bring to the teaching of writing?

AN ATTITUDE

Let your greatest concern be the needs and motivations of your students.—Prator

1. Teachers of writing perceive their students as writers. Students do want to write because the human desire to communicate is a basic need. Writing is frequently perceived as difficult, but students will write, and write well, when the teacher approaches the writing process firm in the conviction that students will achieve success. "Your

42

responsiveness, your genuine excitement and pleasure in the student's writing should never be withheld."[3] This perception of the student as writer is crucial because "the expectations of learners and teachers powerfully influence what happens in school."[4]

Teachers create "communicative settings" with their students in which they never "talk down" but instead "talk across" to their students. They acknowledge openly and comfortably that while some students may have difficulty writing in their second language, they may be successful writers in their first language.

Because they recognize that students are motivated by success, teachers assign students tasks that both the teacher and the student will assess according to clearly defined criteria and which most of the students will be able to successfully complete. In so doing, the teacher can raise the students' expectations of their own writing.

2. Teachers of writing believe in sharing their own writing efforts and writing with their students. Because many students approach writing tasks with trepidation, anger, frustration, and stubbornness, teachers are frequently working with less than cooperative writers! To help students overcome these feelings and develop more positive attitudes, teachers should be sure that students see their teacher's efforts as they approach writing tasks. It is particularly beneficial for students to see their teacher's writing attempts in the teacher's second language. This helps students to recognize that their inability to write clearly and easily may be somewhat universal for all writers when they make their first attempts to write in their second language.

In essence, teachers need to model the behavior they want their students to adopt. Thus, teachers share their own writing with their students so that "each word changed, each line crossed out, each space left on the page shows the teacher's attempts to understand, to remember all those ideas and events not fully articulated or remembered."[5] In so doing, teachers illustrate not only their concern for the value of writing and the effort that it requires but also their belief that revision is central to the writing process, an ongoing part of writing which is both logical and necessary and not an isolated act provided as a punishment for incomplete or unsuccessful writing attempts.

3. Teachers of writing are flexible. We recognize that all students do not enter the writing classroom with the same skills. Furthermore,

writing teachers recognize that the writing process is extremely complex and cannot always be approached in the orderly arrangement of many composition texts. ESL students represent a multitude of backgrounds and abilities; therefore, we need to design programs and individualized lessons which begin where the students *are*, not where the syllabus says they should be. We are prepared to use a wide variety of materials which draw upon the acquired capabilities of students and upon the strategies successfully developed in their first language. Writing teachers realize that no one method will serve as a panacea for all students. Therefore, the successful writing teacher avoids what Prator calls the "pendulum syndrome" in which a teacher sacrifices a variety of successful methods for the use of one method that is currently in vogue.

The flexible writing teacher, then, provides students with assignments and writing opportunities which (1) reflect a broad range of interests, (2) lend themselves to different viewpoints, (3) relate to the students' experiences, and (4) vary in their stylistic complexity.

4. Teachers of writing are sensitive. They recognize that the most successful writing takes place in a comfortable environment—one that is conducive to discovering, creating, and shaping ideas. "Successful composition classes work not simply because the teacher uses a particular technique, whatever that technique may be, but because through that technique the teacher is able to be empathic, self-congruent, and unconditional in his or her regard for students."[6] Therefore, writing teachers create classroom environments that are "characterized by an atmosphere of freedom and writing tasks that are liberating."[7]

In such an environment, the teacher is accessible to students, taking time to listen to students as they discuss their hopes, aspirations, dreams, and frustrations. The teacher recognizes that the students' experiences are the framework of their writing activities. Therefore, the teacher attaches as much importance to *what* a student says as to *how* a student says it. Thus the teacher listens to students and hears not a student with a writing problem or dilemma but a "single human being speaking to another single human being."[8] As a result, the teacher creates an environment in which the student and teacher collaborate to resolve a dilemma. Students are comfortable talking about their writing with teachers because they view the teacher as one who will help them better their abilities and not just criticize them. They feel capable of moving forward and growing from within. They are willing to take a step beyond where they have been, and "each step forward is made possible by the feeling of being safe, of operating out into the unknown from a safe home port, of daring because retreat is possible."[9]

5. *The writing teacher is supportive—encouraging independence.* The potential of each individual is nurtured and enhanced. The teacher meets the particular needs of individual students by discovering what kinds of tasks students will have to accomplish with the language and then creating materials that will develop these specific areas. Because students learn English for a variety of reasons, some academic, some vocational, and some for survival, teachers need to have students do the kinds of writing in class that they are going to be doing in the future. This is crucial because what students do in class is what they will learn.[10]

Students have different learning styles as well as different goals for learning a language. Therefore, teachers must develop activities with which the student is successful. As students experience success with the language, they are willing to experiment with the new language. They will be receptive to experimenting with different learning styles and with planning to work toward the goal of developing the new language into an ordered system which they can revise progressively.[11] The successful writing teacher encourages such strategies so that the students develop the second language as a separate reference system and work toward thinking in that second language.

In sum, the attitude of the writing teacher determines, to a great extent, the success of the teaching and learning efforts in the classroom. The teacher who views language learning as more of an art than a science, who considers the individuality of each human being, experiments with all methods available, and uses all the empirical data supplied from applied linguistics, educational psychology, rhetorical analysis, and a host of other disciplines will create a productive writing environment.

First and foremost, teachers of writing bring particular attitudes to the classroom. But what else must they bring?

A BODY OF KNOWLEDGE

A teacher must be able to break down complicated rhetorical and linguistic operations and teach them separately.—Smith

Wanting to provide a conducive writing environment and *actually providing* that atmosphere are two different issues. Along with possessing an attitude that fosters a sound writing environment, teachers must bring to the classroom a body of knowledge which enables them, after diagnosing the needs of their students, to select from an array of theories and methods those which will work best in their ESL classrooms at any given time. Several broad areas should be at the command of writing teachers in order for them to best meet the needs of their students.

1. *The teacher understands the multiple phases of the writing process.* The very complexity of the writing process demands that the writing teacher break it down into parts so that each aspect becomes manageable for students, enabling them to develop their writing abilities. Recognizing that writing is a creative, active, and recursive process enables teachers to provide activities and design assignments that will stimulate, motivate, and reinforce writers as they move through phases of the process. Thus the successful writing teacher is able to "set forth and classify coherently the categories and functions of the written language."[12] In so doing, teachers help students to be aware of *what* they are going to do and *why* they are going to do it. "Simplification (of a task) has been shown to lead to success, and success attained through routes understood all the way can be its best reward. Motivation coming from increased competence rather than intrinsic rewards thus becomes a dominant factor in learning and leads to further self-learning."[13]

2. *The teacher recognizes the factors involved in second language learning.* Those involved in teaching a second language generally agree on the following three points: (1) learning a second language can be an awesome task for most people, (2) some language learners are more successful than others in an identical situation, and (3) for particular individuals some aspects of language learning are more easily mastered than others.

In her model of second language learning, Bialystok discusses three factors which influence language learning and defines these as input, knowledge, and output.[14] The first factor influencing language learning is exposure to the language, which Bialystok calls *input.* Different people experience or encounter the second language in different ways. Some have a specialized exposure, that of the language class. Others learn the language through books, reading words and phrases and memorizing structures, all the while relying heavily on memory and comprehension skills. Still others engage in "immersion in a culture." They live in a country where the target language is spoken and absorb information about the language through a variety of senses. They hear the sounds of the language, read and/or study in the language, and, perhaps most importantly, interact with others on a day-to-day basis using the second language. Therefore, writing teachers need to be aware of how students have encountered the second language because different experiences with the language require different teaching strategies.

A second factor involved in language learning is the core of information or *knowledge* learners have acquired about the second language and their use of that information to learn the second language more completely and efficiently. Included in this core of language information are grammar rules, pronunciation rules, vocabulary items, and rhetorical principles which students can articulate. In addition, this core of information includes knowledge of other language systems, insights into the world around the speaker, and attitudes students have internalized about the second language.

Teachers who utilize the amount of information the student already has about the language will be more able to expand that student's understanding of the language by building upon an established foundation. For example, the student who articulates a clear understanding of the American concept "time is money" will probably be able to generalize its significance in the writing class where the conventions of presenting (1) a clear thesis statement early in the paper, followed by (2) strong supporting ideas are discussed by the teacher.

Output, the third factor involved in second language learning, is the use of the linguistic information the learner has stored to produce or to comprehend the second language. Bialystok characterizes two types of responses language learners make when using their linguistic information to comprehend or produce language. The factor distinguishing the two types of response is time. Category 1 responses are those which are spontaneous and immediate, such as responding to questions. Category 2 responses are delayed responses given after careful thought, perhaps given after reading additional information, or those spoken after students have had sufficient time to think about the rules they know for the language.

Understanding the output factor enables the teacher to provide a mix of class activities and assignments which will utilize the linguistic information students have. Therefore, students are given the opportunity to develop and use both kinds of

responses in developing their writing abilities. Techniques discussed in Chapter 4 will utilize both categories of responses as a means to initiate the writing process.

3. The teacher is familiar with the variety of learning strategies employed to learn a second language. The wise writing teacher realizes (happily!) that a great deal of language learning occurs beyond the formalized classroom setting. For many students, learning a second language is best accomplished by employing several strategies and using each more or less intensively as the situation dictates.

One strategy students use is practice, or the *conscious* effort of students to increase their exposure to the language. Stern classifies two areas of practice, formal and functional.[15] Formal practice includes those activities students engage in to increase their knowledge of the language code. Students who study from the grammar text to complement class practice or practice pronunciation drills in the language laboratory are exercising a formal practice strategy.

Functional practice involves increased exposure to the language in "real-life" communication settings. That is, learners use their knowledge of the language to communicate or understand information. Such practice occurs in the classroom when a student responds to a teacher's questions regarding reading assignments, produces correct grammatical forms, and uses correct vocabulary words. However, it more commonly occurs outside the classroom when a student goes to a bank and opens an account, reads a newspaper, asks directions to the post office, or watches television. Students communicate because they have to in order to survive. Functional practice is a more subconscious learning strategy. The student focuses more on the *meaning* conveyed than on the *rules* learned to convey the message.

A third strategy students employ to learn a language is monitoring, a strategy in which language learners "monitor," or analyze their written or spoken production according to the formalized information they have about a language. Students engage in a process of self-correction which is evident when a statement such as, "He go, I mean, he is going to Mexico City next week" is made. The student is conveying information in response to a question and is concerned not only with giving the correct meaning-bearing response but also with giving the response in the correct linguistic form. Krashen postulates "that adult second language learners concurrently develop two possibly independent systems for second language performers, one acquired, developed in ways similar to first language acquisition in children, and the other learned, developed consciously and most often in formal situations."[16]

Overuse of the monitor by a student might be one way to account for the fact that some students seem to learn one aspect of a language more easily than another. For example, students who are able to write fairly easily but speak with much hesitancy may rely so heavily on the monitor that they allow themselves little opportunity to practice speaking with others, fearing that they will use incorrect lexical terms or grammatical structures.

A fourth strategy employed by students is the use of inference, a strategy in which they use various bits and pieces of information they have about language to discover some new information about the second language. For example, Spanish speakers learning English are inferencing when they interpret word meanings in English that have a similar or identical meaning in Spanish. They are using their knowledge of first language to develop their second language. Additionally, students who discover new word meanings by applying their knowledge of prefix meanings are making use of inferencing strategy.

Inferencing is also used frequently outside the classroom. The student who notes the hand gestures, the facial expression, and the pad and pencil of the uniformed man disembarking from the blue automobile with the flashing red lights on its roof is about to make an inference. The student decides the uniformed man is not simply stopping to chat as he walks toward the student's car, which just passed through the red light. The student infers that something unpleasant is going to happen as the officer requests a driver's license. The student has arrived at this judgment through the process of inferencing, taking what is already known about uniforms, red lights, and traffic rules and piecing it together to give insight into the present situation.

The teacher who is aware of these different learning strategies and the myriad ways students use them will be more able to design classroom assignments that will allow students to utilize more than one learning strategy, thereby giving students more opportunities to learn successfully.

4. The teacher recognizes the factors which influence successful language learning. Writing teachers are aware that a number of factors such as age, ability, method of instruction, attitude, motivation, and personal flexibility influence individuals as they go about learning a second language. Investigation into the first three factors has not been particularly conclusive. Aptitude seems to be a more important factor in formalized second language learning settings than it is in settings providing direct exposure to the language.[17]

Attitude, motivation, and personal flexibility seem to be more crucial to successful second language learning and as a result are crucial to the ability to write in a second language. Successful language learners have a *positive attitude* toward the language they are going to learn and about their ability to learn the language. They are favorably disposed toward the native speakers of the second language and want to learn the language. They have probably had positive reinforcement from parents and friends regarding their ability and need to learn the second language. They view instructors as resource people who can aid them in their quest for skills rather than as authoritarian figures who will only monitor and correct language deficiencies.

Conversely, unsuccessful language learners have negative attitudes. They may perceive the second language as inferior to their own; they may dislike the speakers of the second language that they have met and generalize this to include a dislike for all speakers of the second language. They may not *want* to learn a second language and therefore may have no internal motivation. They view language learning as a "chore" and develop "language blocks;" "I'm too old to learn another language, I'm not smart enough, the language is too hard," or "The teacher isn't any good." Such attitudes become self-fulfilling prophecies—students have difficulty and the cycle begins again.

Along with attitude, successful language learning is influenced by *motivation.* The student needs a reason to learn the language. Studies by Lambert, Gardner, and others identify two types of motivation—integrative and instrumental. The learner possessing integrative motivation is interested in learning a second language in order to communicate and interact with valued members of the second language community. Learners who possess instrumental motivation have as their primary objective more personal goals. They may be learning the language to get a better job, to enter a university, or to be able to complete a job application form. Of the two types of motivation, instrumental seems to occur more frequently. "The emergence in recent years of the movement to teach English for special purposes underlines the fact that students are learning English for pragmatic, not humanistic goals."[18]

This suggests that teachers need to create writing assignments that are meaningful and useful to students. The student needs to believe that the assignment is important and that *the teacher considers the assignment to be important and valuable to the student.*

Personal flexibility is the third factor influencing the language learner. The student needs to be receptive to other people, other teaching techniques, and other cultures. The student needs to recognize that progress takes the form of a continuum—students may move forward but they cannot be afraid of lapses and the feeling of moving backward. Students must feel they *can* learn. That is, they need to feel comfortable experimenting, using the language to make it meet their needs. They need to feel that it is all right to make mistakes. Students need, therefore, to adapt the child's method of first language acquisition. That is, students need to be less inhibited as they go about learning a second language. They need to develop a degree of "ego flexibility," a receptiveness to the idea of learning. They need to adopt the child's method of language acquisition because "the adult will learn the new language the more easily, the more of these infantile characteristics he has preserved."[19]

In order then to maximize the opportunities for the second language learner, writing teachers consider the attitudes, motivations, and levels of flexibility of their students. They actively set out to create conditions which "make the learner less anxious, make him feel accepted and make him form identifications with speakers of the target language."[20]

5. The teacher possesses a thorough knowledge of the subject. Besides recognizing the complexities of the writing process, the writing teacher is familiar with other aspects of the English language. The teacher is familiar with the origins of the language and is able to use this knowledge to help students arrange and classify information that they have already acquired about the language. Aware of the extensive borrowing in English, the teacher points out similar or identical words to students to help them strengthen their ability to inference from their own language and build their second language capabilities.

In addition, writing teachers are familiar with and comfortable teaching the structure of the language. Teachers recognize the importance of teaching grammatical forms in context and do not rely solely on the use of isolated grammar drills to develop a student's intuitive use of the grammar in writing. Furthermore, teachers recognize the links and interconnections between reading, speaking, and writing. Teachers are aware that reading and writing employ similar skills. To read well, students must be able to generalize, synthesize, compare, and contrast chunks of information. To write well, students must do the same. They must also employ their reading skill to accomplish these tasks successfully.

6. The teacher understands the additional complexities involved in learning the writing process for the ESL writer. Necessary for all writers are the abilities to form ideas, arrange them in an effective manner to convey intended meaning, and state them well using "acceptable grammar, diction, and syntactic structure."[21] For the ESL writer, there are additional tasks to be learned in order to successfully accomplish these three.

To begin, ESL writers must learn the rhetorical structure of the second language. Students have to learn how unity, coherence, and style are "linguistically and culturally coded" because "the ways in which sentences are related to each other in larger lumps of language constitutes something to be taught, not something to be assumed to exist universally across language and culture barriers."[22]

In addition, ESL writers must attempt to master the syntax and lexicon of the new language. The teacher's task is a huge one! Indeed the teacher can create an environment for successful learning and, as Raimes suggests, a context for learning. To create the context for learning, Raimes suggests that the teacher must deal with three points:

1. The content for composition. Because content can be regarded principally as a vehicle to teach grammar and rhetoric, the choice of content is crucial. The teacher chooses interesting and intellectually stimulating material.

2. The rhetorical structure generated by the content. A carefully chosen task will unobtrusively lead students to write spatial order, analysis, definition, comparison, and contrast and other methods of organization. They will not copy a model; they will not be told to use a specific paragraph pattern. They will write and will become aware of the options open to them when they organize.

3. The syntactic structures generated by the rhetorical structures. Certain kinds of organ-

ization lend themselves to the use of certain syntactic structures. For example, a comparison-contrast task will inevitably lead to the use of comparative and superlative structures; a chronological narrative will lead to the use of the past tense; spatial order will generate prepositions of place.[23]

The teacher's task becomes one of selection and prediction. Crucial is the selection of the content. This suggests the rhetorical structure to be generated and the syntactic structure then employed. As Raimes says, "If the teacher chooses the first of these three—the content—carefully enough, thereby predicting the other two, [the teacher] will direct the student towards working on composition by working on invention, arrangement, and style." (1980:386).

7. The teacher utilizes practical observation. Successful writing teachers observe their students closely and note what techniques work. That is, they look at the reactions of their students and their writing efforts, both successful and unsuccessful, and analyze their teaching efforts. They reject methods that seem unproductive and try something else. They do not, however, abandon methods altogether but analyze carefully the conditions under which techniques succeeded or failed. In the future, they work to recreate the former and avoid the latter.

It is clear then that the role of the teacher is crucial to helping students become productive writers. Knowing this, teachers endeavor to constantly increase their body of knowledge regarding the teaching of writing and related language learning. And, besides relying on a broad base of knowledge, the ESL writing teacher brings a third quality to the writing classroom.

SKILL

Teaching is even more difficult than learning . . . because what teaching calls for is this: to let learn. The real teacher in fact—lets nothing else be learned than learning.
—Heidegger

The writing teacher is a skills teacher. Every student is an individual, and the teacher needs to consider what methods and techniques will best develop the potential of each student. The successful writing teacher establishes a program built on the belief that the student is an active participant—a doer. Therefore, the classroom is a laboratory for the teacher and the student. Teachers must have at their disposal a variety of techniques and methods which give students practice with writing. Because students are involved in a discovery method through which they learn to write by writing, teachers consider the following points as they develop a writing curriculum:

- They keep the writing task clear, simple, and straightforward.

- They *teach* the writing *process*.

- They *analyze* and *diagnose* a writing *product*.

- They establish short-term and long-term goals for each student.

- They balance classroom activities, providing some for individuals and some for groups.

- They develop meaningful assignments.

- They provide a real audience: an audience other than the teacher.

- They make student papers available to tudents; they allow students to see their own body of work develop.

- They move from the known to the unknown and utilize the student's previous knowledge.

- They provide writing activities which reinforce reading, listening, and speaking skills.

- They provide heuristics for invention, purpose, and audience.

- They outline clearly the goals for each writing assignment.

- They teach the conventions of spelling, punctuation, and capitalization.

- They teach the principles—rules, conventions, and guidelines of writing—as a means to develop thoughts, order ideas, and communicate these ideas in a significant way.

An attitude, a body of knowledge, and skills are all necessary to the creation of a successful writing environment. They are inextricably intertwined with a fourth consideration which, like the others, continues to expand and flourish with the experiences of each teacher.

INSIGHT

> *Good writing teachers make their presence felt, but do not dominate.* —Irmscher

"Good teachers are good teachers because they have brains, great learning, engaging personalities, and enough experience to learn what to do with themselves," says Charlton Laird in *And Gladly Teche* (1970:VI). Indeed, it is this last characteristic, to learn what to do with themselves, which helps to shape completely the successful writing teacher.

Good writing teachers take the teaching of writing seriously. They want to teach writing because they believe that writing skills are important. They believe that one of their "central responsibili[ties] as teachers of ESL is to teach students to operate effectively in a language which they can at best only partially control."[24] Therefore, their approach to the teaching of writing needs to be centered on concern for making it possible for students to function comfortably when writing English.

Students need to have the confidence to write papers that develop content and express the knowledge and understanding of the writer. For ESL students, particularly, teachers need to adopt practices that foster writing production rather than writing "blocks."

Writing teachers are best able to accomplish this task when they have learned "what to do with themselves." That is, they have identified the strengths of their own personal styles and have modified or developed classroom methods that are complementary to them.[25] They recognize that there is no one ideal teacher personality and no one ideal method to guarantee that students will learn to write well. They do, however, approach the teaching of writing and the development of their own personal style armed with the following insights:

- *Writing can be taught.* Teachers can give students opportunities to discover the basic skills which each writer has to learn and practice while "aspiring to art," says Murray (1968:23).

- *You can't teach writing by talking.* Writing is taught *by writing* with a minimum of talking about writing. The teacher provides guidance necessary to carrying out a task, but the students and teacher are collaborators. The students are with the teacher and their concentration is on-task.

- *Students should write often.* Teachers have their students write often. They recognize that not every paper need be eloquent, graded, or necessarily finished, *but* every piece of writing is practice in writing.

- *Being a good reader does not make one a good writer.* Reading serves to give the writer ideas, data, model sentence patterns, and structures, but a student will be able to become a good writer only by writing. A pianist is not a pianist because he reads about Mozart. He is a pianist because he plays Mozart.

- *Teachers must respect their students.* Teachers must believe that their students have something to say. Furthermore, teachers must respect the integrity of each student. Students need to know what assignments are being graded, how they will be graded, and according to what standards they are being graded. In order to maintain a relationship based on trust, teachers must ensure that students feel the role of the teachers is collaborator not critic.

- *Students need to be encouraged to take risks.* Teachers need to help students move beyond the secure learnings, those which they have already mastered, and try new forms. For the teacher, this means concentrating on the ideas that students are trying to express, rather than on the usage. It means recognizing that what writers want to say should be the master of the way they say it.

- *Students must be praised.* Students need to feel that they are making progress toward a goal. They need to feel the effort is worthwhile; therefore, the successful teacher looks for something good in each piece of student writing, compliments the student in success, and aids the student in meeting further learning needs. Good writing is generated from within, and the successful writer is motivated to pursue the task.

- *Teachers know that learning begun in the classroom is a springboard to the world beyond.* The student who is receptive to learning, who has had positive classroom experiences, will be receptive to learning—anytime, anywhere. Such a student will have greater opportunity to build upon the learning begun in the classroom. Growth will be continued because the student has the tools with which to develop from within. "Students reflect in positive ways a good teachers's sense for exploration, experimentation, discovery, standards, and opportunities of effective expression. Here the effect of the total presence of the teacher as a writer, in a context that enhances rather than suppresses positive, catalytic signals and recognitions, becomes crucially apparent."[26]

The teacher who develops a personal style and a writing curriculum based on these insights will have the tools to create a successful writing environment. The teacher's presence *will* be felt, but the *dominant* force in the writing class will be the *writer*.

3.3 The role of the learner

A student who is not writing cannot improve.

Louis T. Milic

The student-writer needs to be actively engaged in the writing process. Therefore, the student takes an active approach to the learning task and the student-writer *writes*. While writing classes may talk about writing by analyzing representative pieces of writing or gather information by reading and interviewing, the primary task of students in the writing class is to write. As teachers, then, we view the learner "not as a passive slave to habits but as an active agent constructing a coherent view of the world."[27]

In concert with their active participation, student-writers take responsibility for their own learning. Because student and teacher are collaborators, partners in the task of learning to write, students do not passively wait to be *taught* how to write—they take the responsibility to *learn* to write. They do not rely solely on the teacher. They do not always wait for the teacher to explain the next procedure. Good learners, students who will succeed in developing their writing abilities, have a sense of adventure, a willingness to explore for themselves and move beyond the formalized learning setting.

Successful students define goals for themselves and strive to attain those goals with the help of the teacher. As Stern says, the good language learner "faces the language learning task with conscious deliberation and develops his own approach and study habits. . . . He takes deliberate steps to involve himself in the language and to adapt the language learning activity to his own life"(1980:62–63).

Students learn at different rates, use different strategies, and have diverse purposes for learning a second language. Our role as teacher-facilitator-collaborator will be more effective if our students are willing to be active learners in the writing class. What do students need to assume this active role?

A POSITIVE APPROACH

For ESL students, attitude plays a very important role in their ability to successfully develop skill using a second language. Stern details the components necessary to developing a positive approach to the language learning task and states that students will be more successful in learning to *write* in a second language if they—

1. *Want* to learn the second language—see learning as important.

2. Possess a tolerant and outgoing approach to the second language. They should not view the second language as inferior to their native language.

3. Feel a degree of empathy toward speakers of the second language.

4. Are willing to use the second language in real-life communication beyond the classroom setting. They are not afraid of assuming the "child-role" of language learning. That is, they are not inhibited in their attempts to utilize the language. They are not concerned with making perfect responses the first time they speak. They allow themselves the opportunity of making mistakes.

ESL students will be more successful in their attempts to write in a second language when they possess the above attitudes toward second language

50

learning in general, and, the following attitudes toward the writing task in particular:

1. *A motivation to write.* Students more successfully develop sound writing skills when they *want* to write—when they see the writing task as worth doing. The reasons students have for learning English are numerous. Most are learning the language to meet pragmatic goals, some to meet humanistic goals. Each type will be more successful if writing skill is viewed as necessary and important.

2. *The belief that the writing task can be accomplished.* More successful writing students believe they are able to accomplish their goals. Furthermore, they are realistic about the task. They accept that writing is a complex process. They recognize they will not learn to write overnight. They know the learning process is a prolonged one, and they accept the fact that progress will come in bits and pieces.

3. *A curious, questioning, and open-minded attitude.* They are curious about the world around them, its events, its problems, its complexities. They are sensitive—aware of life, caring about people. They are receptive to impressions and ideas. They read, listen, look, taste, and touch. They *engage* the world around them. Successful learners question—their teachers, friends, themselves. They explore issues, beliefs, and attitudes as a means to develop their own particular points of view. They are open to ideas, and by questioning and discovering answers they make connections and develop insights. They are willing to pursue issues so that they can develop content from a variety of sources. They do not believe that they already possess all the information they need to formulate a thesis. They strive for "precision and flexibility in defining, modifying, and perfecting a hypothesis."[28]

4. *Successful developing writers have a concern for completeness.* They are willing to look at all sides of an issue and explore further. They are unwilling to accept partial answers—they are willing to see a task go through many stages. They are concerned with the writing task as a whole and are willing to develop the parts carefully to strengthen that whole.

5. *The learner is willing to practice.* Successful learners practice their craft. That is, they write and write and write again. They view practicing writing positively. They try a variety of writing patterns, sentence structures, and invention techniques to develop their skills. Thus students are willing to revise and rephrase, rethink and reorder information to ensure that a piece of writing does reflect examination of an issue from all sides.

SKILLS

Students possessing a positive attitude have the first basic tool to develop their writing skills. Yet attitude is not enough. Student writers need several skills, some of which are more complex for the ESL writer because they involve learning additional skills which act as complements to developing writing skills.

1. *Students need a degree of control of the language.* Beginning writers need to gain control of the sentence. That is, they need to understand the structure of the sentence and the ways to formulate clear sentences because sentences cohesively tied together are fundamental to developing essays.

Student-writers need, then, practice in manipulating the language—making it work for them. As Widdowson states, "to compose sentences is not the only ability we need to communicate. Communication takes place when we make use of a variety of sentences to perform a variety of different tasks" (1978: 16). Thus student-writers also need skill in formulating and manipulating paragraphs.

Another aspect in control of the language is the control of a subject. Beginning writers need to know (1) what a thesis is, (2) ways to find a thesis, and (3) how to discern what issues should be addressed in a piece of writing. Once writers have grasped the initial control of the subject, they can begin to select the paragraph forms, word choices, and the voice necessary to creating a good piece of writing.

Recognizing the differences between oral production and written production is another means by which students gain control of language. The context or situation which is self-evident in oral settings must be

51

made explicitly clear in written work. The writer must clearly state (1) who is speaking, (2) to what audience, and (3) under what conditions.

While all writers need to be aware of these means to language control, ESL writers need several additional skills to be able to gain control of the language:

a. ESL writers need to develop an understanding of a grammar system that may be quite different from their own.

b. ESL writers need to discern the systematic patterns that exist in the language. They need to have a sense of how the language builds and develops.

c. ESL writers must develop a vocabulary in order to express their ideas in English. They need a degree of fluency which affords them ready access to many words which they can use to express their ideas.

d. ESL writers need to recognize the rhetorical structure of the language. They need familiarity with the rhetorical conventions of English.

2. *Students need reading skills.* Because reading is a "mirror image" to writing, it is necessary that writers read. Students read to gather information, to collect data, but perhaps more importantly, they read their own writing—to strengthen it, evaluate it, perfect it.

They need to use their reasoning abilities and language cues presented in textual material to help them formulate ideas.

APTITUDES

In addition to a positive attitude and particular skills to help them develop as writers, students need particular aptitudes to help them utilize their skills. These aptitudes include:

1. *A degree of decenteredness.* Writers need to have a sense beyond the "self." They need a degree of audience awareness enabling them to move beyond the self and ask: How might A view this example? Would A choose my position for this discussion?

2. *Reasoning abilities.* Writers need to be able to see relationships between ideas, discern shades of meaning, and extract particular points of view. Student-writers need to syn-

thesize and generalize information. Furthermore, they need to make inferences from information to help them develop a "sense" of subject and audience.

In order to accomplish their tasks as language learners, ESL students also need heightened senses of awareness in three specific areas. For the native speaker, these are part of the process of first language acquisition, but they need to be consciously fostered to aid the ESL student in second language learning.

a. Phonetic awareness—an ability to discriminate among sounds and develop an "ear" for the language.

b. Grammatical sensitivity—an awareness of the function of words in a variety of contexts

c. Inductive reasoning as part of language learning—the ability to infer rules from given language forms

Each of the skills, consciously developed and applied by students, will help them use the language to convey information.

WORKABLE METHODS

Students can use language to convey information only when they have strategies to call upon and aid them in putting their thoughts on the page. Most beginning writers are wary of the writing process because, as Shaughnessy says, "The beginning writer does not know how the writers behave" (1977:79).

When students are actively engaged in the writing process, they learn how writers behave; they become designers and builders. They create and shape papers from ideas they have generated for themselves. As teachers we need to continually encourage students as they work on their own pieces of work. "Great emphasis must be placed on the students' own production and its intensive revision. Once produced, the student's writing begets his loyalty and he becomes eager to improve it."[29]

In order to create pieces of writing and improve them knowledgeably and systematically, students needs strategies, workable methods, which will serve them as they work through the writing process. The workable methods a student chooses to use will be dependent upon the personality and purpose of the student. Because the skills and aptitudes of students also vary, teachers need to encourage students to continue to use methods that the students have found to be successful and encourage them to try new methods to replace unsuccessful ones. The workable methods a student employs include—

1. *Making a conscious search for meaning.* Students try to use all the language cues available to them to understand what happens in the art of communication. They analyze content and situation, they seek explanation, they employ trial and error as they go about creating a piece of writing.

2. *Practicing self-monitoring.* Successful students learn from their own successes and mistakes. That is, they monitor their own performance by maintaining a sensitivity to language use. They try to categorize new learnings and incorporate them into their established language system. In this way students continually expand their second language base.

3. *Using strategies of experimentation and planning.* Successful students are unafraid to experiment with the language. They are purposeful and systematic in their writing attempts. They organize information in a variety of ways to suit their particular purposes. They use their knowledge of language structure to select word forms and sentence patterns.

   Successful students ask and answer questions. They know how to phrase questions to others and they know how to use questioning devices for their own purposes of discovering subject and form. This is an important skill for ESL students to develop because they need to feel comfortable acquiring information by the rapid means of oral questioning as well as the more time-consuming method of reading.

4. *Using understanding of first language in order to develop the second language.* Successful students use the "know-how" of their first language to develop their second language. For example, they look for similarities and differences in grammatical structure, lexical structure, and rhetorical form. They look for relationships among elements of language—they become aware of recurring rules and the redundancy in English. For example, they begin to discover the redundancy in the language as they read and write sentences like "Those books are on the table."

Along with a positive attitude, skills, aptitude, and workable methods, all of which must come primarily from within the student, students need an additional component to successfully develop their writing abilities.

FEEDBACK

Students need a clear assessment of their progress. In order for students to successfully develop their writing abilities, they need to know how they are progressing. As part of their strategies of organizing and structuring information about the second language, students learn from their successes and mistakes. They require, then, frequent and selective assessments from their teachers. We need, therefore, to provide our students with objective, straightforward, and precise comments about their progress.

Furthermore, we should channel our comments toward building upon student successes. Helping students see what they have done well enables them to try to repeat successes in future pieces of writing. Students who are told they use a variety of sentence patterns effectively will, we believe, be aware of this skill and try to reproduce a variety of patterns in future papers.

Errors in student papers should be treated as a means to discover the inconsistencies in their learning strategies. In other words, we need to look at the *pattern* of errors and provide students with tools to correct the pattern rather than merely point out the errors that might appear on a page.

Because students can deal with only a limited number of items at a time, we should encourage them "to deal first with those that seem to us most fundamental, leaving others for successive drafts."[30]

Teachers should not be the only source of feedback for the student. Self-provided feedback, whereby students are given a means to measure their own performance on a particular assignment, and peer-provided feedback are excellent sources of feedback for the writer. (The ESL COMPOSITION PROFILE discussed in Chapter 6 is such a means of measurement.)

Coupled with systematic study, extensive practice using the language, and reinforcement for their efforts, students need clearly defined objectives. With each assignment, students will be more able to successfully accomplish their goals if they have a writing context. Students need to know:

- What they are writing about—a subject
- Who they are writing to—an audience
- Why they are writing—a purpose

53

In sum, the writing process as we have defined it is an active one. The teacher and student are working together to develop the student's writing skills. This active approach to the writing process suggests that it is important for ESL students—

1. To use a variety of learning strategies—formal practice, informal practice, and monitoring

2. To be motivated—willing to write and willing to practice writing often

3. To be flexible—willing to experiment with language structures and accepting of speakers of the second language

4. To learn the rhetorical structure of the second language

5. To learn the syntax and lexicon of the second language in order to gain control of the language

6. To develop a phonetic awareness of the second language

7. To develop grammatical sensitivity to the second language

8. To use their inductive reasoning ability

Therefore, students need a positive attitude, an aptitude, particular skills and workable methods, and the raw materials of writing in order to be actively engaged in the writing process.

Notes

[1]C.I.C. Estacio, "A Cognition-Based Program of Second Language Learning," in *The Psychology of Second Language Learning,* ed. Paul Pimsleur and Terence Quinn (Cambridge, England: Cambridge University Press, 1979), 193.

[2]Mary Finocchiaro, *English as a Second Language: From Theory to Practice* (New York: Regents Publishing Co., Inc., 1974), 173.

[3]John Schultz, "Story Workshop," in *Research on Composing: Points of Departure,* ed. Charles R. Cooper and Lee Odell (Urbana, Ill.: National Council of Teachers of English, 1978), 177.

[4]Mina Shaughnessy, *Errors and Expectations: A Guide for the Teacher of Basic Writing* (New York: Oxford University Press, 1977), 275.

[5]Donald Murray, "Internal Revision: A Process of Discovery," in *Research on Composing: Points of Departure,* ed. Charles R. Cooper and Lee Odell (Urbana, Ill.: National Council of Teachers of English, 1978), 92.

[6]Karen I. Spear, "Psychotherapy and Composition: Effective Teaching beyond Methodology," *College Composition and Communication,* 29 (December 1978), 374.

[7]W. Ross Winterowd, "Brain, Rhetoric and Style," in *Linguistics, Stylistics, and the Teaching of Composition,* ed. Donald McQuade (Akron, Ohio: Department of English, University of Akron, 1979), 161.

[8]Donald M. Murray, *A Writer Teaches Writing* (Boston: Houghton Mifflin Company, 1968), 17.

[9]Abraham H. Maslow, *Toward a Psychology of Being,* 2d ed. (Princeton, N.J.:D. Van Nostrand Co., 1968), 49.

[10]Clifford H. Prator, "In Search of Method," in *Readings on English as a Second Language,* 2d ed., ed. Kenneth Croft (Cambridge: Winthrop Publishers, Inc., 1980), 22.

[11]H. H. Stern, "What Can We Learn from the Good Language Learner?" in *Readings on English as a Second Language,* 2d ed., ed. Kenneth Croft (Cambridge: Winthrop Publishers, Inc., 1980), 64.

[12]Robert de Beaugrande, "Linguistic Theory and Composition," *College Composition and Communication,* 29 (May 1978), 134.

[13]Estacio, p. 192.

[14]Ellen Bialystok, "A Theoretical Model for Second Language Learning," in *Readings on English as a Second Language,* 2d ed., ed. Kenneth Croft (Cambridge: Winthrop Publishers, Inc., 1980), 69–83.

[15]H. H. Stern, "Directions in Language Teaching Theory and Research," in *Applied Linguistics Problems and Solution,* ed. J. Quistgaard, H. Schwarz, and H. Spang-Hansen (Heidelberg: Julius Groos, 1974).

[16]Stephen D. Krashen, "The Monitor Model for Adult Second Language Performance," in *Readings on English as a Second Language,* 2d ed., ed. Kenneth Croft (Cambridge: Winthrop Publisher, Inc., 1980), 213.

[17]John H. Schumann, "Affective Factors and the Problem of Age in Second Language Acquisition," in *Readings on English as a Second Language,* 2d ed., ed. Kenneth Croft (Cambridge: Winthrop Publishers, Inc., 1980), 222.

[18]James J. Kohn, "What ESL Teachers Need to Know about Sociolinguistics," in *Readings on English as a Second Language,* 2d ed., ed. Kenneth Croft (Cambridge: Winthrop Publishers, Inc., 1980), 44.

[19]E. Stengal, "On Learning a New Language" (*International Journal of Psychoanalysis)* 20 (1939): 471–479, in *Readings on English as a Second Language,* 2d ed., ed. Kenneth Croft (Cambridge: Winthrop Publishers, Inc., 1980), 478.

[20]Schumann, p. 239.

[21]W. Ross Winterowd, *Rhetoric: A Synthesis* (New York: Holt, Rinehart and Winston, 1968), 15–16.

[22]Robert B. Kaplan, "Composition at the Advanced ESL Level: A Teacher's Guide to Connected Paragraph Construction for Advanced-Level Foreign Students," *English Record,* 21 (1971), 53–64, in *Readings on English as a Second Language,* 2d ed., ed. Kenneth Croft (Cambridge: Winthrop Publishers, Inc., 1980), 55.

[23]Ann Raimes, "Composition: Controlled by the Teacher, Free for the Student," in *Readings on English as a Second Language,* 2d ed., ed. Kenneth Croft (Cambridge: Winthrop Publisher, Inc., 1980), 386.

[24]Barry Taylor, "Content and Written Form: A Two-Way Street," *Tesol Quarterly,* 15 (March 1981), 8.

[25]Spear, p. 374.

[26]Schultz, p. 184.

[27]Loren S. Barrett and Barry M. Kroll, "Some Implications of Cognitive-Developmental Psychology for Research in Composing" in *Research on Composing: Points of Departure,* ed. Charles R. Cooper and Lee Odell (Urbana, Ill.: National Council of Teachers of English, 1978), 54.

[28]David V. Harrington, "Encouraging Honest Inquiry in Student Writing," *College Composition and Communication,* 30, (May 1979), 185.

[29]Louis Milic, "Composition Via Stylistics," in *Linguistics, Stylistics, and the Teaching of Composition,* ed. Donald McQuade (Ohio: University of Akron, 1979), 101.

[30]W. U. McDonald, Jr., "The Revising Process and the Marking of Student Papers," *College Composition and Communication,* 29, (May 1978), 169.

PART II

GUIDELINES FOR TEACHING WRITING

CHAPTER FOUR

INITIATING WRITING—THE RAW MATERIALS

*The good writer is wasteful. He saws and shapes and
cuts away, discarding wood ends, shavings, saw dust,
bent nails—whatever doesn't fit and doesn't work.
The writer cannot build a good strong piece of writing
unless he has gathered an abundance of fine raw materials.*

Donald Murray

*When we begin to represent the propositional
nature of language, we are getting as near as we
possibly can to pure thought, the raw stuff of which
discourse is made.*

W. Ross Winterowd

Only when the writer possesses or knows how to acquire vital and abundant raw materials can the most effective process of writing begin. Writing necessarily involves linking experiences into meaningful new perceptions which a writer can then share by mapping those perceptions into words. The logical analysis and synthesis required in mapping those experiences into words *on paper* must take into account three important elements:

1. Something to say: message/subject
2. A reason for saying it: writer's purpose
3. Someone to say it to: reader/audience

These three elements cannot be separated during the actual writing process, but for the sake of discussion in this text, we will begin with the invention of a subject—having something to say.

4.1 Inventing a subject

WRITER ⟶ MESSAGE ⟶ READER

Invention requires a process view of rhetoric.

Richard E. Young

*Discourse is a process; one idea generates another
in ongoing, openended progression.*

Jacqueline Berke

The process of writing actively engages the writer. Every writer goes through a process of exploration to discover a subject. In order to develop a good strong piece of writing worthy of a reader's interest, the writer must have something to say. Not only must the writer have something to say, the writer must have a commitment, a point of view, to the chosen subject.

UNIVERSALS IN WRITING

Good writing, that which comes alive and arouses both writer and reader, comes from a variety of sources. Central to all good writing, however, is a concern for universals, that is, an awareness of ideas, beliefs, attitudes, expectations, fears, and hopes that are identifiable to all of us. Good writers know that as part of the process of exploration to discover a subject they must ask, "Is this a universal theme?" "Is this topic one which others, besides myself, will care about?"

What is a universal? It is that aspect of a piece of writing that makes a reader say, "Yes, I understand how that could happen." "Of course, everyone has had that experience." Universals are a part of everyone's experience. They include love, anger, hope, fear, pride, sorrow, pity, compassion, desire for peace, understanding, knowledge, freedom, and security. Universals are repetitious; each generation discovers them again. In fact, each succeeding generation believes it has discovered an idea for the first time. Universals are those ideas which bind us together because they are of concern to each of us. Universals are those ideas or beliefs we talk about, think about, fight about, and write about.

We write because of the need to express ourselves and explore within ourselves. A piece of writing evolves much as a tree grows. A tree begins with a seed. The seed grows as it is watered and fed. It sends out roots and develops a trunk. The roots hold the tree in place as its trunk grows and branches develop. As the branches develop, the tree is pruned and fertilized. It continues to grow and evolves into a mature tree with leaves, branches, and blossoms. It is a thing of beauty and a part of nature's ecosystem.

A piece of writing develops in much the same way. It begins with a seed, a kernel idea, something a writer wants to express. The seed is nurtured and developed; it is fertilized by the writer's knowledge, experience, and judgments. As the kernels grow into multiple paragraphs, the writer shapes the content just as the tree is pruned to give it a balance—a sense of symmetry and a means to continue growth. As writers develop and nurture kernel ideas, they add supporting information, the details which are the supports and expansions (the branches) of the thesis. And what supplies the roots of the writing? The "roots" are the universals—those ideas which hold the mind and the imagination of the writer. The "roots" are ideas which send out "feelers" to the reader and produce interconnections with the reader's own experience. The universals provide the unity and stability to hold the main idea in place.

And, like the tree, the piece of writing matures and blossoms, producing fresh insights for the reader and the writer.

Thus writing is rooted in universals. "Great writing, lasting writing, interesting writing concerns itself with universals. That is, it concerns itself with human qualities and experiences which are shared at least potentially by all mankind. ... If the universals are there and the writing is good, the two minds are together, and the reader and the writer are brothers."[1]

How do writers ensure that their subjects are indeed universals? All events bear a direct relationship to human beings; we are social creatures who interact with one another. Events occur which affect us all, and we do not live in a state of isolation, independent of everyone and everything around us. Human beings are indeed unique. They create—life, art, music. They build—machines, dwellings, empires. They invent—rockets, computers, fibers, foodstuffs, bombs. They destroy—societies, environments, themselves. They also write—to affect all these things. We have an idea, a kernel of thought we wish to explore. Thus, for many writers, one way to discover a subject is to consider a topic or idea from the perspective of how it relates to human beings. We humans are self-centered; if writers look at topics from this perspective, they will have a good chance of successfully communicating with their audiences.

Rougier and Stockhum suggest that writers discover the subject, that is the man-universal relationship, when they take "a mental walk around a subject, examine it carefully from as many points of view as possible, associate it with man, and pinpoint any universals that the association reveals" (1970:34).

They believe it is possible to associate any subject to man if writers—

- Stay with what seems to be a barren subject: analyze it from many perspectives.

- View the subject in relation to time: explore values of time; compare with earlier time.

- Look at the origins of the subject: where does it come from? How has it evolved?

- Examine the subject as a problem: what can be done about it? How can we improve, destroy, revitalize it?

Discovering and applying the universals for writing also requires *honesty* on the part of the writer. Honest inquiry into a subject stems from good reading and good writing, that is, from a "questioning and reasonably open-minded attitude but also from workable methods."[2] In fact, one of the most powerful intellectual aids to students is their learning the techniques of rhetorical invention necessary to honest inquiry. For instance, to approach any writing task honestly, writers must be able to "look at many sides of a question, take into account conflicting data, consider relative merits of alternative hypotheses, concede weaknesses and claim strengths in conclusions."[3] They must be able to distinguish probability from absolute truth and present it as such. Further, writers must avoid one-sidedness or bias and misleading proof. At the same time, they must present their convictions and their findings honestly and in a straightforward manner.

To examine universals, honestly, in any material or within themselves, according to Harrington, writers must be able to (1979:184).

1. *Recognize a problem as worthy of inquiry . . .* and then define the problem clearly. The problem usually arises from some kind of clash or uneasy feeling in one's reaction to a situation. It may stem from a relationship between the writer and the reader or the writer and the subject; it may involve some troubling situation, a surprise development, or merely the need to overcome a problem as simple as putting a bicycle together. Finding a solution lies in the writer's possession of reasonable personal experience, observation, reading, or education; his or her ability to achieve original thought by linking old knowledge with new or by making new combinations of old ideas; and the ability to recognize the universal qualities of the problem and to engage the reader's intelligence and experience.

2. *Undergo a subconscious period of incubation* during which new understandings and definitions of the problem develop.

3. *Experience illumination concerning the problem.* Large piles of data are ineffectual and useless without a clearly defined and verified hypothesis. Heuristic devices are important aids for focusing on the problem, for seeing possibilities for solutions, and for verifying those solutions.

In order to carry out a search with honesty—to find the universals in material with honesty—writers must be personally involved, committed to their positions, and aware of their sources of material.

SOURCES OF MATERIAL

Inventing a subject for writing involves two basic considerations: self-satisfaction and fulfillment of the task. The combination of these two considerations, according to Britton, brings the writers' full force of knowledge, attitudes, and language experience to bear on the task (1975:7). And since the composition process "begins in the mind and the way the mind looks *out* upon its subject matter and *in* upon itself, "[4] writers, like the orators of old, are encouraged to read widely and study conscientiously in order to "stock" the mind with subject matter. Material to "prime the mind's pump" comes from three resources classified by Winterowd as (1) the writer, (2) the context, and (3) the message (1975:2).

Writers look first *within* themselves to find material. They analyze their own experiences, perceptions, beliefs, attitudes, and feelings to formulate ideas about which to write. To do this, student-writers engage in interior monologues in which they talk to themselves in order to find themselves. This "talking" may be in the form of "free writing" through which writers record on paper all the ideas that come to mind about a subject. On the other hand, writers may be responding to a picture, a cartoon, a TV ad, a piece of music, or a certain smell. In other words, writers engage in processes of association, "talking" to themselves, relating sensory impressions to previous experiences.

Indeed writers also look beyond themselves to discover subjects; they look *out* on a subject. That is, they look beyond the person of the writer to events occurring in the world "out there." Writers using context, a particular situation, as a resource may (1) interview people to discover their points of view or (2) debate issues with friends around the luncheon table to gain insights into others' values and perhaps contrast their personal experience with that of others. Furthermore writers may analyze events to garner reactions: how will an event affect individuals, a particular country, a culture, or a religion? When writers look at situations as resources, they engage the world around them and interact with others. Their thinking is stimulated by their interactions with others and they begin to establish points of view.

The *message*, or information writers glean from reading, is the third vital resource for writers.

Through reading, writers gather data; they find answers to questions and support for positions, they prove points, and they discover truths. Writers read and discover fresh insights. For example, students may read from an anthology about the Calvinist work ethic and its effect on American society and realize that the work ethic is indeed part of their own personal experience. On the other hand, they may realize that the work ethic is completely alien to their cultural experiences. In addition, students may respond to a piece of poetry that touches an event central to their own experience. Reading then becomes another means through which writers discover their subjects, universals that will touch their readers.

Obviously writers have a wealth of material available to them from these three resources. They may engage in interior monologues, participate in group discussions, debates, and brainstorming sessions, or carry on interviews. In each case they raise questions to which they seek answers. Consciously or unconsciously, their questions fall into patterns which Young, Becker, and Pike (1970:94) describe as questions of—

- *Fact*—Who? What? Where? or When?

- *Process*—How was it done? How did it happen?

- *Relationship*—How does a system relate to another system in terms of:
  a. *Value*—Is it better than or worse than?
  b. *Cause/effect*—What would happen if?
  c. *Consistency*—What causes it? What logical patterns can be ascertained? Do the pieces fit together?
  d. *Probability*—What should be done about it?

When writers use such questions, we see them developing techniques—developing methods of inquiry to satisfy their needs to discover subjects.

HEURISTICS

Topics should not shackle the mind. They should liberate.—Winterowd

For stocking the mind and exploring the world—for looking *in* and looking *out*—writers need heuristic aids.

Inventio (Latin) is the equivalent of *heuresis* (Greek). Both words originally meant "invention"

or "discovery"; however, we will take the definition of heuristics one step further. Orators in ancient times were trained in heuristics: techniques which, then and now, set the mind in motion, entreat thinking, stir memory, and coax imagination.[4] They are methods of "solving problems; a series of steps or questions which are likely to lead an intelligent analyst to a reasonable solution of a problem."[5] "A heuristic ... provides a series of questions or operations that guides inquiry and increases the chances of discovering a workable solution."[6] The same heuristics used by the ancient orators, and many adaptations of them, work quite successfully today for speakers and writers alike. To bring order to the process of discovery and to help writers originate and clarify their ideas is the underlying purpose. Aristotle codified invention procedures into four broad categories, or "topics," that could be used for analyzing a subject matter on any occasion. All heuristics incorporate one or more of these categories.

HEURISTIC CATEGORIES

1. Degree—the question of more or less

2. Possibility—the possible and the impossible

3. Probability—past fact and future fact

4. Size—the question of greatness or smallness

The treatment of these four categories was originally a formal one, but as they are currently used, heuristics can be both *formal*, the "systematic inquiry into a subject matter and into one's mind as well to discover the best possibilities for discourse,"[7] or *informal*, free-ranging explorations into one's store of knowledge and experience and into other's perspectives on a subject as well.

However formal or informal they may be, heuristics have three main functions as identified by Young, Becker, and Pike: (1) They aid investigators in retrieving relevant information. (2) They draw attention to important information investigators do not possess but can acquire. (3) And they prepare the investigating mind for the intuition of an ordering principle or hypothesis (p. 120). In this last function ESL writers need additional guidance when this intuition has not been fully developed. Thus, to encourage students to discover for themselves as they search for a topic (an activity many ESL writers have rarely engaged in) teachers need to provide for students time to ask the right questions, to rephrase, restate, and summarize, and to experience maximum feedback in finding, defining, and analyzing subject/problem/solution/situation/purpose and audience.

Further, teachers need to be sure the heuristics they offer students meet certain criteria.[8]

Criteria for heuristics

- A heuristic should be broad enough to cover all subjects so that it can be internalized and used repeatedly.

- The writer should be able to move freely within the heuristic, working from middle to beginning to end and back again.

- It should be flexible enough for the rhetorical situation in general—reader, writer, situation, and purpose.

- The model should be highly generative, triggering new insights and synthesis of information.

- It should be simple and clear enough for writers to use as an *aid* to writing rather than a device which might cause writers to get bogged down in the technique itself. (Irmscher says a heuristic should consist of no more than five to nine questions because the mind cannot efficiently and effectively handle more.)

All heuristics, regardless of form or function, are most effective when they conform to these criteria.

Within these criteria are many specific heuristic patterns, each serving different functions—from individual self-discovery, to group activities for stimulating thought and developing awareness of audience expectations, to questioning in order to discover gaps in information or flaws in reasoning. Developing writers should be acquainted with many types of heuristics, since some specific methods may work better than others for a given writer. In addition, writers frequently need the help of more than one heuristic to develop a writing task fully. The main idea is to get writers to internalize the heuristics so they can be used for subsequent invention.

Types of heuristics

Some of the heuristics we have found to be most helpful to ESL writers are classified according to Kinney's "ways of knowing" about a subject.[9] Compatible with the way the mind works and with the natural ways in which writers develop information, they are first the *exploratory/intuitive* heuristics, which are used primarily for finding or creating the subject for a piece of writing. These are concerned with "knowing as nonlinear immediate understanding" (in complement to the inferential ... ordered sequence of rational thought). These heuristics combine right-brain thinking with left-brain terms, ultimately bringing full consciousness to writing. They are characterized most often by what we call "flashes of intuition," "inner reflections," "felt sense," or "flights of imagination" such as those used by the English Romanticists and the American Transcendentalists. Brainstorming, free association, free writing, diary keeping, and journal writing typify the intuitive heuristics.

Next are the *position taking/empirical* heuristics which are concerned with "knowing through the senses, through direct physical experience." In other words, these heuristics involve students' learning by performing a task, by taking an action, by participating in a project, by experiencing sensation. Often aligned primarily with descriptive and narrative writing, these heuristics, developed from the active exchange of thoughts and views, can also be used to develop reports of all kinds as well as persuasive writing. Debate, interview, dialogue, role play, and observation/experiment typify these shaping and developing techniques and require writers to see, hear, practice, and actively participate in finding out what works best with their audiences. The direction and feedback of real audiences help ESL writers learn how to *write* to each other as well as how to communicate orally.

Third in the classification are the *information gathering, form giving/rational* heuristics for which according to Kinney "all that is knowable is so through the exercise of reason working sequentially from general premises" (1979:352). These heuristics promote the development of specific information, show writers how to examine various aspects of a subject, give specific form to specific information; that is, they give more emphasis to rhetorical conventions. Further, they more often involve linear, step-by-step procedures in which the logical structure ties everything together as the writer works through the creative process. Burke's Pentad, Larson's Questions, Pike's Tagmemics, the Classical Topics, and problem-solving formulas typify the rational heuristics.

Features of Heuristics

To use heuristics most effectively, students need to understand these important features:

1. Heuristics are a *private matter:* they are basically for discovery of what the writer will eventually put into final shape for an audience. Therefore, messiness and informality do not count at this point.

2. The *goal* of a heuristic is to simplify and clarify thought.

3. Heuristics are like test models; that is, they should be flexible and revisable like an architect's blueprint.

4. Heuristics help writers develop and limit major propositions or points.

5. Heuristics help writers arrange material logically for an audience.

6. Heuristics help prevent the tedious, lengthy work of unnecessary writing.

Individual or group use of heuristics— Specific applications of heuristics may entail individual activities during which the writer uses "self" and "message" as sources in discovery of ready knowledge about a subject/problem, purpose, and/or reading audience. Individual discovery processes can take place simply by the writer's exercise of "inner reflection" or stream of consciousness: questioning, answering, testing, analyzing, and always reading. Eventually, the process will also involve the writer, with pen and paper as well.

But because writing is a "synthesis between the personal and the social,"[10] other applications of heuristics are more empirical in nature and lend themselves to group activities or situations which promote discovery and generation of ideas by doing. When writers work in groups, several things can happen: they develop greater responsibility for their own learning, and they become active participants in the task; teachers become facilitators rather than "all-knowing" authority figures. Further, through the interaction created by generating topics and discussing ideas and issues, developing writers begin to (1) internalize audience expectations, (2) calibrate their own views against the alternate or opposing views of others, and (3) learn style and conventions. In addition, they (4) make new connections in their own minds, thereby gaining new

perceptions, and (5) find out not only what they know but also what they need to know.

Through questioning, listening, and observing, teachers also discover individual student's needs, the group's needs, and how best to provide information and advice to each. Most activities can be set up so that they lead students inductively through the creative process, and in so doing, the teacher enables students to build confidence that they really do have something to say and a means of saying it. To quote from Hawkins, "While we may be self-centered in our quest for knowledge, we must also rely on the direction and feedback we can elicit from our fellows, real or imagined" (1976:4).

Using heuristics. Most heuristics allow writers to develop thoughts without critical review by an outside observer or judge. This is particularly important for writers using the *exploratory/intuitive* techniques because they are basically unstructured and allow for the free range of a writer's thoughts. The intuitive techniques are also especially helpful for unblocking the writing barriers for ESL students because of the relative ease with which writers can initially record their thoughts with key words rather than having to monitor the correctness of grammar and sentence structure. Many of these heuristics help writers escape "confusion and panic by seeing patterns in the jumble of impressions."[11] In fact, most of these heuristics help writers quickly determine the direction of their thoughts. Following are samples of the heuristics we have found to be effective with ESL writers. With the exception of the journal, each one can be used with groups of students as in-class activities, or each can be used individually.

EXPLORATORY/INTUITIVE HEURISTICS INVOLVE

Getting started—drawing on personal knowledge, experience, and feelings to help writers discover what they have to say . . . capturing and recording ideas quickly.

Brain pattern

The brain pattern is a free-association technique which brings both the logical and creative sides of the brain into play and which helps writers get started.[12] It is a hand-eye-brain process by which writers quickly record for 5 minutes whatever they know and feel about a subject, using single words stemming from a central idea. Since the pattern is for

64

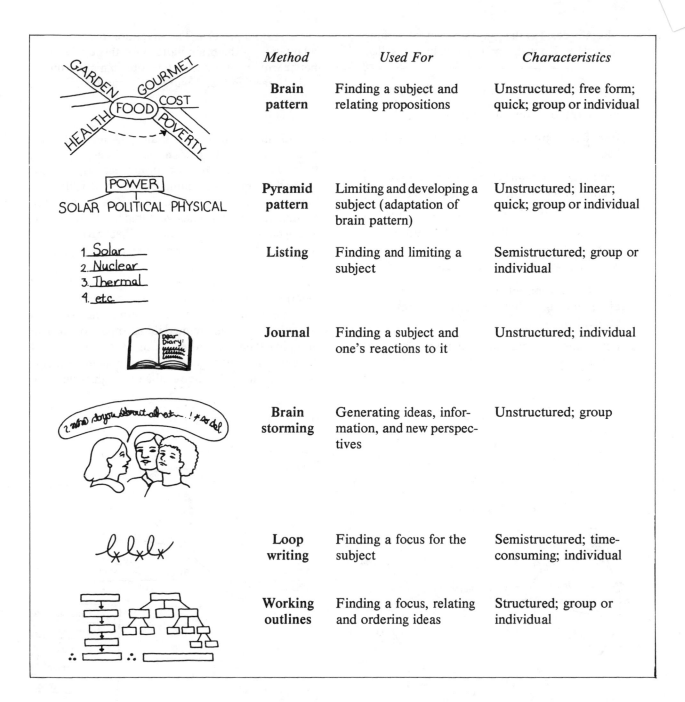

	Method	Used For	Characteristics
	Brain pattern	Finding a subject and relating propositions	Unstructured; free form; quick; group or individual
	Pyramid pattern	Limiting and developing a subject (adaptation of brain pattern)	Unstructured; linear; quick; group or individual
	Listing	Finding and limiting a subject	Semistructured; group or individual
	Journal	Finding a subject and one's reactions to it	Unstructured; individual
	Brain storming	Generating ideas, information, and new perspectives	Unstructured; group
	Loop writing	Finding a focus for the subject	Semistructured; time-consuming; individual
	Working outlines	Finding a focus, relating and ordering ideas	Structured; group or individual

the writer alone, it can take whatever form appeals to the writer's sense of creativity. It usually results in rough notes which require additional limiting and expansion. It is a highly unstructured heuristic, which can be used effectively by either individuals or groups. However, when students share their patterns with each other, they have an opportunity to experience another person's perception of the subject. With this method writers quickly focus on main ideas and levels of importance, space permits the easy addition of new information, and key concepts or propositions are easily linked. Features especially helpful to ESL students are that the pattern—

1. Requires only single words which allow ESL writers to capture their thoughts on the subject *in English* more quickly than if they were also required to think about and grammatically structure them.

2. Reinforces (a) the physical act of writing words in English and (b) vocabulary skills.

Suggestions for creating the Brain Pattern

- Begin in the center of the page.

- Print words in capital letters for easier read-back.

- Print words on lines with each line connecting to another line or to the center circle for basic structure.

- Write without stopping to think in order to let the subconscious mind generate ideas. Keep the pen or pencil moving at all times.

- Don't spend too much time trying to think of just the right English word to express a concept.

- Let order and organization take care of themselves.

Pyramid pattern. The invention pyramid is an adaptation of the brain pattern for those who work better with a pattern that develops in a more linear, orderly fashion (see Figures 4.2 and 4.3).

Listing

Listing is also an initiator—a technique for finding a subject. It can be a free-association technique or it can be more controlled. An age-old method for recording numerous ideas quickly, this heuristic can be used by an individual or a group. Listing helps writers discover what is on their minds and what they know about a subject. By "paying attention" to their responses, they can also discover how they feel about the items on their lists. As a result, they are able to limit their choices and determine the best approach to the subjects they ultimately select. Writers can discover their subjects by noting how many related items appear on the list, grouping them according to the associations that develop, and then questioning the item or items selected. This heuristic results in rough notes from

---

FIGURE 4.1 shows Russell's version of a brain pattern about reading skills.[13]

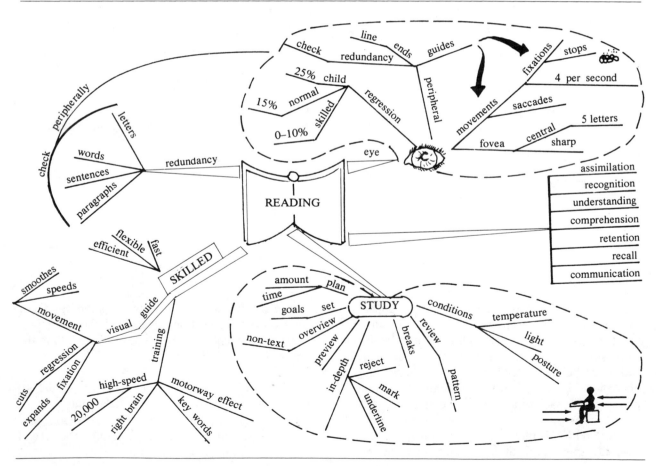

FIGURE 4.2 INVENTION PYRAMID. WRITER 1

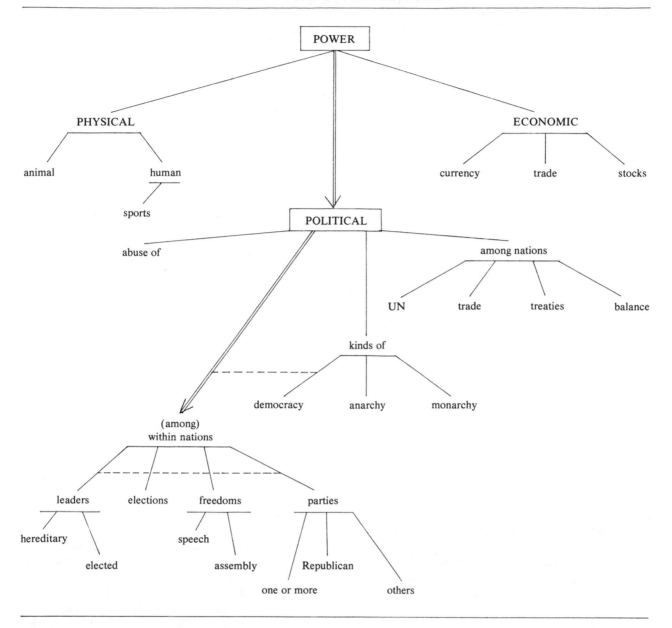

which the writer builds. It is advantageous for ESL writers because of the rapidity with which they can record their thoughts *in English,* and because of the somewhat structured format for further defining their topics.

Suggestions for using Listing

- If there is a general (or specific) purpose for writing, write it at the top of the page.

- List quickly and briefly (no more than 10 items).

- Relate concepts by grouping similar items.

- Pay attention to which item or items create the most interest, reaction, conflict, or appeal.

- Set limits to the one most interesting, or most important, or most amusing item.

- Allow the most vital idea to grow by using a question/answer technique.

FIGURE 4.3 INVENTION PYRAMID. WRITER 2

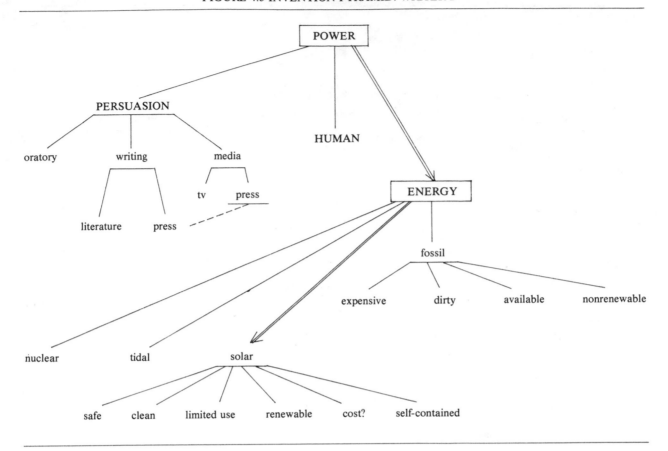

A writer cannot and should not try to use all these questions at one time (notice that this writer used only 7 from the sample); in fact, a writer may need other questions not listed here to complete an investigation of a subject. The questions help the writer direct attention to what needs to be developed about the subject and to the most conventional or logical approach for its development.

Journal keeping

Journal keeping is an unstructured and totally individual way for writers to record their thoughts, observations, and experiences on a daily basis—what interests, troubles, pleases them. Writers are often reflective in this kind of writing, and the pressureless situation of knowing they are recording only for themselves allows more ideas to surface. Further, a quick, unjudged, daily writing task helps dispell the fear of the blank page or the cry, "I have nothing to say." When students think they are devoid of ideas, or experience writer's block, they can go to their journals for inspiration, for a starting place .. to find a subject.

Advantages of journal keeping are that writers get to know themselves and their reactions to situations. Daily recording helps them sharpen their powers of observation, develop an awareness of problems with which they might be struggling or questions which they might have. The journal provides an opportunity for writing out those problems, which often helps solve them or at least helps put them in perspective. Therefore, it serves to clear the mind for other business. Features of journal writing which are especially advantageous for ESL writers are that students must write something every day; thus they learn to write by writing—and their language skills in general improve. The fear of writing in another language is lessened. In addition, it provides an opportunity for student-teacher rapport to develop beyond what is possible in the more formal classroom; it allows the teacher to give encouragement and to monitor students' progress without grade-related assignments. Most importantly, journal writing provides ESL students with a steam valve, an outlet, for the emotions and frustrations which second language

1. List (8 to 10) items about

music	*ways in which I spend my leisure time*
*sports	most important things in my life
reading	most interesting issues, activities, etc.
drawing	most important problems facing me, my nation, the
art	world
food	most important beliefs
family	etc.
walking	
*archery	

2. Limit   (the subject in as many of these ways as possible).

Sports   a specific kind—Archery

                      time—11th century to 19th century to
                           present
                      place—Japan
                      number
                      thing/person/*concept*—spiritual training
                      type—cultural heritage
                      aspect
                      example—7 steps
                      experience—requires discipline and
                         concentration

3. Question[14]   (Answer as many of these questions about your item as possible.)

Question	*Method of Development*
✔ 1. What does X mean?	Definition
✔ 2. How can X be described?	Description
✔ 3. What are the component parts of X?	Simple analysis
✔ 4. How is X made or done?	Process analysis
✔ 5. How *should* X be made or done?	Directional analysis
✔ 6. What is the essential function of X?	Functional analysis
7. What are the causes of X?	Causal analysis
8. What are the consequences of X?	Causal analysis
9. What are the types of X?	Classification
10. How does X compare with Y?	Comparison
11. What is the present status of X?	Comparison
12. How can X be interpreted?	Interpretation
13. What are the facts about X?	Reportage
14. How did X happen?	Narration
15. What kind of person is X?	Characterization
✔ 16. What is my personal response to X?	Reflection
17. What is my memory of X?	Reminiscence
18. What is the value of X?	Evaluation
19. How can X be summarized?	Summary
20. What case can be made *for* or *against* X?	Argumentation

(The paper developed from this sample heuristic exercise appears in Section 4.4.)

students often experience as they struggle to master the language. This is especially true for students who have only recently arrived in the country and are trying to deal with issues such as separation from home and family or unfamiliarity with a new culture.

Suggestions for Journal Keeping:
Students should—

- Write briefly—unless inspired to do more.

- Write *something* every day.

- Write only for themselves.

- Journals should never be graded; however, it is often helpful for the teacher to respond to the message.

Sample entries from an ESL student's journal:

Sept. 26th 1980

have a
In my country we ~~get~~ well-organized public transport system. Our train service and the bus service belong to the government. Most of the employees, as well as the school children, travel by bus or train. The govt issues beneficiary season tickets to all the government employees.

for
~~Beecause of~~ this reason only very few people maintain their own vehicles. It is comparatively cheaper to use the state transpor*tation* facilities because the price of one gallon of gasoline is more than two dollars now. Since the income capacity is also
ss
very low, it is impos*i*ble for an average man to maintain a car for his own use.

There are passenger trains as well as the good trains. Still we do not have an underground train system. It will take some more time for us to get all the modern transpor*tation* systems.

Teacher response:

It sounds well developed already. We desperately need more public transportation in most parts of our country, too.

Oct. 14th 1980

Sri Lanka is famous among the European and Asian countries because of the polite people. Sri Lankans have a nice way of greeting other people and becom*ing* friendly with the others in a short period of time. We show very high respect to any elderly person any person we greet with a smile. Even within the country people are so attached to each other. When a person is in trouble, there are many others to help him to overcome his problem. Our people always maintain very pleasant neighborhoods.

Palitha Wickramasinghe

Teacher response:

That explains why you are all such fine people— and students.

Were this student to develop a "writer's block," he could go to his journal to find a subject about which he is knowledgeable or concerned. Either of these entries could easily be developed using other heuristics.

Brainstorming

"The relationships of talk to writing is central to the writing process."[15] Brainstorming is a spontaneous verbal activity excellent for generating a subject or for expanding ideas and perceptions about a subject. This group activity is an "ice breaker" which helps students relax and also see that each of them has something to contribute to a subject. Because of its unstructured format, students can speak out about whatever the brainstorming activity triggers in their minds. The rapid exchange allows for exploration, clarification, interpretation, explanation, and insight into different opinions. Since brainstorming is a *sharing* of ideas, it helps students develop an awareness of other points of view in an uncritical setting, as well as an awareness of their own personal points of view. It establishes an in-class rapport among the writers, a rapport which is essential when they read each other's papers and give feedback on them. However, because of its free-associational format, a facilitator or moderator should be chosen to help keep the flow of ideas "on track." To be most effective, this activity requires a whole class period.

For ESL students, brainstorming is especially valuable for (1) gaining insights into others' views, (2) reinforcing conversation and listening skills,

(3) note taking practice, and (4) relaxing and developing rapport within the classroom.

Suggestions for Brainstorming
- Make clear the noncritical nature of the discussion.

- Keep the discussion "on track" with a facilitator or moderator.

- Establish the subject to be discussed.

- Encourage the practicipation of *all* class members.

- Encourage participants to take notes as ideas are suggested.

Loop writing

Loop writing, adapted by Cowan and Cowan (1980:9) from Peter Elbow's approach to free writing, is a more complex heuristic which involves writing to find what one wants to say and to find one's point of view. It is a semistructured, individual activity which requires "wet ink" writing, that is, writing for a certain period of time without stopping. The writer writes the first loop on a "given" subject for 10 minutes without stopping, changing, or correcting. Then the writer reads what he or she has written and takes the kernel idea from this 10-minute loop as the starting point for the next 10-minute loop. This procedure is repeated a third time with the main idea of the second loop as a starting point for the third loop.

Because this method for finding a subject and developing a focus will take a 1-hour class period, teachers should allow for that discovery time. Since this activity is often an exhausting exercise for native English writers, it can be even more so for ESL writers; therefore, it is better to use this form with an energetic, enthusiastic group or an advanced class, or wait until later in the semester when the prospect of such intensive writing will not be so frightening. However, since practice in free composition can and should begin at the sentence level, the 10-minute time limit could easily be changed for a group working at such a level.

The advantages of looping are that writers learn to write by writing. They are forced to write without editing, which frees them to discover and explore thoughts, feelings, and perceptions in their data banks. It is helpful in developing thesis statements as key concepts begin to emerge from each loop. And

perhaps most importantly, it reinforces for ESL students the idea that they do indeed have knowledge of a subject *in English* and that they can write about that subject *in English.*

Suggestions for using Loop Writing
- Make clear that the goal is to write "lots" rather than "well."

- Begin with a specific subject.

- Write for a set time without stopping . . . no matter what comes.

- Make no changes or corrections.

- Sum up what has been written in each loop and write that kernel idea as a heading for the next loop.

Following are two ESL student examples of looping exercises.

Student A—Maria

Loop 1

I believe in God, I believe in freedom, I believe in, I believe in, I believe in reincarnation, I believe that something we are doing is producing cancer, I believe in. I believe in, I believe in, I believe, I believe in, I believe that people should be sincere, I believe that lies always become with more problems, I believe that if a person is suffering for a disease we could let him die without any medication, I believe that, I believe that if we know the bad side of the things then we can know the good side, I believe that if we suffer then we are able to know what happiness is, I believe in, I believe that no one have the right to interfere with other human right, I believe in . . .

Loop 2

I believe life is not an easy thing. If you read about the things I wrote before you will notice that all of them are base on life. All the problems that we know are related with life, we haven't heard yet that a dead person have had problems.

Loop 3

If you read the paragraph before, you will think that I like to be dead, that is not true. I have had some beautiful times, also I have had some terrible times, but it is because for this terrible times that I have learned to know what beautiful times are. For example, I know that . . .

Student B—Julio

Loop 1

Because I arrived late to class I am very sorry but I had to talk with a person of Mexico who is going to come to study here the next month and I opened my house and help for the time he will need to find a home for he and his family. Then I came running to class. And I am writing same thing I did yesterday.

I received a cassets I bought and I was listening to some of them I am very happy with the music I bought and I enjoyed listening to Chakovsky's 1812 simphony, the best of the classics played by the most famous piano player Liberace in which he plays the always beautiful Tehowcorsky number one concerto. Also a bought another about jazz . . .

Loop 2

I like music because is a kind of communication.

Music was used for our ancestors to express their feelings in situations such as religion, war, love, etc., and music is still used for the same purposes now a days. For example, you can know the feelings of Schuber when you listen to some of the famous Schuber's senatos which are blue and become you sad.

Music is used also to express protest about political situations. For example, "The Jolckloristas" which is a latin american music group, sing several songs against the situation in Chile, Argentina, etc.

In my opinion these are some of the reasons for which I consider music a kind of communication and for this reason I use music to communicate my feelings too by means of songs I wrote to my father, my mother and my wife . . .

Loop 3

What do you need to listen music?

You need just be quiet for a minute and you can hear your own music which can tell you if you are sad or happy. This can result you so funny that you aren't going to try but think, which music a deaf and dumb person listen to? You can answer any music because they don't know how to produce it: they don't know the noise. Nevertheless I tell you they have their own internal song, their heart, stomach, etc. they can feel more than us because we have more noise outside that is impossible we hear the beautiful song our heart play when he works.

We can listen to a beautiful music authors play but I recomend you try to be quiet for a minut during your busy day and get a chance to heard your heart sing when he works it will be the best of all experiences you can hear our all fascinating musics there are in the world.

Working outlines

Working outlines are pictures of writing or graphics which help writers see the basic skeleton or form of what they plan to write. With this form, writers tie ideas together: they pinpoint and order main ideas, see where main points need further development, and realize where supporting information needs to be added. These outlines are structured, yet flexible, in that they can be easily revised or reworked completely. They can be developed quickly and can be used by individuals or by groups. Such an outline most often results in a rough tentative outline of a writer's ideas, an overall plan that the writer can see at a glance. Writers can also apply these outlines to other pieces of writing to see how they were developed.

Working outlines are especially helpful to ESL writers in the early stages of writing because they contain elements of rhetorical structure that ESL student-writers must learn in order to communicate successfully in English. Those structures involve some of the conventional forms for organizing ideas, including development of a thesis; beginning, middle, and end of a paper; and methods of developing and arranging supporting points. The universality of the graphic or picture form helps students visualize the parts of writing more easily.

The following five working outlines illustrate how a student worked through part of the writing process to discover, generate, and limit ideas for a paper on the subject "space travel." More than one invention technique (heuristic) can often be used to develop a subject.

Sample 1

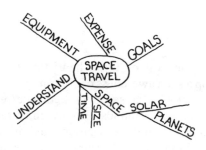

Sample 2

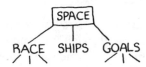

This *linear outline* provides a form or framework for the main support points for the thesis.

Sample 3

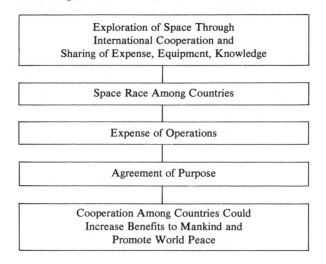

73

Sample 4

Purpose—To Heighten General Awareness of the Cost and Duplication of Space Operations
Audience—General, Unknown—Written in the Form of an Editorial for the Readership of an Urban Community

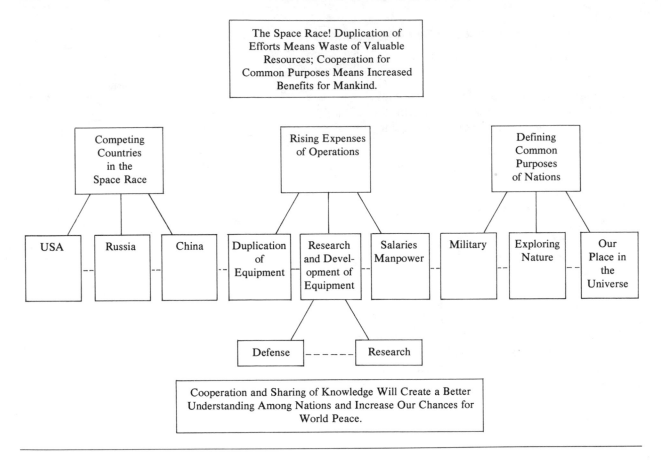

The *pyramid outline* above provides a framework in which the writer can add development of the main support points with example, detail, comparisons, facts, etc. The outline in Sample 5 is the formal sentence outline developed from other invention techniques. It too is subject to change.

The *position taking/empirical* heuristics are shapers and developers. Most of them require the writer's active observation, experimentation, testing, development, discussion, or research of the material about which they will write. Most require verbal participation as well which reinforces the vocabulary, listening, and conversational skills of ESL writers. Because they must research positions for debate and read scripts for role play, writers also reinforce their reading skills, which require them to generalize, synthesize, and elicit specific infor-

mation. Several of these heuristics help writers develop a keen awareness of differing points of view, thus developing a sense of audience/reader expectations and demands. Finally, most require the participant to take a position; and in so doing, writers have an opportunity to develop their persuasive skills.

POSITION TAKING/EMPIRICAL HEURISTICS ARE

Shapers and developers—which build an awareness of audience through exposure to new and different attitudes . . . which generate information and ideas by "doing."

74

A spirit of international cooperation in the space race will be beneficial to the community of nations because it may serve as a catalyst to better understanding between people.

   I. At present countries compete against each other in their efforts to explore outer space.

   A. The United States competes with Russia to get the first manned outpost into outer space.

   B. Both the United States and Russia develop programs enabling them to achieve the goal of being the first nation to establish a space colony.

      1. The United States works to develop the space shuttle.
      2. The Russians work to develop manned space laboratories.

   II. The rising costs of the space program will prevent future expansion unless there is international cooperation.

   A. Presently there is much duplication in areas of exploration between countries.

      1. The United States sent satellites to the moon.
      2. Russia sent satellites to the moon.

   B. The development of equipment is channeled into two extremely expensive areas for each country.

      1. Defense equipment is developed individually and countries are spending large sums of money developing the same equipment.
      2. Research equipment is being developed individually at great expense to individual countries when the purposes for the equipment often overlap.

   C. Because vast numbers of people are employed in each facet of the space program, large sums of money must be spent to train employees.

   III. Greater international cooperation would enable nations to focus their space exploration for common purposes in specific areas and exchange knowledge about those areas.

   A. Joint programs could be established to share knowledge that has already been accumulated by individual nations.

   B. Programs could be established to avoid duplication of effort in developing research programs that would meet a common need.

Increased cooperation, sharing of knowledge, and better understanding of ourselves increases the chances for world peace.

Experiment/observation

Experiment and observation emphasizes the situational context. Writers learn something about how they identify with various situations and the objects and/or actors in those situations. This technique generates information and brings into play writers' powers of observation, which in turn promotes accurate description and reporting of factual information. This serves to point up for writers the differences between the use of fact, what *is* true, and opinion, what *seems* to be or what we want to be true. By observing and experimenting, students learn to tap yet another available resource for material ... especially when they are writing from the position of expert or reporter.

	Method	Used For	Characteristics
Fertilizer	Experiment/observation	Gathering information; description; problem solving. Awareness of situation	Flexible as to structure and time limits. Group or individual
What do you think? / *I think...*	Interview	Gathering information; questioning; discovering alternate views	Semistructured; flexible time requirements; 2 or more people
Point 1...	Dialogue	Discovering one's own as well as others' position on a subject	Unstructured; flexible time requirements; 2 people
	Debate	Developing one's position; gathering proof; practicing persuasion	Structured; time-consuming; group
Howdy, mah name's Tex.	Role play	Developing appreciation for audience position and one's own position. Awareness of situation	Structured; time-consuming; group

Outside the classroom, in the "real world," this heuristic usually requires longer periods of time than would normally be available in a classroom situation; however, observations and experiments can be practiced in a shorter time period in a simulated classroom situation (e.g., coffee making, films, field trips).

This heuristic can be used as either an individual or a group activity. With a group, students benefit by comparing what each observed or found with what their fellow classmates observed in order to discover different perspectives. Further, experiment and observation reinforce students' abilities to generalize, predict, and synthesize material. Thus they provide *specific* experience and information for a writing task and are helpful as well in developing descriptive powers necessary for comparison-contrast, classification, definition, and process, empirically revealing various aspects of a subject, issue, event, problem, or object. They promote the acquisition of these skills (rather than the learning of them) because the focus is on the event or activity rather than on the writing task itself. They are especially advantageous to ESL students because they replace the inhibitions created by a formal classroom atmosphere with a more relaxed realistic setting.

Suggestions for using
Experiment/Observation

- Use all your senses of observation: look, smell, feel, taste, hear.
- Notice changes in the object or situation.
- Be thorough.
- Make notes.
- Cull irrelevant information.
- Report conflicting findings or observations.

76

Interview

Interview is an information-gathering, generative heuristic. It is a method of talking with and/or questioning someone to discover that person's knowledge of and views about a given subject. This technique is usually an individual activity that involves novice or uninformed writers seeking responses from participants, observers, and experts in the area being researched. Writers must analyze the subject/problem in order to know who to approach for information and what to attempt to find out. They should also take notes on the responses they receive. This heuristic is usually somewhat time-consuming, but it can be used as an out-of-class activity. It can also be used in the class by having members of the group interview each other on subjects about which they are knowledgeable.

Advantages of this method are that it develops skills in formulating effective questions; and because it places students in real-life situations, it reinforces all language skills—speaking, listening, vocabulary, and grammar. Further, it promotes the synthesis of information and note taking. In addition, ESL students are provided an opportunity to become acquainted with the community and with members of the community. Interviewing works best when the interviews stem from *real* problem-solving situations, and when students have a real concern for the issue at hand (e.g., Is the mass transit system in X community effective in serving the needs of the student population? If not, can it be changed? How can it be changed?) Important decisions to be made using this method include: Who should be interviewed? What questions should be asked? When and how long should the interview be?

Suggestions for Interview

- Analyze the problem/subject to determine what information is probably needed.

- Decide who to interview.

- Frame questions for the interview.

- Contact the interviewees to set up an appointment. Give them time to gather information.

- Take notes on the responses to the interview questions.

- Synthesize the information and decide what is valuable and what is irrelevant to the subject.

Dialogue

Dialogue is the communication of ideas between two people on any subject. "Writing [too] is communication [and] if we don't talk to each other we will be writing in a vacuum."[16] And further, "talk permits the expression of tentative conclusions and opinions; it gives writers an opportunity to try out ideas."[17] Like interviewing, dialogue is the free exchange of ideas and information about a subject/problem/issue, etc. However, it is usually less formal or structured than interview. It involves "I think . . .," "You think . . .," "But what about . . .," and "On the other hand . . .," a kind of picking-the-brain activity. It is an unstructured discussion which can lead a writer or writers to see just what it is they want to say on a specific subject or an assigned subject. It can help them find a universal stance on whatever subject they are required to address; that is, it will help them find a method of approach to that subject and determine what might interest an audience. Dialogue can provide a *quick* activity for seeking diverse opinions.

Writing groups can and should carry on dialogues orally for immediate response value and then abstract the exercise by writing two-way dialogues individually in question-and-answer sessions with themselves. Such an exercise helps students learn to anticipate audience response.

Special advantages for the ESL writer are reinforcement in the skills of questioning, analyzing, listening, and conversing. This heuristic also serves as an ice breaker and helps student-writers relax in an uncritical, pressureless situation. It tends to provide a workshop as opposed to a formal classroom atmosphere.

Suggestions for using Dialogue

- Establish the subject to be discussed.

- Assure a relaxed atmosphere.

- Encourage all participants to engage freely in the dialogue.

- If using dialogue in a classroom, set some time limits.

- Have participants share views with other members of the class.

Debate

Debate is a more highly structured group activity. Though it is time-consuming (it takes at least two to three class periods for preparation and delivery), it is valuable in helping writers develop and express specific points for persuasion. It involves collecting, evaluating, and using factual information and proof. Writers as well as speakers must be able to support and substantiate controversial or general statements with facts, figures, and logical thinking. The participants in this heuristic have immediate feedback for their positions from the opposing debate team and thus develop a keen awareness of audience response. Unlike interview and dialogue, this is a critical activity: the audience requires specific proofs, and students therefore learn to deal with opposition. From this feedback, students also develop an awareness of strengths and weaknesses in argument or in presenting any position. Further, this activity requires attention to a specific subject; it requires taking a definite position (position taking is not always easy for ESL writers who often want to present both sides of a question); researching information in support of that position; presenting the information in a clear, concise form—within established time limits.

This debate heuristic is especially helpful to students for developing persuasive (or argumentative) writing skills. It teaches students how to utilize available resources—interview, reading, etc.—and how to adopt or discard roles and views. For ESL students, it reinforces almost all language skills—reading, listening, speaking, note taking, research, analysis, vocabulary, and grammar.

Suggestions for using Debate

- Be sure the task is realistic and based on a universal theme.

- Agree on the issue to be debated, e.g., "Nuclear power should/should not be available to all countries."

- Thoroughly research both sides of the question.

- Students can defend one position during a class session and then switch and defend the opposite position in a subsequent class session.

- At the end, analyze and evaluate the success of the points presented and the reasons for their success.

Role play

The role play heuristic stresses the situational aspect of writing. It forces writers to imagine themselves in a particular situation or having to solve a special problem, much like many real-life situations when business or technical requests place a writer in the position of having to respond quickly and knowledgeably from a given position. Writers must analyze the variety of possible solutions to a problem. Thus writers examine different aspects of the subject depending on their role as well as the role of the given audience. If writers have trouble identifying with their audiences (the readers of *Popular Science* magazine, for instance), they quickly become aware of the need to learn more about that audience. Writers learn about how they identify with various roles or situations, making them more acutely aware of others' views and of detail and approach in their own writing.

This heuristic is somewhat more complicated than dialogue or interview. It could be used early in a semester with an advanced class, but for less advanced levels, it would probably be more successful if it were used later. It is also somewhat time-consuming, taking at least a 1-hour class period.

Advantages of role play are that it helps develop position taking, perspective, audience awareness, and persuasive skills. Other ESL skills are reinforced as well, especially reading, listening, conversation, and vocabulary.

Suggestions for using Role Play

- Establish situation clearly.

- Be sure situation is one familiar enough to the participants so that they can actually participate.

- Emphasize the need for each participant to stay in character—no matter how much they may agree or disagree with that stance.

- Have students analyze the attitudes that surfaced during the role play.

The third group of heuristics, *information gathering and form giving/rational* clearly demonstrates the overlapping nature and interaction between invention or generating ideas—and shaping or form giving. These particular methods (1) promote the development of specific information, (2) show writers how to view subjects and problems from various aspects, and (3) provide appropriate form to the material. As such, they are more highly structured than the first two groups of heuristics, and some are more time-consuming. However, they are an equally important investment for ESL students, since techniques to improve mastery of the structure of the English language are especially important for those who don't necessarily have an intuitive feel for the English conventions of writing.

Concerned for the most part with critical analysis, these heuristics utilize the context "situation" and the "message," thus exercising the writers' experience and reading skills. They are rational in that they all lend themselves to tying ideas, concepts, and propositions together through step-by-step, logical processes.

INFORMATION GATHERING/FORM GIVING/RATIONAL HEURISTICS ARE

Directors and expanders—which aid in the discovery and generation of material and form . . . which tie ideas together through step-by-step, logical processes. Most are variations of classical invention.

Journalistic

The journalistic approach simply asks *Who?* U.S., Russia, China. *What?* race. *When?* present/future. *Where?* in space. *How?* ships, satellites. *Why?* knowledge, military.

	Method	Used For	Characteristics
	Journal-istic	Gathering surface facts and information	Structured; quick; group or individual
	Drama-tistic	Multidimensional analysis of the facts and the interactions of the situation	Structured; time-consuming; group or individual
	Questions	Finding specific information about a subject; defining an approach . . . a form	Structured; flexible time requirements; group or individual
	Cubing	Finding different aspects of a subject . . . a focus	Structured; quick; group or individual
	Classical invention	Exploring what one knows and needs to know about a subject; developing argumentation	Structured; time-consuming; group or individual
	Tag-memics	Examining and solving problems by looking at many aspects; gathering information; developing a focus; organizing	Structured; time-consuming; group or individual

79

It is a quick and efficient, structured heuristic for initiating a subject and getting out the essential objective surface information necessary in almost any expository or persuasive writing task. Writers can use it most effectively when they are working with time pressures such as in an exam situation.

For ESL writers it is particularly effective in reinforcing the formation and use of questions and answers. Further, since it is quick, clear, and simple to use, it is especially helpful for beginning to intermediate ESL writers.

Dramatistic

The dramatistic approach, borrowed from Burke's Pentad,[18] is a more complex heuristic than the journalistic one because it functions at a multidimensional level. It doesn't just ask "Who?" and "What?" but rather it combines the terms to ask, *"How does Who affect What?"* It gets at the *motives* and *interaction* of a situation; it analyzes far beyond the surface-level facts. The dynamics involved in the interaction call for more of the writer's subjectivity, judgment, and opinion; they stimulate more ways for the writer to see and think about the subject. Burke uses interaction between and among Agent, Purpose, Act, Means, Scene. For ESL students these terms might be adapted to a series of questions which clearly spell out the interactions or relationships:

How does the *Agent* (U.S., Russia, China)
           Who

affect the *Purpose* (getting into space)? How
           Why

does the *Means* affect the *Agent*? The *Purpose*?
    How   Who   Why

and so on.

This heuristic is recommended for use with more advanced ESL groups when a complex situation needs to be analyzed. Also its adaptation to fit the level of the group is advisable. It will usually require a class period for completion if it is used with a group.

Questions

There are a variety of "question format" heuristics. These can be time-consuming or quick; but whatever amount of time they take, we see that "when the topics are posed in the form of questions ... they seem to work better for students as generating devices, perhaps because a question by its very nature stimulates a response."[19] Systematic questions *answered by writers themselves* force them to become familiar with facts and the relationships possible among them, and with the experiences worth writing about. They must examine the facts underlying concepts important to them and the content of propositions which they may want to write. Not all questions produce useful answers for every situation or for every subject; as a result, writers need to practice with questions to learn which ones work best and when. Berke's Twenty Questions are included in the listing heuristic, and an adaptation of Larson's questioning heuristic is included here. ESL teachers and students need to remain aware that many of the questions will not apply to every given situation and thus should use them accordingly. To do otherwise could cause confusion and frustration for developing writers. In many cases, especially with beginning to intermediate students, the teacher may expect to cull the questions before presenting them to the students as a heuristic.

Questions

A. *Physical Objects*

1.	What are the object's characteristics: shape, dimension, materials?	Description
2.	What sort of structure does it have?	Classification
3.	What is it similar to?	Compare/Contrast
4.	How does it differ from other things that resemble it?	Compare/Contrast
5.	Who or what produced it?	Cause/Effect
6.	Who uses it? for what?	Process

B. *Events*

1.	Exactly what happened? (Who? What? When? Where? Why?)	Definition
2.	What were its causes?	Cause/Effect
3.	What were its consequences?	Cause/Effect

4. How was the event like or unlike similar events?	Compare/Contrast
5. To what other events was it connected?	Association
6. How might the event have been changed or avoided?	Analysis

C. *Abstract Concepts* (e.g., democracy, justice)

1. How has the term been defined before?	Definition
2. How do you define the term?	Definition
3. What other concepts have been related to it?	Association
4. In what ways has this concept affected the lives of people?	Cause/Effect
5. How might the concept be changed to work better?	Cause/Effect

D. *Propositions* (statements to be proved or disproved)

1. What must be established before the reader will believe it?	Definition, Description, Cause/Effect
2. What are the meanings of key words in the proposition?	Definition
3. By what kinds of evidence or argument can propositions be proved or disproved?	Proof—facts
4. What counterarguments must be confronted or refuted?	Proof—facts
5. What are the practical consequences of the proposition?	Cause/Effect

Adapted from Cowan and Cowan (1980:33).

Cubing

Since "the turning point in the whole cycle of growing [in writing] is the emergence of a focus or a theme,"[20] writers can most effectively use cubing (Cowan and Cowan, p. 21) as a quick means for identifying focus for a subject and a workable form as well. This heuristic works best for looking at a subject from all angles for the purpose of setting limits. It, like most of the "rational" heuristics, is an adaptation of classical invention, a simplified method which asks students simply and quickly to—

1. *Describe* —by using one's senses to look at color, size, shape; to feel; to smell; to touch; to hear.

2. *Compare* —what it is like or unlike.

3. *Associate* —it with whatever it brings to mind, similar or dissimilar.

4. *Analyze* —how it is composed, what it is part of, what is part of it.

5. *Apply* —it in whatever way it can be used or done.

6. *Argue* —for it or argue against it, and give reasons for taking that position.

Students should write about all six sides of the cube, working consistently (3 to 5 minutes or more for each side). This structured and quick heuristic is excellent for ESL students because of its simplicity. At the top of page 82 is an example of an ESL student's cubing exercise. It was based on the topic, "Law," a universal subject. The final paper appears in the Appendix. Other heuristics and rough notes for this paper appear in Section 4.4.

Describe it—Law cannot be considered as a stable aspect. It has no color, size, shape, or smell. It changes from country to country and from time to time.

Compare it—Laws and rules are alike in that they both present the things to be done or not to be done, or general sequences of events. But every law can be considered as a kind of rule, while it is not possible to consider every rule as a law.

Associate it—Law is the rules of conduct established by the authority or custom or a nation. People are supposed to obey law.

Kernel idea for the students' final paper { Analyze it—There are two kinds of law. First kind of law is established by the authority of a nation and guarded by the armed forces of the nation. Any citizen goes to court if he doesn't obey this law. The second type of law is called social law, which is established by the society. Social law is a function of time, tradition, character of the national, geographic settlement of the nation, etc.

Apply it—Although education is very important for the society to obey rules and regulations, law is essential to prevent these rules and regulations from destruction.

Argue it—Actually, rules and laws are determined by human beings, and it can be said that in the future human beings will be able to live without law. On the other hand, it seems impossible to live without any regulation and law because they are the social control for human survival.

Classical invention

Classical invention is the forerunner of many other forms of heuristics. It was originally developed for orators as a device for guiding the logical development of their arguments. Based on Aristotle's four categories, the topoi, or "common topics," helped speakers explore the "regions of

their minds" for what they knew and needed to know. The topics work in the same way today for modern writers of English in developing arguments.

topoi (Greek) = *loci* (Latin) = *place* or *region* (English)

In rhetorical terms, the *topoi* are the places where one looks to find something to say on a given subject; they are a part of the method for probing one's subject in order to discover possible ways of developing the subject. As such, they are form givers. The various forms produced by the topics are not distinct and separate from each other, however. Rather, each one uses elements of each of the others to complete itself. Actually the forms become, in a sense, the purposes for writing or the ways of giving particular emphasis to the subject/problem.

The common topics consist of examining X (the problem, object, situation, issue, etc.) in five ways:

Definition — What is X? Classify and divide it.

Comparison — How or what is X like or different from? How much is it like or different from it?

Relationship — What caused X? What effect does X have on ____? What came before X? What will follow X? What is contrary to X? What restricts X?

Circumstances — What is possible? Is X possible? What about X is possible? What is not possible? What are past facts about X? What can we predict about X for the future? (probability)

Testimony — Where did the facts originate? (famous person, expert, theories) Who says so? What statistics are available? What time-tested theories, maxims, laws support X?

Classical Invention: An ESL writer's questions about "the space race" used to develop a referential paper

Definition:

1. What is the space race?

2. What countries are involved?

Comparison:

1. How are the aims of the United States and Russia similar in regard to space exploration?

2. What pieces of equipment already used by each country are similar?

3. In what way are the motives for space exploration different for the two countries?

4. What areas of common development exist between the two nations?

5. In what areas are the two superpowers most able to achieve an agreement or compromise in their development?

Relationship:

1. Why do people want to explore space?

2. What is the effect of spending billions of dollars for a space program?

3. What are the positive effects of space exploration?

4. What are the negative effects?

5. What are the financial consequences of space exploration?

6. What is contradictory about the space program?

7. What are the consequences of a mutually sponsored space program?

8. What are the results of a mutually sponsored space program?

Circumstances:

1. In what possible areas of research could the United States and Russia collaborate?

2. In what areas and situations would it be impossible for the United States and Russia to cooperate?

3. What has occurred as a result of individual space exploration in the past?

4. What is the most feasible future situation if nations cooperate in the space race?

5. If they do not cooperate, what will happen?

Testimony:

1. What have respected famous scientists said about cooperative space efforts?

2. What evidence is there to support the idea of cooperative effort?

3. What percentage of the government supports joint programs? What would be the financial savings in joint programs?

4. What laws or maxims support the concept of joint exploration?

(After deciding these issues, the writer determines what modes of writing will best develop the information so that the purpose can be achieved.)

Students using classical invention should examine each topic thoroughly, questioning whether they need what that topic would help them produce, questioning whether that particular line of development will add anything significant or substantial to the subject. They should also make written notes as they work in order to capture what is valuable to them and to know in what areas to generate more information.

Tagmemics

Particle/Wave/Field. This tagmemic approach is an adaptation of Kenneth Pike's more complex particle/wave/field theory.[21] (See also Vitanza, 1979, and Irmscher, 1979a.) This heuristic can aid writers in seeing things in relation to other things. It can be used at the paragraph level or for writing whole compositions. It provides various ways of viewing experience and helps writers determine whether to focus on a "particle" of the subject or on the larger picture of "how the particle relates to the wave or the field" or the situation surrounding it. Thus it develops the writer's ability to change perspectives. The writer can begin to perceive unit characteristics of contrast—how the subject can differ from other things; range of variation—how much the subject can change and still be itself; and distribution—how the subject fits into hierarchies of larger systems. It helps writers to see that any paper or approach to a subject could have taken a different form, or even countless different forms, depending on the writer's purpose. Example: *Particle*—Sadat, the man. *Wave*—Sadat as husband, father, friend, or brother. *Field*—Sadat as leader in Egypt, in the Middle East, in the world.

TRIPSQA. Another tagmemic heuristic, this also adds form and structure to a writer's efforts because it can be used for analysis of other expository pieces of writing or as a guide for the working writer.

Becker's form-oriented topics or schema (for expository or referential writing) embody three identifiable patterns of rhetorical structure:[22]

> T R I — Topic (X),
> Restriction (although),
> Illustration (for example)
>
> + P S — Problem, Solution
>
> + Q A — Question, Answer
>
> ─────────────────────
>
> = T R I P S Q A
> = the form of any expository paragraph

All English expository or referential writing contains *one or some combination of these three* patterns of development. The universality of the mathematical format of this structure is often helpful to ESL students in learning how to arrange their materials. For instance, a thesis paragraph may develop for ESL writers more easily if they can follow the formula (P S + T R I) or (Q A + T R I + I + I). This, in turn, sets the pattern for the rest of the composition. With this heuristic, developing writers also have the opportunity to see that beginning with a problem/solution rather than a question/answer develops a completely different approach and serves a different purpose. For example, in the P/S stance writers focus on offering a solution; while in the Q/A stance they are probably seeking an answer or solution, or offering a problem for general consideration.

Problem:

    He could not live forever.

Question:

    Now that he is gone, who will maintain the balance in that part of the world?

Solution:

    Old/new, wise, reasoning, leadership must be cultivated.

Answer:

    Perhaps a new universalist, peacekeeper will come forth.

Topic:

    The death of Sadat, a widely respected political figure, leaves a gap in world leadership.

Restriction:

    Although he had had arguments and disagreements with some of the Arab nations recently,—

Illustration:

    For example, Begin-Sadat relationships, etc.
            Iran-Sadat
            U.S.-Sadat

4.2 Establishing a purpose

WRITER → *MESSAGE* → *READER*

Invention is not the mere creation of novelties, but rather the modification of existing knowledge in response to a specific intention and goal.

Robert de Beaugrande

Communication would not exist unless intention had initially brought it into being.

James Britton

We naturally seek meaning and purpose. The question WHY? is as inherent to our nature as the question HOW? In fact, psychologically and rationally, questions of connection (why?) are prior to questions of implementation (how?).

Caroline D. Eckhardt, David H. Stewart

Why? Why? Why? Why? The best way to find purpose in writing is to continually question why. Why do we write? What are our purposes?, our intents? What is to be accomplished by writing? Why? Because . . . Why? It is essential to know why we write because, after all, writing requires effort, extended concentration, and commitment. Outside an academic setting, most people write only when they have a clear and pressing reason to write. But all writers, even those in the ESL composition classroom, need a reason to write and a purpose. Our task is to help writers recognize and clarify their reasons, to help writers recognize universal purposes and use "language to its best possible effect: to teach, to delight, to win assent, to "energize" the truth, to move an audience to an action—not ill-chosen or precipitous action, but considered and significant action."[23] Students with no understanding of *why* they are writing or no personal commitment to *what* they are writing become bored and turn out sloppy or mediocre work. Even worse than that, they become "turned off" to learning. But since writers with a purpose more clearly see how writing relates to the "real world," it is crucial that student-writers have the opportunity or latitude, whenever possible, to choose their own subjects and define their own reasons for writing. When free choice of subject matter is not possible, teachers need to involve the writer in the process by causing them to take a position and by assuring that the assigned purpose is clear and appropriate.

So—writers need to identify a purpose. However, when writers do identify or establish what they think is their primary purpose for writing, they may, consciously or unconsciously, be fulfilling a number of other purposes. Reasons for writing are as varied as the hues in a rainbow, ranging from the need for self-expression—catharsis and aesthetics—to the desire to stir people to immediate action, to solve problems and clarify issues, to the wish to be remembered in the annals of history. And further, all the purposes overlap and intertwine like the tendrils of a vine.

Researchers (Britton, Kinneavy, Winterowd, D'Angelo, Smith, to name a few) have proposed that for most writers the primary purpose is to satisfy themselves; only when they have achieved self-discovery or self-expression can they successfully communicate to someone else. That is, writers must be clearly acquainted with themselves and their own purposes in order to make the leap from self-expression to communicative effectiveness. Berke describes that leap in terms of reader expectations. Purpose must be clear to the writer because "those (seeking) such information should have reasonably easy access to it, which means that written instructions should be clear, simple, spare, direct, and most of all, human: for no matter how technical a subject, all writing is done *for* human beings *by* human beings. Writing, in other words, like language itself, is a strictly human enterprise" (1976:9). Consequently, a duality of purpose exists in that writers write for self-expression as well as for public audiences.

The ultimate writing purposes of most ESL writers will usually be to share experience and demonstrate knowledge. Their major purposes are what we have traditionally called exposition and argument, or in modern terms, referential and persuasive forms of discourse. These purposes both involve audience to some degree, and ESL writing will therefore generally fall into the category of public writing: mostly for academically oriented audiences for the present; for business, political, or technical audiences later. In this situation, "A *reader* constitutes a purpose, provides a focus."[24] Thus we see reader and purpose are inevitably entwined in writers' considerations.

Assuming that a reader is involved in a writer's purpose, the writer's objective concerning that reading audience will be one or more of the following:

to narrate   to emote   to entertain
to inform   to question   to inspire
to convince   to change

"The decision made here, whether conscious or not, will control all choices subsequently made by the writer as to tone, choice of subject, point of view, selection of evidence, style, organization, and so on."[25] It will also determine considerations of audience and the final shape of the subject. The writer's objectives are ways of clarifying and identifying their purposes.

How then do we further define purpose? What Kinneavy terms "aims of discourse" and D'Angelo calls "forms of discourse" are essentially writers' purposes, both personal and public. These purposes differ significantly from the "techniques" that are frequently offered to students as "reasons" for writing. Techniques (definition, description, classification, cause and effect, comparison and contrast, analogy, and so on) are merely tools writers use to achieve their purposes. However, techniques are not separate entities from purposes but are actually incorporated in the purposes. Furthermore, students should know how to use the various techniques and know when to use each to their best advantage in accomplishing a purpose.

"Thus, the purpose of the piece of writing becomes paramount; and writers select whatever tools, instruments, and tactics seem most functional to that purpose, given the writer's sense of style and subject matter, and the audience."[26] One is the *why* of writing—the purpose or the goal. The other is the *how* of writing—the means for achieving that goal. As Winterowd says, "The purpose is catalyst to schema" (1975:6). When writers have identified what they want to accomplish, they can decide what technique will best help them accomplish their goals. But first, they must decide what they want to accomplish. The general forms purposes take are shown below (adapted by D'Angelo from Kinneavy, 1976:146).

	PURPOSES			
DISCOURSE FORM	AIM is to	FOCUS is on		EXAMPLE
Literary	create text/message	internal ordering	overlap—overlap—overlap—overlap	drama, poetry, songs, comedy, jokes
Expressive	express oneself	writer's attitudes		diaries, journals, letters, protests
Referential	convey reality/ situation	real world/context		articles, texts, histories, analysis, theories
Persuasive	convince/persuade	audience/reader		political, oratory, editorial, propaganda

LITERARY DISCOURSE

The writer's purpose is to create literary discourse when the aim is to create a language structure "worthy of appreciation in its own right."[27]

It is characterized by internal ordering in keeping with literary traditions: the finely honed sentence, precise word choice, and crystal-clear expression of terms, ideas, and beliefs. The focus, or emphasis, is on the written form itself, on the presentation of the subject. Poetry, novels, epitaphs, and ballads all carry cultural meaning within their forms. Among the invention techniques for developing this purpose are intuitive journal writing, stream of consciousness, and meditation. Writing literary discourse is rarely an ESL writer's purpose unless the writer is extremely proficient in English, or unless a teacher has imposed such a purpose—writing task—in an English literature class. *Reading* literary discourse is helpful to ESL writers, nevertheless, as a means of becoming familiar with the genre, the conventions of the language, rhetorical patterns, and reader expectations.

EXPRESSIVE DISCOURSE

Expressive discourse provides a means to display the writer's attitudes and can be defined as a more personal form of communication. Since writers use this form to discover more about themselves, it can often be a final form, an *end* in itself, in the writing process. Yet it can also be an exploratory form of writing—a *means* of discovering self, subject, purpose itself, or audience, and it is especially helpful to ESL writers in this particular sense.

Rather than trying to influence an audience in expressive discourse, writers' aims are to articulate their points of view. The writer may need a steam valve, a way to express feelings, ideas, insights—perhaps to clarify a position or a hypothesis, perhaps to identify a problem or to define a concept more thoroughly.

Characterized by less formal structure and form, expressive writing tends toward more abstract and poetic forms. Imagery frequently conveys content, and content relies more on feelings and beliefs than on facts and figures. The focus in this genre is on the writer's self. This form overlaps literary discourse, since much of literature is also based on writer's feelings, experiences, and beliefs.

Techniques most useful in developing expressive discourse are the exploratory/intuitive ones.

REFERENTIAL DISCOURSE

When writers' purposes are theoretical, technical, scientific, exploratory, or informative, they create referential discourse such as that frequently used in the worlds of academia, science, technology, and business. The aim of this kind of writing is to designate or reproduce reality—real situations— and to convey truths. Characterized mainly by the communication of factual material, referential discourse is comprehensive in scope and employs the careful use of inductive and deductive reasoning. Writers do much of their cognitive problem solving under the umbrella of what is called "referential discourse." Writers are most likely to want their readers "to know . . ." "to understand . . ." "to learn . . ." Thus they must be aware of what their readers already possibly know and what they want them to know about the subject.

In referential discourse the subject itself is the primary focus; thus the purpose can be most thoroughly developed by using the rational heuristics such as classical invention, cubing, reporter's questions, and the tagmemics. Of all the writing purposes, ESL students probably have a need for this one most often.

Because so much of the writing ESL students do focuses on the real world, and because much of the writing originates from real life situations requiring the problem-solving techniques used for reports, research papers, letters, and so on, ESL students especially need a general heuristic for problem solving. Writers can use this heuristic to find the nature of a problem/subject.

HEURISTIC FOR PROBLEM SOLVING

State the problem: _____

  Define the problem: that is,_____

    in other words, _____

    Although, _____

Give reasons for or the origin of the problem:

1. because
2. for example
3. as a result,
4. at first. . . but now

Identify for whom this is a problem: _____

  Why is it a problem for them (you)? _____

State a solution to the problem (if you have one): _____

  State alternative solutions (if any): _____

Demonstrate how the solution will change the problem:

1. for instance,
2. first,
3. if,

Or ask for a solution (open-ended)_____

PERSUASIVE DISCOURSE

The purpose of persuasive discourse may be (1) to substantiate and recommend factual information—*logos*, (2) to present an emotional position regarding a situation or an issue—*pathos*, or (3) to present oneself as a moral and intellectual representative of a position—*ethos*. Its aim, by definition, is to induce some practical choice or prompt an action from its audience. In the classical sense, physical, emotional, moral, and intellectual relationships develop between writer and reader.

Since the focus is directly on the audience, writers must climb into the reader's shoes—they must see through the reader's eyes. Writers employing persuasion or argumentation operate from the stance, "I want them to do . . ." or "I want to convince them that . . ." Yet, writers must understand the reader's biases and beliefs, must play devil's advocate to both sides of the question, before they can persuade the audience to a new point of view. The writer's *commitment to the audience* is vital. While being acutely aware of those whom they are addressing—the reader's knowledge, experiences, beliefs, and feelings—persuasive writers must also be *true to themselves,* honest in their approach, and committed as well to their own beliefs. "If a strong sense of the person behind the paper comes through, we're more likely to be convinced of the paper's point."[28]

Writers must also pay careful attention to the arrangement of material because "without order the force of even the best material, though chosen with keenest discretion, will be weakened."[29] Inductive and deductive reasoning are critical skills for using the rational appeal in argument. The traditional arrangement for argumentation is as follows:

ARRANGEMENT FOR ARGUMENTATION

1. Introduction—statement of *what many people think* is the solution.

2. Statement of the *writer's case.*

3. Outline of the *points* in support of the case.

4. *Proof* of the case and alternative courses of action.
   Refutation of the opposition and reasons for the refutation. Support of *one position.*

5. Conclusion—summary of the arguments and recommendations.

"Inexperienced writers," according to Corbett, "need nothing so much as simple, definite principles to guide them in arrangement of material" (1971:36), and this traditional pattern sets forth clear principles of organization. However, writers should also be aware that the pattern is flexible. All parts need not always be used, and it can be rearranged to the writer's advantage. For example, writers can use an inductive or a deductive pattern to develop an argument. Quintilian's questions can help writers determine which patterns are most effective for arranging their material.[30]

---

1. When is introduction necessary and when can it be abbreviated or omitted?

2. When should statement of facts be continuous or broken up?

3. Under what circumstances can statement of fact be omitted?

4. When should the writer deal with the opponent's argument—first, last?

5. When should the writer present the strongest, weakest argument—first, last?

6. Which arguments will the audience readily accept? Must the audience be induced to accept?

7. Should the writer deal with the opponent's argument as a whole or in detail?

8. How much ethical appeal is required?

9. Should the writer use emotional appeal—at the end—or throughout?

10. What evidence and documents should be used and where will they be most effective in the discourse?

Effective arrangement of material will help persuade or convince an audience of the worth or benefits of a certain idea, position, product; prove to or substantiate for them that the writer's thesis is valid and should be accepted; move the audience to action; or, at the least, gain the audience's attention and entice them to experience the writer's point of view.

Writers should also be aware that at times the best form of persuasion, depending on audience and situation, may in fact be getting the readers to entertain and experience a point of view through literary discourse, as Orwell did when he wrote *Animal Farm* or as Jonathan Swift did in *A Modest Proposal* or through referential and expressive forms.

Invention techniques best suited for developing persuasive discourse are rational ones such as classical invention, debate, role play, or any of the heuristics that heighten a writer's sense of audience. ESL writers will often find a purpose for persuasive discourse both in academia and in the real world.

Writers should not naively think at this point that they will choose one or another of these purposes and then follow a set pattern for writing, because writers' purposes are often dual or even multiple. They may find a reason to concentrate on both the message or context of reality and on the reader. In fact, what began as self-expressive clarification of a concept may become a routine referential lab report about the results of an experiment which, in turn, may become a persuasive statement about the superiority of those results over what is currently known or believed and a strong recommendation for acceptance of those results. One purpose builds on and incorporates another. Thus, in choosing what they think are their primary purposes, writers may, indeed, fulfill several overlapping purposes through commitments to themselves, their messages, their readers, and their situations.

In sum then, "purpose in discourse is all important. The *aim* of discourse determines everything else in the process of discourse."[31] Writers with an established purpose have a strong commitment to their writing.

A CHECKLIST TO
HELP WRITERS IDENTIFY PURPOSE

LITERARY

I. I want to write a poem, a novel, etc., in a certain literary mode _____ .

EXPRESSIVE

II. I want to satisfy a *personal* desire (or need) to express *my* feelings _____ *my* ideas _____

REFERENTIAL/EXPOSITORY

III. I want to tell someone about something __✓__

I want them to understand it __✓__ to know about it __✓__

I want to solve a problem _____ to question _____ to find an answer _____

I want to convey: a truth _____ an idea _____ a concept __✓__ new information _____ how to perform an operation _____ how something was done or made _____

I want to compare: show differences _____ show similiarities __✓__ show superiority of one over another _____

I want to analyze: a situation _____ a concept _____ an object _____ to show causes _____ to show effects _____ to understand the composition _____

PERSUASIVE/ARGUMENTATIVE

IV. I want to convince someone about something _____

I want them to agree with my position _____ to take action _____ to change their opinions _____

I want to argue this point because _____

I might cause _____ to happen _____ to change _____

I am addressing _____

I will affect _____

How will it affect them? _____

_____ exists now.

I want _____ to exist.

Am I qualified to argue? _____

Do I have enough facts? _____

Is _____ the best approach?

THE THESIS

By the time writers have fully determined their purposes for writing, they should also be able to make statements about that purpose. The statement, which we call a thesis, becomes the writer's promise to or contract with his or her readers as to the purpose for writing. The thesis sets the framework for the content of the message, thereby tying all three elements together.

From the checkmarks on the preceding list, we can see how Sami Shaker, an Egyptian student, began to develop his purpose for writing, and thus his thesis: "As human settlements are one of the major impacts of civilization, their study will reflect some characteristic elements of ancient Egypt." (See the completed paper in Chapter 7.)

In making a contract with the reader, writers move beyond their own personal desires and needs for writing and attempt to convey thoughts to an audience. Who then is this audience?

4.3 Identifying an audience

WRITER ⟶ *MESSAGE* ⟶ *READER*

Nothing should ever be written in a vacuum.

Jacqueline Berke

The first consideration in writing is deciding if one has something to say, and then to whom it is to be said.

Thomas Hawkins

The primary audience is always the writer.

Frank Smith

My task . . . is, by the power of the written word, to make you hear, to make you feel, . . . to make you see.

Joseph Conrad

While having something to say and a purpose for saying it are paramount to the writing process, knowing who one is addressing and how one wants to affect that particular audience are equally crucial. To accomplish these tasks, writers need an active sense of—

1. Who they are as writers

2. Who the readers (audience) are

3. Why they are addressing those readers and on what occasion

4. Their relationship to the subject matter

5. How they want their readers to relate to the subject matter, that is, what effect they want to have on them[32]

Not only is good writing therefore dependent on the writer, the purpose, and the reader, but also "Good writing is adapted to achieve the *desired effect* on the *desired audience*."[33]

Question: What is the desired effect a writer wants to have on an audience?

Answer: Effect is determined by a writer's purpose for writing and thus by the distance established between the reader and the writer.

As Elbow says, "Different kinds of writing [purposes] imply different distances from an audience" (1981:191). And we can easily see in the established purposes—literary, expressive, referential, and persuasive—important differences in distance from the reader and therefore, in effect on the reader.

For example, when the purpose is expressive, writers are their own audience. The writer's distance from the subject and the audience is almost nonexistent, and the effects of the writing are often immediate. Writers explore universal truths for

90

themselves in that they are honestly attempting to examine what they know, feel, and believe about their experience. Perhaps they are calibrating those experiences with some new ideas or experiences or perhaps in relation to what they think others know, feel, and believe.

Reexamine the journal entry in Section 4.1 to see how Palitha was rehearsing in his own mind the fine qualities of his countrymen—a pleasing thought for him in his isolation from his homeland (exactly the effect he intended to create for himself)—or his identification and clarification of the Sri Lankian transportation system and its future developmental needs. The effect? To carry him purposefully into the future. Examine Julio and Madeline's loop writing examples, in that same section, to see how these writers, serving as their own audiences, were able to clarify their thoughts about life—good and bad, suffering and happiness, music as communication and its effects on others. The effects these writers were seeking for themselves were those of catharsis, aesthetic creation, clarification, identification, and discovery.

When writers' purposes are literary, they are writing not only to please themselves but also to synthesize life experiences and studies in order to create a *form* for their expression that will appeal to a specific kind of audience. A writer interested in using an art form for communicating a controversial political philosophy will probably choose the novel in order to reach a wide audience, since it is a more popular literary form than poetry, for instance. Since writers may not always be able to clearly identify exactly who the audience will be, or when, in time, the effect will be realized, there is distance between writers and their audiences. Nevertheless, whatever art form the writer chooses, the reading audience must have some understanding of the specific literary genre in order to fully appreciate the form in which the message is conveyed, as well as the message. In other words, the desired effect is to attain audience appreciation of a written art form as well as to convey a message.

But when writers' purposes are referential (as they often are for ESL writers whose goals are usually pragmatic rather than humanistic), the effect they want to have is to make readers *understand* what it is the writer has to say. Indeed, in most cases, it is a bonus if the reader *agrees* with the message, but in referential writing that is usually not necessary. The purpose is to convey factual, objective information or to work out a problem; its intended effect is to make readers see, hear, and understand, and also to illustrate the writers' own understanding of the information. In other words, writers first express themselves; then they consider adaptation of the material for an audience. They are often removed in time and distance from their audience and seldom are able to gauge their immediate effects upon the audience.

A reading of Nilufer's paper about the "Social Laws of Turkey" in Appendix C clearly demonstrates her intent to affect the reading audience by adding to their knowledge and appreciation of her country—nothing more, nothing less.

On the other hand, the effect writers want to achieve when they write persuasively is to make their readers not only see, hear, and understand, but also feel, experience, agree, and act. If the audience already agrees with the writer's position wholeheartedly, the writing is not persuasive. If there is anything left to tell or add to what the audience presently knows, the writer is strictly conveying information. Thus the purpose and effect are referential. But if the writer knows that the audience is undecided about an issue, or even hostile to the writer's position, then the desired effect, indeed, is to convince them or to change their position on the issue at hand. As a result, writers must keep their audiences in the mind's eye from the very beginning, remaining constantly aware of how they might be affected by the argument. This is quite a different matter. Writers must bring themselves quite close to their audiences. While the effects of the other writing purposes may happen to persuade an audience to accept some point, it is not as crucial to the success of the writing task as it is in persuasive writing. To compare differences in approach, read Maria's argument concerning woman's role in the military.

In addition, writers quickly discover that there are a number of different techniques or devices which may successfully persuade or help create the desired effect. For example, a writer may find the best means of moving an audience is through a well-written satiric poem. But that depends on the composition of the audience, the message, and the purpose, as well as on the writer's ability to use the form. Conversely, the writer may find the effects of a straightforward argument most successful with an objective, open-minded audience; or an experiential presentation, "put yourself in my place," may have the most desired effect on a hostile audience.

Whatever the desired effect on the audience, "good writing comes through the adoption of a strong rhetorical stance: the balance of which is achieved between writer, work and audience." In fact, "the stance should be one which is suitable to all three and to the purpose at hand."[34] Walker Gibson also believes that there exists "a constant shifting and interplay of relationships" among writer, subject, audience in argument as well as in other types of discourse and that the "total impact of any communication is surely more or less an amalgam of all three" (1979:xi). By examining purposes, especially referential and persuasive, and the effects they are intended to have, writers become acutely aware of the close link between purpose and audience. In fact, by discovering one, writers often discover the other.

But do writers always *have* an audience? An audience implies some degree of willingness on the part of the receiver, the person to whom the message is being sent. Are writers' audiences always willing?

Question: What is the difference between *requested* and *voluntary* writing?

Answer: It is the difference between being the honored speaker at a banquet or being the orator of the day on the speaker's corner in Hyde Park.

Requested writing is that which is done when writers have been specifically asked, or at least expected, to communicate about some subject. The potential reader has said "please tell me . . .," or "I want to know, what you think or know . . ." In this situation, the reader is willing to take the role of audience and writers usually know something, perhaps even a great deal, about the subject at hand or they can find out about it. They usually know what kind of information the audience expects, why they expected it, and also who the reading audience will be. For example,

Mother and father request a letter from school.

A friend wants a description of your university and its environs.

An advisor/professor asks for a report on a research project.

A professor assigns a term paper or gives an essay exam.

A business superior requires a recommendation report or a procedures manual.

A professional journal invites you to submit an article.

In other words, the audience is "buying" or "has placed an order for" what the writer has to say. The audience is either personally known to the writer or identifiable, and the writer is usually acquainted with how much knowledge or background the audience has, and how much needs to be supplied. Further, since the writer is certain of his or her role in the writing task, he or she can more easily achieve the expected goal.

Voluntary writing, by definition, originates with the writer. It may take form in a journal entry and the writer may be the sole audience; or it may develop because the writer feels the need, the desire, the inspiration to communicate to someone else, in which case there is usually no ready and willing audience on hand. The situation may be one in which—

A scientist wants to publicize a newly discovered theory of physics (but no one has asked him to).

An aspiring young professor needs to improve her position by contributing to a journal in her field.

A teacher contributes new or updated materials to fill a curriculum gap.

A new writer tries to get a first short story published.

A student requests admission to a higher course level or applies for a scholarship.

A graduating senior applies for a job.

An enraged citizen submits an editorial protesting unreasonable increases in apartment rents.

In most of these situations, writers are not certain *how* their efforts will be received, or even *if they will* be received. The potential reader is under no obligation to become an audience when writing is voluntary. Thus writers of uninvited, unrequested, unexpected discourse need to consider even more carefully (1) who the audience might be, (2) how they can initially capture the attention of that audience with considerations such as—deciding where to try to publish, what form to use, etc., and (3) how that audience will respond to the message if they do indeed consent to read it. In other words, writers are selling, but they don't know whether the audience is buying; therefore, they must design, package, and market their products as well as they can for the audience they have identified as their target. (See Peter Elbow's book *Writing with Power* for a scintillating discussion on this point.) But before writers can design, package, and market, they must know something about the market; in other words, who that market is.

Question: Who is the desired audience?*

Answer 1: It is oneself.

The primary audience is always the writer (because he or she is the first person to interact with the text in the act of writing). Then the writing is available to others. —Smith

As their own audiences, writers find truths, making discoveries that many others before them have also found and made. By comparing, sharing, calibrating their ideas with those of others, writers find the universal concerns of human beings and thus of other writers. In their interaction with their own writing, writers may discover that, just as they themselves react positively or negatively to some stimulus, or just as they can convince themselves of a new position or stand firm in their established position, so will their reading audiences. By recognizing and analyzing their own reactions to externals, perhaps they can anticipate those same reactions in their audiences. As Murray states, "The writer is on a search for himself. If he finds himself, he will find an audience because all of us have a common core" (1968:4). Murray further states that writers develop their own truths and then put them into terms which readers will understand by designing writing "in such a way that it will effectively carry [their] thoughts into the reader's head" (p. 5).

Question: Who is the desired audience?

Answer 2: It is others, present and known to the writer.

When writers move away from themselves as audience and into the public arena, they begin to adapt their writing to the person or persons whom they are addressing, to "make adjustments in writing to diverse audiences."[35] "A highly developed sense of audience," says Britton, "must be one of the marks of the competent mature writer, for it is concerned with nothing less than the implementation of his concern to maintain and establish an appropriate relationship with his reader in order to achieve his full intent" (1975:58). A highly developed sense of audience, like much of the rest of the writing process, does not just happen. It comes about by practicing on and getting to know "real" audiences. Therefore, audience is also those who are known to the writer, who are immediate or present. In fact, after self, the best testing ground for a writer's words is a known, personal audience. What demands does this audience make on writers that they would not make on themselves, and how can this audience be helpful to developing writers? Usually, this audience wants the writer to be very clear and logical; however, they also *want to understand and to agree* so they are often more accepting, more forgiving, more tolerant, and, probably more honest. When not sure of the reader's expectations, the writer can ask what they are because the audience is available for feedback. Further, readers can respond to the writing efforts by actually telling the writer whether or not they understood the message and whether it had the intended effect. Moreover, they can tell the writer why or how the communication succeeded and also how, why, or where it broke down. The reader can say to the writer "this is what I think you told me . . .," and the writer can respond, "Yes, in part, but I also meant. . . ." The opportunity to gain a sense of audience and to practice clarification of one's message is invaluable, since it rarely occurs outside the classroom. Indeed, we *do* teach writing.

Again the role of the teacher and the peer group is crucial because feedback within the classroom environment in a nonthreatening and supportive atmosphere can teach the writer what to expect. Furthermore, the stakes are not quite as high—if the writer has not communicated to or convinced the reader, there is still opportunity to revise. However, if the message is misinterpreted by *an audience removed in time and distance,* the opportunity to "sell" the idea may be lost.

Elbow says that if writers get enough feedback or reactions from enough people—teachers, classmates, friends, and colleagues—they finally begin to develop "a trustworthy sense of the effects of [their] words" and learn "the feel of real readers" (1973:126).

However, Elbow also states, *"Teachers are not the real audience"* (1981:220). McDonald adds that teachers are only "a tryout audience" (1978:167). For many teachers, reading student writing—in the role of real audience—is impossible because, as teachers, they are also continually monitoring linguistic and mechanical factors. Thus

---

*See Britton (1975) on "sense of audience" for a thorough discussion of this point.

teachers have difficulty responding only to the message. Occasionally, teachers can and do become real audiences when students' actual writing purpose is to persuade them on a real issue. However, even though teachers cannot usually fill the role of real audience, they do have a vital role as readers.

As readers, teachers can become advisers or coaches to writers who are addressing another real audience. They can guide writers in such ways as helping them discover why a different approach might be more successful with a specific audience and indicating where points are or are not clear, where logical connections have or have not been made, and where more evidence would strengthen a position.

Teachers can also become collaborators in the writing process. Since most students, themselves, view the teacher as a "tester" or "a mirror to instruction,"[36] their writing takes on a stilted or unnatural feeling when they know teacher is audience. Further, Mina Shaughnessy suggests that the student "is aware that he leaves a trail of errors behind him when he writes. He can usually think of little else . . ." (1977:7) and as a result, the writer expects the teacher to read only for the sake of error correction. To overcome this fear and to become a collaborator, teachers must put themselves into the writing process along with their students. When teachers actually become working members of the group: writing with the group, being evaluated by the group, as well as evaluating others' writing, they can work with students on a basis of shared experience and learning and thus can collaborate and, perhaps, on occasion, even become a real audience.

But, all in all, the best way for students to learn is to write for real audiences, preferably first for their peers and then for others.

According to Britton, "good teachers make students responsive to each others' efforts" (1975:71). By giving and receiving responses to their writing efforts, writers learn that they cannot please everyone. And, further, they discover that the readers' *perceptions of* and *experiences with* their words are more important than the readers' *judgments* of them.[37] Thus, writers learn to maintain their own standards and their honesty, and only to *test* the readers' *understanding* of their words.

Elbow sets forth a number of reasons why student readers usually make better audiences than teachers (1973:127–132):

1. They are more open.

2. They miss more meaning and, consequently, give better evidence of what is unclear.

3. They indicate where the message is weak or confused by too many other messages.

4. They often know less about the subject (than the teacher), which is useful because it allows them to show the writer where communication problems exist. Expert to expert is of little help here. (An addendum: In many writing classes, ESL and otherwise, we should not assume that the teacher is always more expert than students in certain areas. When students are experts in their fields, they can sometimes use the ESL teacher as an interested, but uninformed audience, writing to him or her in an explicit fashion about their subjects. Thus, more context is supplied, and less implied, than if that student were writing to a peer who is also expert in the same field.)

In addition,

5. The writer learns by simply listening and attending to reader's reactions. (This is often easier with one's peers.)

6. Readers can hear messages in the text that writers did not intend to send such as: their fear or dislike of the task or the audience, an expectation of failure to achieve the intended goal, or a feeling that they really don't believe what they are saying.

By becoming aware of some of these writing blocks, writers can remedy them. But without feedback, this task would be far more difficult, if not impossible.

Thus, "writer-based prose is capable of transformation," say Flower and Hayes, ". . . when the writer develops the ability to take readers and *their purposes for reading* into account" (1980:293).

While all writers need to discover a sense of audience, it is this aspect of the writing process that presents additional complications for ESL writers. They can use heuristics to discover a subject and heuristics to discover a purpose, but using heuristics to discover an audience is often not enough. The ESL writer needs practice in discovering not only who the audience is and what their expectations are but also what rhetorical patterns used in English best satisfy audience expectations. Therefore, ESL writers must learn not only a sense of audience, as indeed native speakers must, but also the rhetorical expectations embedded in the culture of the language.

They must know that readers expect writing to be straightforward; they expect it to be simple, not in ideas, but in presentation; they expect the writer to take a certain role in relation to them as audience; they expect logical reasoning and order, precision and detail, and honesty; they expect a certain tone or appropriateness of language for the specific audience; and they expect to find the material interesting as well as to have whatever questions are in their minds answered by the writing; they expect to be addressed in terms they can understand; and they expect to be talked across to, never down to.

In his concern with how writers can write prose which will make sense to the majority of readers, Hawkins found that "structured peer group interaction has important implications for the teaching of standard English composition to speakers of nonstandard English" (1976:7). He says that in the group "speech and cultural differences become identified, understood, and valued by all; [therefore] oral language is freed to serve its prime function as a shaper of ideas and attitudes." We find that the same is true for ESL writers, in that group interaction frees them to discover the conventions or audience expectations necessary to written communication *in English*. The ESL writing classroom can and should be one of the most comfortable places for writers to experiment with the language and with audience expectations before trying them out on strangers. In the classroom teachers can make demands on their students while still encouraging and supporting their efforts. It is like the situation Maimon describes when she writes, "The child learned to speak only when the mother learned to role-play, to make some of the communicative demands that strangers might make."[38]

Question: Who else can be a desired audience?

Answer 3: It is others, perhaps more distant, yet known to the writer.

When writers become comfortable and secure writing for a group of peers or classmates, they can begin to branch out and write for more distant, objective, and professional audiences whose demands and expectations are still known to the writer: colleagues, people in related fields, local newspapers, and so on.

Writers begin to realize that they have made assumptions with an immediate audience which they can no longer make. Writers cannot so easily ask their audiences what they want to know or what they already know. They must begin to make some educated guesses or calculations regarding those factors. Further, they must take into consideration specific conventions recognized by various disciplines. These special conventions are rarely explained to students. Usually they must learn them by talking with colleagues and by reading journals and texts written within the discipline or field. "When we write within our own fields, we are not really talking to total strangers but are talking to colleagues who share assumptions and standards with us," says Maimon (1979:365). Thus, with this kind of audience, writers usually know something about their audience's educational background, general vocabulary terms in the sense of what needs to be defined or explained and what does not, and so on. But what about those audiences with whom the writer has no known, shared experiences or standards?

Question: Then who is the desired audience?

Answer 4: It is others; strangers removed in time and distance, abstract, general, and unknown to the writer.

"How many of us would ever talk in print to strangers about our new ideas if we had not first talked to friends?" questions Maimon (p. 368). Few of us indeed. We know that collaborative learning and sharing of ideas nurtures ideas and helps them grow. And yet writers must learn to talk to strangers because much of their writing, in the real world, will be for strangers. To master written communication to such an unknown and distant audience requires what Elsasser calls a "critical shift in the consciousness of the learner . . . from an immediate audience that shares the learner's experiences and frame of reference to a larger, abstract, and unfamiliar audience" (1977:358).

But the most critical questions are—how do writers accomplish this shift? How do they discover the "requirements of those absent strangers who will read their messages?" (Maimon, p. 365). How can writers "ensure that what [they] write can be understood without further help from [them]"?[39]

First, they must perceive or imagine the audience based on the knowledge and experience they have had within their peer groups and in writing to other known, but more objective audiences. They must make inferences from what is known to what is unknown. They consciously identify and examine the universals and the cultural specifics they may have unconsciously acquired through working with real and present audiences. Based on these past experiences, writers can question:

QUESTIONS TO DETERMINE AUDIENCE

1. Who is the audience? What do I know about them?

2. What is my role in relation to them?

3. What is the occasion for my writing?

4. Will my writing be published and, if so, where?

5. How do I feel about my subject? Will the audience agree, disagree, or be apathetic?

6. What questions might they want to ask me?

four people, all of whom related what they saw quite differently and in the best light for themselves. Such is the fate of a piece of writing that goes to an unknown audience. "Since demands made by one type of audience differ from those made by another" (1975:116), says Britton, it is crucial that the writer identify this audience as clearly and concisely as possible and convey the message to them in a manner which is most compatible with and complementary to their own experiences. The audience is in one role, says Britton; the writer "must be in a complementary role" (p. 62). Role play, one of the empirical heuristics described in Section 4.1, is an effective way for writers to begin to move from "ego-centered" positions to "decentered" positions from which they can more easily identify their audiences.

In fact, any "information about the intended audience acts as a cue to the writer to decenter from the content and to consider additional requirements of the writing."[40] Such cues may consist of the writers actually writing out or checklisting their own role in relation to the reading audience (see Checklist below).

Second, writers become aware that all readers bring their own experiences and perceptions to the reading of a piece of writing and therefore all will read the message differently, as it specifically relates to their needs, expectations, or advantages. Akira Kurosawa's *Rashamon* illustrates this phenomenon: it is the story of a crime witnessed by

---

WRITERS' RELATIONSHIP CHECKLIST*

WRITER

I am—

- an expert
- a classmate, peer, colleague
- a student
- a citizen, a voter
- a resident of a community
- an employee
- a writer
- _____ (other)

READER

writing for—

- interested, uninformed laymen
- other experts
- equals who share my interest or concern
- a teacher
- (to) a senator or representative
- (to) the city officials, news media
- (to) or (for) an employer
- a magazine, journal, publishing house
- _____ (other)

*Developed and adapted from Britton, p. 62.

Writers begin to develop their stance with such cues as these, yet beyond this identification they need to know more about the specific but unknown audience. What are other distinguishing characteristics? What are, as Ede says, the "general properties of the group" (1979:294) or their demography? Writers may also need to analyze their audiences based on demographic qualities such as—

age ___   income ___   marital status ___

sex ___   residence ___   politics ___

religion ___   occupation ___   education ___   etc.

Finally, writers may take cues from more "purpose-oriented" analysis, that is, information based on the needs of writers as they make decisions concerning content and the desired effect of the message. So we have come full circle, back to the inevitable connection between audience, writer's purpose, and the message. Flower and Hayes have developed an extremely useful model which can help a writer bring all these factors together. It addresses the rhetorical problem to be solved, the writer's own image or role in relation to the audience, and the effect of the message to be conveyed (1980:23–24).

Assignment: Write about your job for the readers of *Seventeen* magazine, young teenagers. You are an English teacher.

THE RHETORICAL PROBLEM

Elements of the Problem	*Examples*
The Rhetorical Situation	
Exigency or assignment	Write for *Seventeen* magazine. "This is impossible."
Audience	"Someone like myself, but adjusted for 20 years." (changed later to fashion consumer.)
The Writer's Own Goals involving the	
Reader	"I'll change their notion of English teachers."
Persona or self (voice)	"I'll look like an idiot if I say . . ."
Meaning	"So if I compare those 2 attitudes . . ."
Text	"First, we'll want an introduction."

It is clear that successful writing is closely linked to writers' achieving a comprehensive understanding of their audience. The clearer the image of the audience in the writers' eye, the easier it will be to take that crucial next step—of putting writing on paper. Writers will discover the form of what they have to write, its length, its tone, when they know to whom they are speaking.[41]

4.4 Putting it on paper

A thesis is a promise to the reader, which the essay fulfills. It is a proposition—which the writer carries out, or defends. . . . It is a challenge— to the reader to see a subject as the writer does; to the writer to make the reader see, make him understand.

Harry Rougier and E. Krage Stockum

After writers discover subject, audience, and purpose, they are ready to commit their ideas to paper in more formalized form. That is, they are ready to organize the ideas which they have generated in their minds and in informal jottings on paper into a meaningful, more conventionally organized discussion on the page.

Writers should consider this first formalized writing as an "exploratory draft," one in which they map out their papers, test hypotheses, develop positions. *It is a completely flexible draft. It is meant to be altered, rearranged, and rethought.* "In writing, as in few other endeavors, hindsight can clarify foresight."[42]

The following words of advice can help writers effectively get ideas from the mind to the printed page, to create a useful "exploratory draft."

Do's and Don'ts For Writing
an Exploratory Draft

1. Do schedule writing time—set it aside and use it.

2. Do make a rough plan for a piece of writing.

3. Don't expect to write an essay in one sitting.

4. Don't be overawed by the rough plan—be willing and able to adjust it.

5. Don't let ideas escape—keep a separate page for jotting down additional ideas that come as the writing develops.

6. Don't believe you have to begin at the beginning—ignore the idea that you must completely finish each point before you begin something new.

7. Do overwrite—it is easier to pare down than to build up.

8. Don't become bogged down in minor choices—you may lose your main train of thought. Write a draft first and then go back and make word choice, sentence structure decisions.

9. Do become the reader and ask questions to stimulate new ideas especially if ideas won't come.

10. Don't erase, obliterate, or destroy anything yet—you may use it later.

11. Don't recopy yet—spend your time generating before shaping.

12. Do leave space, for revision—have scissors, extra paper, colored pens, and tape available to help you reorder and reformulate.

The paper which follows is a student's first effort to get her ideas on paper. Now that she has written an exploratory draft, she is ready to shape or fine-tune her work. (This paper, completed after she analyzed her sentence structure, word choices, and word forms, appears in Appendix C.)

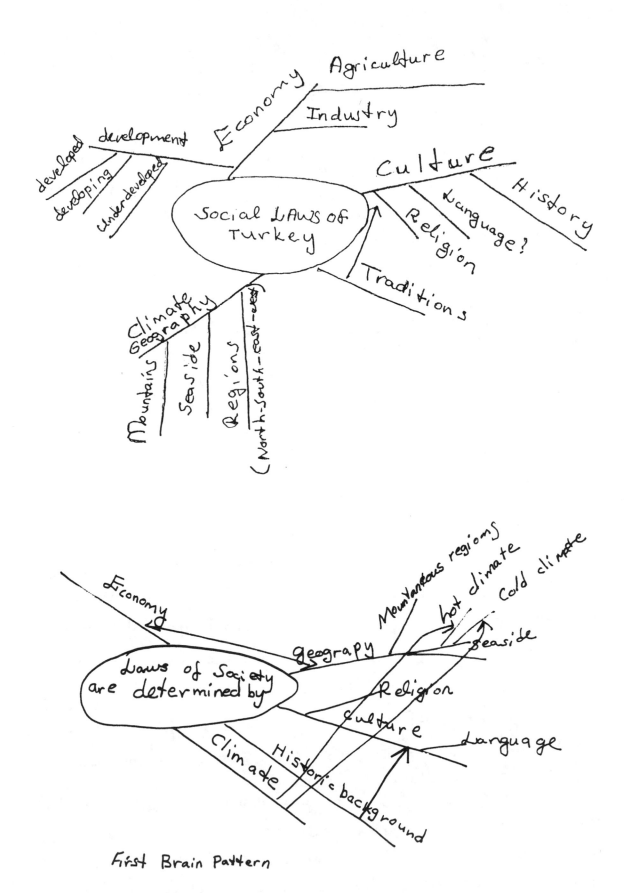

First Brain Pattern

99

SOCIAL LAWS OF TURKEY

Although a country seems to be ruled by only
the laws that are established by authority, there is
another kind of law, called social laws that cannot be seen on the
papers but it is felt everywhere, and it determines
the human relations, way of life (life style) and social values
in the society. Social laws of Turkey can be
classified into those determined by: culture, economic
structure, and geographic location.

Social laws determined by culture is composed of
traditions originated from historic background and religion.
In the history Turks had many wars, therefore today's
society shows nationalist characteristics. To be a member
of army is a respected status. When young people, when
they are 18 years old, go for their military service it is
a custom to celebrate the event in the neighbourhood.
Hospitality is another social law coming from
history, and it is originated from the Nomadic
society in old ages. Another social law coming from
history is respect for old people. In the family,
in every kinds of meeting, old people are always
respected. Religion is the other determinant
of the social laws determined by culture.
Since more than 99% of the population is Muslims,
it is customary that people visit each other, give
presents and candies to children, and rich help
poor in religious holidays of Islam religion.

Economic structure is the second determinant of social laws of Turkey. Turkey is a developing country. She shows characteristics of an agricultural society in rural areas, and characteristics of an industrial society in urban areas.

In rural areas, families are large, relationships between relatives and neighbours are very close and people are dependent on each other. In urban areas families are smaller, a big? proportion of women are working, education is more important.

Social laws of Turkey are also affected by the geographic characteristics. Turkey is in the warm climate region (?) of the world. Therefore, it shows the general characteristics of that region. But, the country shows a variety of climates an land structure within the limits.

Notes

[1]Harry Rougier and E. Krage Stockum, *Getting Started—A Preface to Writing* (New York: W. W. Norton & Company, Inc., 1970), 28.

[2]David V. Harrington, "Encouraging Honest Inquiry in Student Writing," *College Composition and Communication,* 30 (May 1979), 182.

[3]Harrington, p. 182.

[4]Jacqueline Berke, *Twenty Questions for the Writer: A Rhetoric with Readings*, 2d ed. (New York: Harcourt Brace Jovanovich, Inc., 1976), 10.

[5]Beth Neman, *Teaching Students to Write* (Columbus: Charles E. Merrell Publishing Co., 1980), 456.

[6]Richard E. Young, Alton L. Becker, and Kenneth Pike, *Rhetoric: Discovery and Change* (New York: Harcourt Brace and World, Inc., 1970), 120.

[7]Berke, p. 18.

[8]Janice M. Lauer, "Toward a Metatheory of Heuristic Procedures," *College Composition and Communication,* 30 (October 1979), 268.

[9]James Kinney, "Classifying Heuristics," *College Composition and Communication,* 30 (December 1979), 352.

[10]Thomas Hawkins, "Group Inquiry Techniques for Teaching Writing: Clearinghouse on Reading and Communication Skills," National Council of Teachers of English (1976), 1.

[11]Donald M. Murray, *A Writer Teaches Writing: A Practical Method of Teaching Composition* (Boston: Houghton Mifflin Company, 1968), 3.

[12]Tony Buzan, *Use Both Sides of Your Brain* (New York: E. P. Dutton Publishers, 1976), 83.

[13]Peter Russell, *The Brain Book* (New York: E. P. Dutton Publishers, 1979), 210.

[14]Berke, p. 20.

[15]James Britton, Tony Burgess, Nancy Martin, Alex McLeod, and Harold Rosen, "The Development of Writing Abilities," *Schools Council Research Studies* (1975), 28.

[16]Hawkins, p. 13.

[17]Britton, p. 30.

[18]Kenneth Burke, "The Five Key Terms of Dramatism," *Contemporary Rhetoric,* ed. W. Ross Winterowd (New York: Harcourt Brace Jovanovich, Inc., 1975).

[19]Edward P. J. Corbett, *Classical Rhetoric for the Modern Student* (New York: Oxford University Press, 1971), 163.

[20]Peter Elbow, *Writing without Teachers* (London: Oxford University Press, 1973), 35.

[21]Young, Becker, and Pike, p. 26.

[22]Alton L. Becker, "A Tagmemic Approach to Paragraph Analysis: The Sentence and the Paragraph," National Council of Teachers of English (1966).

[23]Berke, p. 3.

[24]Frank Smith, "Demonstrations, Engagement and Sensitivity: A Revised Approach to Language Learning," *Language Arts* (January 1981), 15.

[25]Sharon Crowley and George Redman, "Why Teach Writing?" *College Composition and Communication* (October 1975), 281.

[26]Caroline D. Eckhardt and David H. Stewart, "Towards a Functional Taxonomy of Composition," *College Composition and Communication*, 30, no. 4 (December 1979), 339.

[27]James L. Kinneavy, *A Theory of Discourse* (Englewood Cliffs, N.J.: Prentice-Hall, Inc., 1971), 39.

[28]Crowley and Redman, p. 39.

[29]Corbett, p. 299.

[30]Corbett, p. 301.

[31]Kinneavy, p. 48.

[32]Berke, p. 9.

[33]Richard Fulkerson, "Four Philosophies of Composition," *College Composition and Communication,* 30, no. 4 (December 1979), 346.

[34]Crowley, p. 281.

[35]Britton, p. 58.

[36]Britton, p. 69.

[37]Elbow, p. 126.

[38]Elaine P. Maimon, "Talking to Strangers," *College Composition and Communication,* 30, no. 4 (December 1979), p. 365.

[39]Donn Byrne, *Teaching Writing Skills* (London: Longmans Group, Ltd., 1979), 1.

[40]Lisa S. Ede, "On Audience and Composition," *College Composition and Communication,* 30, (October 1979), 293.

[41]Murray, p. 4.

[42]Rougier and Stockum, p. 52.

CHAPTER FIVE

SHAPING WRITING

The change from maximally compact inner speech to maximally detailed written speech requires what might be called deliberate semantics—deliberate structuring of the web of meaning.

Lev Vygotsky

In putting the finishing touches to any piece of writing, one becomes aware, once again, of the twofold nature of the whole process—the need to meet the demands and satisfy the reader, and the need of the writer to satisfy himself, to do what he wanted to do.

James Britton

Composition does have an underlying structure which gives unity and coherence to the field . . . that structure can be conceived of in terms of principles and forms.

Frank J. D'Angelo

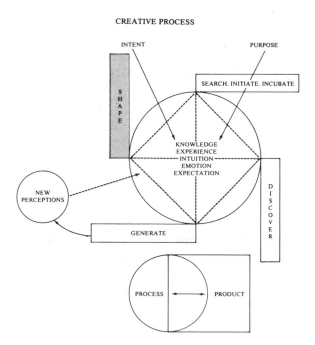

CREATIVE PROCESS

Inventio (generating ideas) and *dispositio* (arranging ideas) are inseparable parts of the whole writing process, except for our purposes of analyzing and teaching that process. Thus, finding form or shaping one's ideas is an integral part of the discovery process and not just an exercise in applying set patterns to available material.

"No two people can ever write exactly alike," says Britton, "either in generating ideas or in shaping or arranging them" (1975:47). Thus, we find that there are as many variations in the forms and structures as there are individual writers. And further, to quote Kinneavy, "there is no neat organizational formula" (1976:164) but many ways of discovering, generating, and shaping material.

Shahn says of shape and content that they are inseparable. Form is formulation—the turning of content into a material entity, rendering a content accessible to others, giving it permanence, willing it to the race" (1957:53). He advises the artist/writer: "Form is not just the intention of content; it is the embodiment of content. Form is based, first, upon a supposition, a theme. Form is, second, a marshaling of materials, the inert matter in which the theme is to be cast. Form is, third, a setting of boundaries, of limits, the whole extent of idea, *but no more,* an outer shape of idea. Form is, next, the relating of inner shapes to the outer limits, the initial establishing of harmonies. Form is, further, the abolishing of excessive content, of content that falls outside the true limits of the theme. It is the abolishing of excessive materials, whatever material is extraneous to inner harmony, to the order of shapes now established. Form is thus a discipline, an ordering, according to the needs of content" (p. 70).

Shahn's six conditions for finding form in art generally apply to writing as well:

---

1. Determine a theme.

2. Gather material.

3. Set limits—"outer shape."

4. Relate inner parts to outer shape.

5. Eliminate material not directly related.

6. Order the whole to meet the needs of the content.

Once writers have generated a theme (a thesis) and the raw materials for writing, (subject—purpose—audience), they are ready to begin putting the finishing touches to the piece of writing. To do this, they must turn to their *knowledge of the language* in order to set the limits, relate the parts, and delete, change, and order the whole to meet the

needs of the content. What writers must have now are the tools for making the message accessible to others, that is, the techniques, the strategies, the "know-how" to accomplish their purposes. True, ideas can be expressed, even understood, without attention to form and structure, but to communicate most effectively and to assure success in reaching a goal, writers cannot afford to neglect these elements. They are what carry the writer's meaning to the audience. When writers neglect shape, readers are often forced to backtrack in order to understand what the writer is saying—an exercise most readers (other than writing teachers!) are not willing to perform.[1] Further, since the shapes writing may take are as varied and diverse as the number of individual writers, readers and writers alike depend upon a common ground for understanding: the principles of writing which govern the shape of a piece of writing and guide both reader and writer.

What are those principles of writing upon which understanding is based? When writers shape their discourse, they are making choices by applying certain expected sets of rhetorical, linguistic, and mechanical criteria—rules, conventions, and guidelines—to their writing. "Some [of these] principles," says d'Angelo, "are assumptions, some are self-evident, some are based on observations of repeated events, and some are derived from theory" (1975:144). They are all concerned with the overall design of a piece of writing, the shape and structure which ready it for someone else. When writers apply the principles to their writing, says Britton, their writing becomes more explicit, supplies more context, reflects concern for accurate and specific reference, seeks organization most effective to the task, and excludes the personal (1975:83).

5.1 Rules, conventions, and guidelines—the principles of writing

We have divided the principles of writing into rules, conventions, and guidelines. *Rules*, as we define them, are hard-and-fast laws governing the use of the language. Expected, even demanded, by readers knowledgeable in the language, they have to do with honesty of expression and correctness of language use. "Rules are probably the major organizing factor,"[2] and when writers ignore rules, their communication often fails or is severely

impaired. These "rules can be learned directly or by inference through experience," says Rose, and "... students can be trained to select, to know which rules are appropriate for each [of the writing] problems" (1980:400). There is no question but that writers need to have clear rules, yet Rose advocates that rules and strategies of writing be characterized by flexibility rather than rigidity. They should be functional so that they aid writers' purposes rather than block the flow of their ideas. In fact, there are few rules which can be rigidly followed without restricting creativity.

Conventions are the forms, shapes, and structures that readers expect. They are customary. They increase the "relative readability" of a piece: that is, they help writers frame their discourse so that it is conveyed to the reader with the least possible interference. They are important to the successful communication of a message because they are practices which have been established by use of the language over a long period of time. Although they are not hard-and-fast laws, like the rules, and although they can be bent and changed to achieve a particular purpose, writers should know that readers expect writers to observe most of the conventions so that they can read along easily without backtracking in search of meaning.

Guidelines, on the other hand, are reminders or suggestions for using the language. Not necessarily expected or established by long use, they are viewed more as helpful hints for working with and within the language. They are techniques that make writing clearer and more effective. Guidelines have different purposes for different kinds of writing. As such they allow varying degrees of flexibility and at times are even vague.

Thus, even as we categorize rules, conventions, and guidelines, we emphasize the idea that there must be flexibility and a flow among them. What is a convention in one case may be a guideline in the next, depending upon the writer's purpose, audience, message, intended effect, and even the discipline for which the piece is written. Figure 5.1 sets out the major rules, conventions, and guidelines helpful to writers as they shape their discourse.

Let us look briefly at the special considerations for ESL writers in dealing with the principles for shaping their writing in English. Bringing order to the myriad of thoughts about a subject is not always easy, even for native English writers who possess an intuitive sense of order learned over the period of time it took to acquire the first language. In fact, Colette Daiute tells us that even experienced native

FIGURE 5.1

	RULES	CONVENTIONS	GUIDELINES	
RHETORICAL	Be aware of a thesis	State your thesis clearly	Consider the reader	
	Be honest	Have a beginning, a middle, an	Consider the situation	
	Be truthful	end	Have a firm purpose in mind	
	Be brief—be	Choose a suitable design for	Make the writing alive	
	straightforward	paper and stay with it	Define	
	Be accurate	Make paragraphs the unit of	Think about	
	Be relevant	the composition	Design a plan for	the subject
	Be aware of an audience	Give an order for information	Make notes about	
	Be curious, questioning	—e.g., least important—	Talk about	
	and open minded about	most important	Look up information about	
	your subject	Use topic sentences to focus	Redesign	
	Must communicate	each paragraph	Write, rewrite, revise, edit	
	Limit your subject		proofread	
	Be thorough			
LINGUISTIC	Use clear and correct	Use devices which provide	Use active voice	
	sentence structure	coherence and cohesion	Use consistent verb tense	
	Use clear reference	Avoid non-committal	Avoid loose sentences	
	Use correct word form	language	Keep related words together	
		Avoid ambiguous word order	Word sentences positively	
		Establish a tone		
		Cut out the deadwood		
		Use suitable sentence		
		structure		
MECHANICAL	Use correct punctuation	Use !—? sparingly	Make the final message neat	
	Use correct spelling	Use transitional words,	in appearance	
	Make your paragraphing	phrases and sentences to	Use diagrams, charts, and/or	
	clear	signal paragraph changes	headings whenever	
		Follow one stylistic form	appropriate	
		consistently		

105

speaker/writers have syntax errors in their first drafts which they correct as they revise, and she strongly recommends, even for them, a clear separation of production and editing in the writing process (1981:20). But ESL writers obviously have even less intuition or acquired sense of the order of written English. What most ESL writers do have with regard to the principles is a body of consciously "learned" knowledge which they monitor as they work. Kroll found that "when students think their writing is going to be judged primarily for its adherence to form, . . . they are quite likely to rely heavily on what they see as their learned systems, trying to follow 'rules' of discourse which they may have incorrectly or incompletely learned. Many more errors may occur than if their acquired mastery were being called upon" (1978:180). Further, Britton states, "When the external constraints are strong, the fluent process is often interrupted by the need to make conscious choices—to select the appropriate word, to make sure of the punctuation, to keep the tone and level of formality consistent, to decide about the intricacies of grammar and syntax" (1975:41).

We must realize that ESL students have many constraints, that they do not automatically know how to shape a piece of writing in English, that they are constantly monitoring, and that the choices become even more difficult if they are uneasy about their mastery of what is acceptable. Therefore, we need to assure them that it is O.K., even necessary, to get thoughts down first, in any form, and then revise for purposes of shaping. Further, we need to show them as clearly as possible how to go about shaping discourse for their particular purposes. We should be mindful in presenting the principles that we do so in such a way that they become a part of their language acquisition. When writers apply form and structure to their already developed ideas, it becomes a matter of pride, a challenge, for them to present their thoughts as well as they can in English. Thus we encourage writers to become "optimal monitors," that is, to use their monitoring skills to their *best advantage.* "The optimal [L$_2$ monitor] user is an efficient editor or reviser who knows when and where and how to use the full resources of learned and acquired systems," says Kroll (1978:181).

The graphic manner in which the rhetorical patterns for organizing content are presented in the following pages has proved helpful to ESL writers for several reasons:

1. Students have a "picture" in mind which they can call up whenever they need the pattern to help them accomplish a writing purpose.

2. Students actually develop the writing patterns for themselves; thus they are learning by doing.

3. Students learn that the patterns are flexible guides to their writing.

5.2 Rhetorical shaping—organizing content

My literary tasks kept me fully occupied: my apprenticeship at the altar of technique, craft; the devilish intricacies of paragraphing, punctuation, dialogue placement. Not to mention the grand overall design, the dread demanding arc of middle-beginning-end. One had to learn so much, and from so many sources: not only from books, but from music, from painting, and just plain everyday observation.

Truman Capote

Content comes first, form follows, dependent upon the aim and purpose of the writing and dependent upon the audience.

William Irmscher

Such writing is a means to some end—its organization will be on the principle of efficiency in carrying out that end.

James Britton

Audience, purpose, and subject matter determine the particular organizational form content will take in a piece of writing. As Shahn suggests, writers find form by first determining a theme, then gathering material which substantiates and develops that theme. Writers need a clear focus, a thesis, before they can go about organizing information so that the message they wish "to communicate to readers is organized into a written text and made manifest to readers."[3]

The writers' task, then, as they work at communicating, is to strive to develop the universals— "to find and use points of agreement between [writer and reader] or shared assumptions, or shared values rather than viewing the person being addressed as an adversary, separate at a distance."[4]

"The writer needs to design his writing in such a way that it will effectively carry his thoughts into the reader's head."[5] As teachers, we must provide our students with a "set of explicit and workable strategies of expression which guide effective text production in a given situation and context."[6]

How does the writer go about ordering content? How does a writer "build a thought on the page which is so well constructed that the reader will accept it as his own?"[7] Writers often discover rhetorical form as they use heuristics to discover a subject. They are not always conscious that this aspect of discovery is occurring, but as Perl and Egendorf suggest, "The order of a set of ideas may be allowed to emerge from the clarifying of them, rather than being rigidly imposed at the outset . . . 'planning' and 'writing' overlap and interact: what was planned may need to change in the writing of it" (1979:129). Because of this overlapping and interaction, students need to discover that flexibility of form and structure is inherent in shaping discourse. We can lead our students to this insight by having them discover their rhetorical form as they "discover" their subjects.

Young, Becker, and Pike discuss a heuristic technique, a "playing with the unknown," which enables students to discover rhetorical form as part of the process of discovering their subjects. In "playing with the unknown," writers are successively classifying and reclassifying it (the unknown) as a question of (1970:44):

FACT
—requiring that the answer isolate and identify (Who? What? Where? When?)

PROCESS
—requiring that the answer describe an activity or prescribe a set of actions (How did it happen? How can it be done?)

RELATIONSHIP
—involving systems or units within systems. Questions of relationship explore issues of:

1. Value—ask about the relative positions of units in a value system (Which is better?)

2. Cause/Effect—What caused it? What is its probable effect?

3. Consistency—questions of logic and classification (Does the conclusion follow from the evidence? Do units have enough in common to be grouped in one category?)

4. Policy—questions or discussions prescribe actions (What should be done?)

Rhetorical patterns emerge quite naturally from the answers to these questions. Writers not only discover rhetorical purpose but also begin to see ways in which to structure content to suit their particular purpose. Writers may find themselves using several of these patterns to develop a paper, or they may employ one or two patterns more extensively depending on the purpose of the discourse. The writer's task begins with isolating and identifying a subject. Writers may work through the series of questions above beginning with questions of FACT. A natural means to begin such an exercise is to classify information, that is, to organize it into groups according to common characteristics, qualities, or traits. To do this, writers may employ a heuristic in which they answer the following questions.

- What are the types of X?
- What are the component parts of X?
- What are the common qualities of X?
- What distinguishes that X from another X?

From the answers to these questions, a pattern of organization begins to emerge. Figure 5.2 is a diagram of such a classification pattern.

Development of such visual patterns is particularly useful to ESL writers because they can "see" the structure in an overall sense before they begin to work on the actual sentence and paragraph construction necessary to the paper. A sense of order begins to emerge from the chaos of ideas.

Student-writers need to follow rules and guidelines as they begin formulating clear and precise pieces of writing. Students need to consider the following strategies as they develop a classification pattern for a piece of writing:

Goal of the classification:

Successfully group into a complex entity similar parts or pieces which illustrate the relationship between the parts.

Rules:

Be certain categories do not overlap. Be sure classification principles are clear to the reader:

1. What is the group composed of?
2. How was it decided what makes up a grouping?

Treat (in most cases) only the principal groups and subgroups. Too many groupings may confuse the reader.

Guidelines

Choose and use a single principle of classification. A logical whole should emerge from the parts.

Clearly state the guiding principle at the beginning of the paper to give clarity and purpose to the subject.

FIGURE 5.2 CLASSIFICATION PATTERN

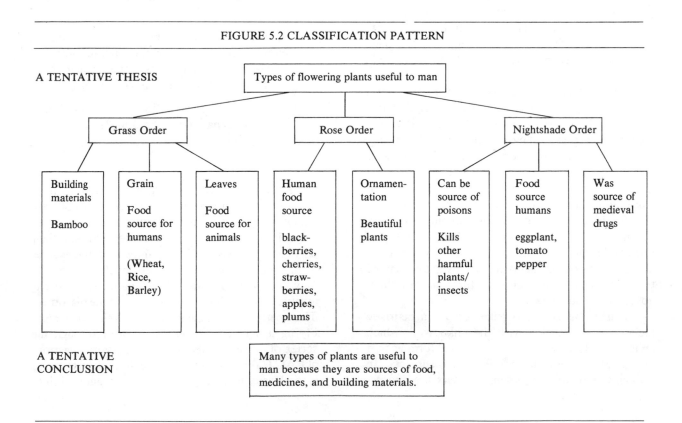

A TENTATIVE THESIS — Types of flowering plants useful to man

Grass Order | Rose Order | Nightshade Order

| Building materials

Bamboo | Grain

Food source for humans

(Wheat, Rice, Barley) | Leaves

Food source for animals | Human food source

blackberries, cherries, strawberries, apples, plums | Ornamentation

Beautiful plants | Can be source of poisons

Kills other harmful plants/ insects | Food source humans

eggplant, tomato pepper | Was source of medieval drugs |

A TENTATIVE CONCLUSION — Many types of plants are useful to man because they are sources of food, medicines, and building materials.

108

Choose a limited group as a subject. Do not attempt to classify *mankind*.

Try to choose a group with three or more subgroups.

Make your classification reasonably complete.

Introduce subclasses as necessary.

Depending on whether presentation of facts or opinions is your goal, incorporate a personal and original pattern in the classification.

Select a pattern of logical ordering to suit your purpose—sequence, order of importance, general to specific information, spatial order.

Besides using heuristics to isolate a subject, writers also identify a subject. As they do so, a pattern of *definition* develops. Writers seek, as they define, to explain the nature or essential qualities of a word, function, concept, or method. Furthermore, fixed boundaries are defined, enabling the writer to gain further control of a topic, and in so doing, strive for clarity in the communication. Questions writers can ask as they seek to define are:

- What is X?
- What are the characteristics of X?
- What is X like?

- How is X different from Y?
- What caused it?
- Who uses it?

Figure 5.3 shows a definition pattern that a student developed as she answered questions to discover a subject. The student was then able to flesh out each aspect of this definition to develop a detailed paper discussing cyclones.

As student-writers work with a definition pattern as part of the overall rhetorical form of a paper to explain a subject, they should keep the following strategies in mind:

Goal of the definition:

To explain a term or class of objects or concepts to which a term belongs.

Rules:

Do not include the term, concept, object being defined in the definition. *Roast duckling is a duck that has been roasted.*

Differentiate the term from others—establish its precise meaning using synonyms, antonyms, examples.

FIGURE 5.3 DEFINITION PATTERN

_____*A cyclone*_____ is _____*a storm which occurs in the Indian Ocean*_____.

That is, _____*the form and behavior of a cyclone*_____.

(It) is like _____*the hurricanes of the western Atlantic and western Pacific.*

For example, _____*in the fall of 1970, a cyclone swept across the Ganges delta, flooding thousands of villages*_____.

It contains qualities of _____*high winds, heavy rains*_____ and/or characteristics of _____*clockwise and counterclockwise motions. The winds are small at first but grow as they feed on hot, moist air.*

It is not _____*a tornado—it is not like the inland tornado of the Wizard of Oz* nor is it like _____.

It is caused by _____*a convergence of trade winds* or originated from _____*the northern and southern hemispheres which form an updraft.*

As a result (of it) _____*floods are frequent, villages are destroyed and numerous people are killed.*

Therefore, _____*efforts are being made to tame such storms by meteorologists.*

109

Illustrate the origins of the term.

Explain in terms of personal definition. Do not use dictionary definitions as the sole source of explanation.

✓ *Guidelines:*

First duty is to define—provide an *expansion* of the basic definition.

Define a generic rather than a specific term—define "automobile," not "Buick."

Develop definition fully by using expository methods—description, narration, classification, cause and effect, analysis, negation.

State differentiating characteristics precisely.

Do not define single terms using "is where," "is when."

Use the principle from "known to unknown." Use language that is clear and familiar to your audience.

As students shape content, they will note that in writing a definition, other methods of development will also be employed—comparison, classification, cause/effect, and so on. The writer observes that while one pattern may be dominant, other patterns are necessary to develop the definition effectively and completely.

As writers work to classify and reclassify an unknown, they employ questions of PROCESS in addition to questions of FACT. With questions of process, the writer attempts to explain a procedure: how it is done, how it happened, how it evolved. The writer's primary aim will not be to categorize or classify but instead to *explain* a procedure by (1) giving specific directions to an audience about something they presumably want to do or (2) giving general information about a procedure, method, or event. The first implies the use of specific directions and the second the use of general information supported by details. For example, directions to make a chocolate mousse require clear, brief, but complete details, and a logical ordering of information. However, a discussion of the evolution of the automobile industry in America would require more detailed description of major events that occurred over the long term. Like direction giving, a logical ordering of information is crucial.

The questions of process that a writer asks as a means to shape a subject include:

- Why is this process important?

- What do we do first to complete the process?

- What follows the first step, second step,. . .?

- What is the effect of the process on people? places? things?

- What tools are needed to complete the process?

Figure 5.4 illustrates the pattern of development for an instructional process. The writer added a thesis statement and a concluding statement *after* working out the lines of the pattern.

FIGURE 5.4 PROCESS PATTERN

TENTATIVE THESIS | Planting blackberries is an exacting process.

Importance—of planting at the right time of the year
First, prepare the soil and assemble equipment
Do not—allow stock to dry out
Second, set plants 4 inches deep in soil
After—plants are established, cultivate them
Next, assure good drainage of the soil
Then, use fertilizer and herbicide
Finally, harvest berries

TENTATIVE CONCLUSION | Your planting efforts are all worthwhile when you enjoy blackberry pie, blackberry jam, or blackberries with sugar and cream.

From the material begun on the process diagram, a student is able to develop a completed paper. As students begin to develop a paper, they need to consider the following rules and guidelines:

Goal of Process Explanation:

To explain a procedure by (1) giving explicit directions to an audience whose goal is to carry out the procedure or (2) telling an audience how something actually occurred without having them carry out the exercise.

Rules:

Direction-giving requires extraordinary clarity —the reader must be able to accomplish the task correctly.

110

All steps in the process must be discussed completely and logically. A statement as to the importance of the procedure should be stated early in the discussion.

Guidelines (Direction-giving process):

Writer should have personally performed the process.

Give complete details. The audience is those who do not know but wish to learn the process.

Define terms carefully. If necessary, provide synonymous words. Give reasons (briefly) for the process. Tell why as well as how.

Tell the reader what *not* to do, and include the consequences.

Use illustrations to make directions definite and concrete. A picture is worth a thousand words.

Guidelines (Information-giving process):

Be thoroughly familiar with the subject. Know the details.

Select the details for presentation carefully. Do not weigh down the reader in minutiae.

Order the procedure logically.

As writers work to develop the process pattern, they also begin to perceive another aspect of rhetorical form, that of logical arrangement. Working with a process highlights the need for a particular arrangement of ideas, and writers discover that a definite order is necessary to successfully communicate to the reader. Logical arrangement is essential, for example, to the correct completion of the direction-giving task. While sequential order was most suitable to the process illustrated in the process pattern, other logical patterns of arrangement may also emerge depending on the *purpose* of the writer. Logical arrangement applies to all patterns of development; writers select the pattern most suitable to their purposes. Figure 5.5 shows various patterns for logical arrangement.

Another way of "playing with the unknown" involves answering questions of RELATIONSHIP. The writer works to discover similarities or differences between events, people, concepts, . . . as a means to relate systems or elements within systems. Patterns of *comparison and/or contrast* become a means to ensure clarity of ideas because they allow the writer to set up ideas which the reader can then

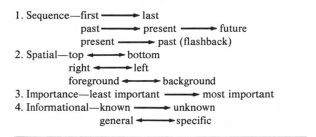

FIGURE 5.5 LOGICAL ARRANGEMENT PATTERNS

evaluate. Comparison and contrast is a means to present choices and possibilities from which readers can establish a point of view.

The questions of comparative relationship that a writer asks include:

- How is A like B?
- Is A better than B? How is A better?
- Is A different from B? How is A different?
- How is A's function different from B's function?
- How has A evolved differently from B?
- Does A produce the same effect as B?

Figure 5.6 illustrates the question/answer process a student might engage in and the rhetorical form that emerges as a student "plays with the unknown" answering questions of relationship. The functional section of the comparison is not detailed because it was not applicable to the writer's purpose. Given another topic of interest, the writer could fill in this area.

From the information obtained in Figure 5.6, the writer has the material necessary to develop a paper comparing the dolphin and the shark. The ordering of information also provides the writer with possibilities for a thesis statement. In this particular case the writer arrived at the following tentative thesis: *Unique features enable dolphins to protect themselves from their deadly enemy, the shark.*

The following rules and guidelines need to be considered by the student in shaping a paper using a comparative arrangement.:

Goal of the comparison:

Examining detailed information to emphasize the similarities or differences between or among things.

111

FIGURE 5.6 COMPARISON-CONTRAST PATTERN

_____A dolphin_____ is similar to _____a shark_____ in terms of:

Physical characteristics:

	A	B
size	body size—large	
type	several different species	
speed	capable of high speeds for a short time	
weight	grow to similar adult size	
color		

Behavioral characteristics:

	A	B
Social habits	Both are found in all seas	
temperament		
eating habits	eat the same basic food—fish	

Functional characteristics:

	A	B
Use		
Design		
Performance		

_____A dolphin_____ is different from _____a shark_____ in terms of:

Physical characteristics:

A (dolphin)	B (shark)
dolphin is warm-blooded	cold-blooded
better vertical swimming ability	less developed vertebral column because
because of vertebral column	of being cold-blooded
able to sustain muscular effort	doesn't get enough oxygen to sustain
for a longer period of time	long-term muscular activity
smaller jaw	larger jaw
smaller, pointed teeth	sharp-pointed teeth are capable of tearing

Behavioral characteristics:

A	B
has higher intelligence	limited intelligence
can "communicate" with other dolphins	rarely "communicates"
travels in groups	travels alone
highly organized group structure	usually found with other sharks only
	when feeding on a kill

Functional characteristics:

A	B

Rules:

To ensure clarity, be consistent in making comparisons—state features of A and compare with the same or similar features in B.

Provide sufficient detail in the comparison to ensure that similarities or differences are properly emphasized.

Guidelines:

Limit the comparison. Do not make the field of comparison too large; for example, do not compare 20 types of automobiles.

Organize the overall comparison according to your purpose and subject:

- Consider a point-by-point comparison. This alternating pattern emphasizes specific details within a larger category. This is useful for short papers. For example:

  Category of comparison—dolphin and shark behavior
  Point of comparison—eating habits
  Specific details—eating habits of shark
  —eating habits of dolphin

- Consider an overall comparison. This opposing pattern presents *all* the main points of one component of the comparison and then *all* the main points of the second component. This pattern is useful for emphasizing whole concepts. For example:

  Overall comparison: *Behavior of sharks and dolphins*

  Shark behavior:
  1. Physical features
  2. Geographical distribution
  3. Eating habits
  4. Social habits

  Dolphin behavior:
  1. Physical features
  2. Geographical distribution
  3. Eating habits
  4. Social habits

- Consider combining both the alternating and the opposing patterns. This method is useful for extended pieces of writing. It requires very careful paragraph arrangement.

- Use balanced sentence structures. To illustrate *similarities,* use parallel and coordinating constructions; to *illustrate* differ-

ences, use subordinating constructions and antithesis.

Writers also discover *causes and effects* when they answer questions of relationship. From the answers to such questions yet another rhetorical pattern emerges. The cause-and-effect pattern is a method to explain the "hows," or reasons, for particular events, attitudes, beliefs, and behaviors. For example, a writer might ask what causes pollution. In developing such a paper, a writer might address several causes of pollution, perhaps classifying them into groups of natural causes and manufactured causes.

On the other hand, a writer might wish to address the *effects* of a particular event rather than its causes. The writer's goal now is to explain "what will happen" or "what has happened" as a consequence of a particular event, attitude, belief, or behavior. Using pollution as a topic, a writer might focus on the result of a particular kind of pollution (air, water, noise) in a particular place (a town, city, country).

Questions writers ask to determine cause-effect relationships include:

- What causes X? At present? In the past? In the future?

- What are the consequences of X?

- What would happen to X if . . . ?

- What is the effect of X on . . . ?

Figure 5.7 illustrates the question/answer process a writer might engage in and the rhetorical form generated as a writer "plays with the unknown" to discover relationships.

From information generated in the cause-effect pattern, the writer can begin to shape a paper employing a cause-effect rhetorical form. These rules and guidelines should be considered:

Goal of the Cause-Effect explanation:

To examine the factors which have caused a particular result(s).

Rules:

Be certain the relationship between the cause(s) and effect(s) is clear.

Be certain the causes and/or effects are sufficient to convince the reader.

113

FIGURE 5.7 CAUSE-EFFECT PATTERN

EFFECT		*REASONS (CAUSES)*	
House plants are unhealthy	because of:	1. *water conditions*	
	cause:	*too much water roots rot*	(effect)
		too little water roots dry out	(effect)
		2. *light conditions*	
	cause:	*too much light leaves burn*	(effect)
		too little light leaves can't grow	(effect)
		3. *temperature factors*	
	cause:	*too hot stems and leaves wilt*	(effect)
		too cold stems and leaves freeze	(effect)
		4. *fertilizer factors*	
	cause:	*too much soil becomes acidic*	(effect)
		too little roots can't develop	(effect)

CAUSE		*RESULTS (EFFECTS)*		
What are the	*effects of hurricanes* on:			
	individuals:	*(1) inconvenience, (2) injury, (3) death*	?	cause
	a country:	*mass destruction of property, population*	?	cause
	a region of the world:	*property loss—food shortages*	?	cause
What are the	*effects of hurricanes* in terms of:			
	physical environment:	*destruction of life, property*	?	cause
	emotional environment:	*fatalistic attitude, humans cannot control nature*	?	cause

Establish an order for causation—Is X a primary cause or secondary cause? immediate or remote cause?

Discover true causes or actual effects. Do not rely on coincidental occurrences or effects. For example, Bill could not withdraw money from his checking account because his balance was zero (true cause) not because he arrived at the bank without a withdrawal slip (coincidental cause).

Guidelines:

Be sure to examine *all* pertinent causes of an effect. Frequently, many causes produce an effect.

Be aware of contradictory effects—(hurry up and slow down). If necessary, qualify causes—plants need water but not too much.

When appropriate to the writing purpose, present the secondary causes or effects which influence the primary cause-effect relationship (e.g., Chemical spraying reduces crop loss [primary effect], but it may also cause human illness as a result of persons' inhaling chemicals which are poisonous to them [secondary effect]).

After writers have discovered their subjects and begun preliminary shaping of content by employing these questioning techniques, they are ready to determine the "outer shape" of their papers. Students begin this phase of the writing process armed with note cards, lists, quotations, looping exercises, and rhetorical patterns—all the bits and pieces, the nuggets of writing they have already completed as part of the writing process. They are ready to organize these nuggets to create a skeletal framework or tentative blueprint upon which to structure their main ideas.

Figure 5.8 helps students see the *overall organization* of a paper—the *beginning, middle,*

FIGURE 5.8 OVERALL ORGANIZATION. From Lee J. Martin/revised by Harry P. Kroitor, *The Five-Hundred Word Theme* (Englewood Cliffs, N.J.: Prentice-Hall, Inc., 1974), 121.

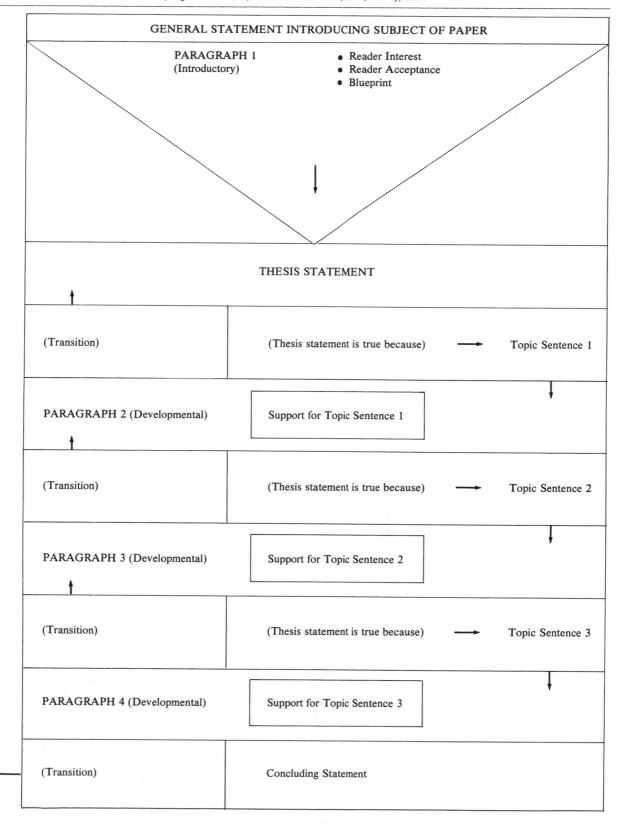

and *end*. Once a purpose for writing has been established, it is also a means to help determine how to effectively develop the rhetorical form for each individual paragraph.

As students arrange main points, they can arrange key words or phrases into a formal sentence outline which further organizes the composition. Students are encouraged at this point to write their ideas as complete thoughts.

Thesis:

I.

    A.
    B.

       1.
       2.

          a.
          b.

II.

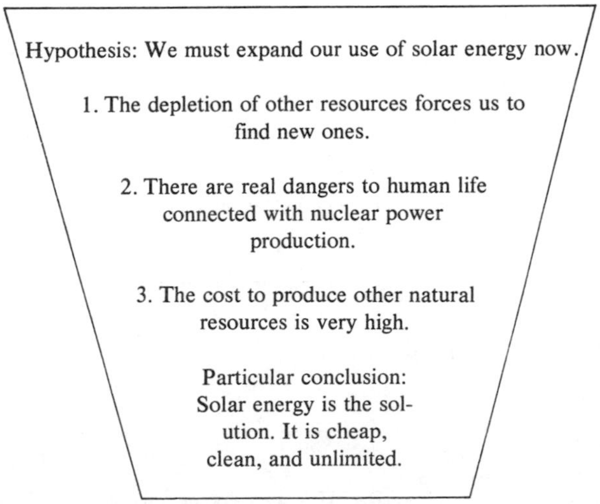

In the process of organizing material students develop a sense for an overall pattern of development. Depending on the purpose, audience, and subject matter of the paper, writers may select an inductive or deductive pattern of development.

Using an inductive pattern of development, writers present particular points which lead to a general principle or thesis. For example, the writer of a paper on "house plant care" might use the inductive pattern in Figure 5.9 to illustrate the importance of proper plant care.

Using a deductive pattern of development, writers present a general hypothesis first and then support it with specific proof leading to a particular conclusion.

Having established an overall structure for their papers, students can then develop each particular point using the rhetorical pattern which seems most appropriate. Comparison might be used, for example, to develop point 3 of the solar energy ideas illustrated in Figure 5.10. A cause-and-effect pattern emerges quite naturally in the development of point 2.

As writers design and develop a piece of writing, they need to be aware that a "shared context builds up between writer and reader as the piece proceeds, so the chances of losing, confusing, misleading or frustrating a reader are at their greatest in the opening sentences."[8] Aware of this fact, writers need to develop the introductions to

FIGURE 5.9 INDUCTIVE PATTERN

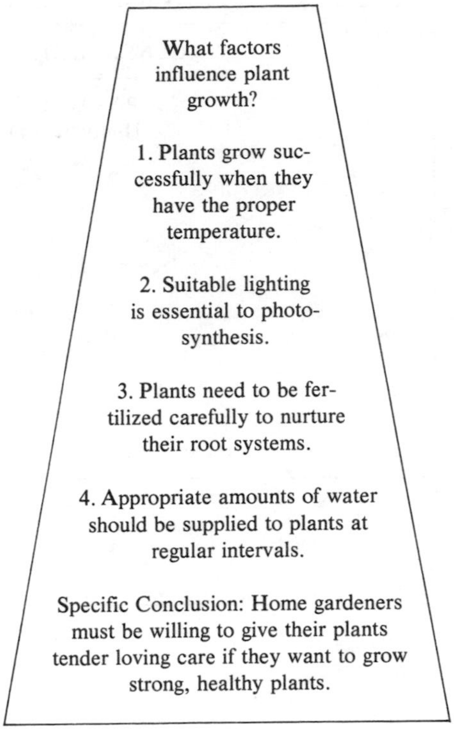

What factors influence plant growth?

1. Plants grow successfully when they have the proper temperature.

2. Suitable lighting is essential to photosynthesis.

3. Plants need to be fertilized carefully to nurture their root systems.

4. Appropriate amounts of water should be supplied to plants at regular intervals.

Specific Conclusion: Home gardeners must be willing to give their plants tender loving care if they want to grow strong, healthy plants.

FIGURE 5.10 DEDUCTIVE PATTERN

Hypothesis: We must expand our use of solar energy now.

1. The depletion of other resources forces us to find new ones.

2. There are real dangers to human life connected with nuclear power production.

3. The cost to produce other natural resources is very high.

Particular conclusion: Solar energy is the solution. It is cheap, clean, and unlimited.

their papers carefully. Students are now ready to work on the "fine tuning" of their papers, the development of successful introductions.

Writers need to know that while well-developed content, reliable sources, a clear purpose, and a well-defined audience are necessary to creating a successful paper, *originality* in presentation serves to further hold the readers' attention. A paper may be technically correct in both content and organization, but without originality of presentation, a writer's message may be lost and a shared context may not build between writer and reader.

Writers therefore need methods to help them create introductions which—

- Arouse the reader's interest.

- Inspire the reader.

- Introduce the thesis to the reader.

- Suit the writer's purpose and audience

WAYS OF DEVELOPING INTRODUCTIONS

IN THE BEGINNING... Want to catch your reader's attention? and hold it? Ask a question, or use any variation of the techniques listed below. The idea, of course, is to entice your readers to begin and make them want to continue reading.

INTRODUCTORY PARAGRAPHS
may hold more appeal for an audience if they

- entice with a rhetorical question (?)

- present a startling fact (!)

- develop background or historical perspective

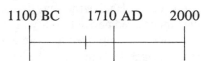

- use a quotation which illustrates or makes a statement about the subject "..."

- narrate an interesting, funny, sad, unusual ... incident

- appeal to the reader for an action or change in action

- illustrate the importance of the topic

The following examples illustrate how writers aroused reader interest by using one of the methods of introduction listed.

1. *A provocative question:*

There is much discussion today about the value of "natural foods." Supporters of the "natural food" movement criticize supermarkets for selling a majority of foods containing preservatives, suggesting that such foods are unhealthy. Yet, what would happen if food manufacturers stopped using preservatives in baked goods, frozen vegetables, breakfast cereals, and canned foods? Is the American homemaker prepared to deal with storing foods without preservatives? Preservatives are necessary for the majority of American homemakers.

2. *A startling statement or statistic:*

Physically and psychically women are by far the superiors of men. The old chestnut about women being more emotional than men has been forever destroyed by the facts of the two great wars. Women under blockade, heavy bombardment, concentration-camp confinement, and similar rigors withstand them vastly more successfully than men. The psychiatric casualties of civilian populations under such conditions are mostly masculine, and there are more men in our mental hospitals than there are women. The steady hand at the helm is the hand that has rocked the cradle. (Adapted from Ashley Montagu's *The Natural Superiority of Women.*)

3. *A statement which provides historical details about the subject:*

Many people believe that the Women's Movement began in the mid-1960s with the creation of the National Organization of Women. However, the causes of women can be traced back to 19th century America. The first Women's Rights Convention was held in Seneca Falls, New York, in 1848. A "Declaration of Sentiments" was presented which outlined the views of women concerning the injustices which they faced.

4. *An appropriate quotation:*

Thomas Jefferson said, "The way to prevent error is to give the people full information of their affairs." If we believe this statement, censorship of our media cannot be permitted.

Citizens can make informed judgments only if they are aware of all the facts relating to a given situation.

5. *A short anecdote:*

Pham Dung, from Thailand, was the only surviving child from a family of eight children. He survived because of the efforts of two American doctors who came to work in his country to overcome the problems of starvation. Dung, now an important businessman, remembers how he and his family went out each morning to beg for food because they didn't have even a crust of bread. He was just one of the millions of people on the verge of starvation owing to an inadequate world food supply.

6. *Appeal to the reader for an action or a change in action:*

Unless each citizen immediately begins working to conserve our natural resources, daily life for each of us will be extremely different by the dawn of the twenty-first century. Each of us must use less fuel, less electricity, and less water in our daily lives. Wasteful consumption can destroy our society as we know it.

7. *Appeal to the reader regarding the importance of the topic:*

With all the wealth, power, luxuries of life, and abundance of food in the United States, it might surprise people to learn that Americans rank only fourth in the world as the best fed and only sixth in terms of longevity. There are several reasons for this surprising record, but the main one is directly related to the eating habits of the American people.

As these introductory paragraphs illustrate, writers tap varied sources of information to develop introductory paragraphs, finding material in—
- Themselves—personal experience.

- Situations—the world beyond the writer.

- Written words—data from books, diaries, magazines, newspapers, and journals.

Another aspect of "fine tuning" a paper is creating an effective conclusion. Writers need to

bring a piece of work to closure. The conclusion gives writers one last opportunity to ensure that a shared context, a sense of agreement and understanding, has developed between writer and reader. The conclusion enables the writer to tie the ideas presented in the paper into one final point of contact with the reader.

THE END ... Concluding paragraphs are meant to create a feeling of finale. What is presented here is probably what the reader will remember best. Therefore, based on their results and proofs, writers must use their creative talents in this most important part of the composition to—

- lead to the thesis for the first time.

- emphasize the thesis or main points with
  a. a summary, or
  b. an enumeration.

- draw a conclusion.

- make a judgment—recommend an action to be taken.

- express an opinion and/or

- pose a question to
  a. provoke further thought, or
  b. indicate further possible development of the topic.

Each of the following paragraphs serves as the conclusion of an essay. Each writer has used one of the techniques mentioned above to unify the paper. The particular methods employed to write effective introductions (see page 117) may also be employed in writing conclusions.

1. *Lead to the thesis for the first time* (from an essay discussing the need for alternative forms of energy):

The world supply of oil, coal, and natural gas is diminishing more rapidly than scientists ever expected. Furthermore, nuclear power has proved to be dangerous to human life. Its use in various parts of the world has provoked violent protests and a sense of fear. What is the solution to the worldwide energy crisis that grows more complex each year?

The solution is solar energy. It is cheap, clean, and most important, unlimited in supply. A worldwide effort must be made to develop this most essential energy source.

2. *Summarize the main points presented* (from an essay discussing the need for mass transit):

What will make the quality of life better in our city? An efficient mass transit system. By providing mass transit, we can decrease the amount of gasoline consumed daily. We can decrease the air and noise pollution created by too many automobiles. And finally, we can decrease commuting costs for the majority of men and women in our city. We all want to improve our quality of life. To do so, an efficient mass transit system is vital to our city.

3. *Draw a conclusion from the examples which have been presented* (from an essay discussing world population problems):

No longer can inadequate food supply be considered a problem of the Third World only. Continuing food shortages are rapidly becoming an issue for half of the earth's population. The resulting problems of starvation and rampant disease pose a threat to all mankind. The problems of insufficient housing, inadequate health care, and exhausted natural resources increase daily. Inadequate food supply is the number one social problem worldwide.

4. *Recommend an action to be taken* (from an essay discussing the high illiteracy rate existing in many sections of the world):

We must act on this crucial problem NOW. Citizens throughout the world must realize we cannot tolerate illiteracy and the problems that it breeds. To solve the problem, countries can begin by allocating more funds to provide teachers for areas with few or nonexistent schools. Second, countries must establish nationwide campaigns to recruit adults as well as children to enroll in literacy programs. Most important, government leaders must make a firm commitment to eliminate illiteracy. Only through government support and financial commitment will the menace of illiteracy be destroyed.

5. *Express an opinion and (6) pose a question* (from an essay discussing revolution as a means of change):

Revolutions are important for us because they are a means of change. Indeed they can be either a positive or a negative means of change. They are a change for the better in the case of technological and industrial revolution and a change for the worse in the case of political revolution. For my country, revolution has meant blood and death. For others, revolution has meant scientific and technological advancement. Let us use revolution positively to secure our species and solve our problems peacefully.

Why not work to change for the betterment of mankind? Why not use revolution positively to secure a better life for every man?

After writers have developed and shaped their content by determining suitable rhetorical forms and creating effective introductions and conclusions, they are ready to complete another aspect of "fine tuning" a paper, the linguistic shaping. Coupled with rhetorical shaping, linguistic shaping is essential to ensure that writers fulfill completely point three of the axiom—

Writing well is at the same time perceiving well, thinking well, and saying well.—Buffon

5.3 Linguistic shaping

Syntax and rhetoric are different aspects of the writing process; improvement of one does not imply improvement of the other.

Vivian Zamel

Students . . . do not possess "coherence" as a primary force for the creation of meaning until we teach them about such matters as connecting words and transitions.

William Stalter

Grammar is to a writer what anatomy is to a sculptor, or the scales to a musician. You may loathe it, it may bore you, but nothing will replace it, and once mastered it will support you like a rock.

Nevil Chute

Linguistic shaping is the fine tuning in discourse which clarifies, links, directs, and carries the deep structure of meaning to the reader. It is largely influenced by the writer's purpose, message, and audience, and also by the rhetorical forms the writer has chosen as an outgrowth of the other three. All these elements influence writers' decisions about which words and structures to use and how to use them to their own best advantage. Further, even though rhetorical and syntactical improvements do not directly affect each other, improved syntax does aid the reader in interpreting the message. Thus, fine tuning is directly related to reader expectations as to what they expect to find when they entertain a piece of writing: unity of expression, coherence, and cohesion. In other words, it is further relating the inner parts to each other and to the outer shape and "ordering the whole to meet the needs of the content." It embodies the *arrangement and interrelationships* of thoughts, grammatical constructions, and words, in addition to *lexical considerations* of the form, use, and choice of words themselves. In sum, as Stalter states, "Structure is most effectively defined as that set of relationships between the parts which create the whole—in the case of written composition, the meaning of the whole" (1978:341).

UNITY AND COHERENCE

To achieve unity and coherence in a piece of writing, then, writers will first examine the structure—arrangement—of the larger parts, or units, of writing. Writers will determine that—

1. There is an overall design.

2. A thesis, or main idea, controls the piece of writing.

3. Each main point and its support are developed as a paragraph unit.

4. The main point of each paragraph relates to the thesis.

5. Each sentence in each paragraph relates to, adds new information to, or supports the main idea of that paragraph.

6. Each paragraph relates logically to each succeeding paragraph until closure is made.

The next illustration (Figure 5.11) shows how each of the points made in a single paragraph could be developed into new paragraphs which support the thesis that "early colonists settled America for a variety of reasons."

Beyond the unity and coherence achieved from the preceding arrangement of ideas are many compex and intricate structures of the language. Raimes says that of the "additional problems that our ESL students have over and above any native speaker's difficulties. . . . The most obvious and pressing problem is that of errors in sentence structure and grammar (1979:46). However, few

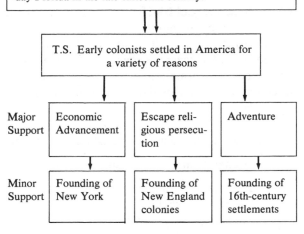

FIGURE 5.11

The early colonists settled in America for a variety of reasons. The Dutch came largely for economic advancement. They founded New Amsterdam, now New York City, and by the mid-17th century, it was a thriving trade center in the New World. Many English colonists came to America to escape religious persecution. They founded colonies in New England based on the ideals of religious freedom and tolerance. The early Spanish explorers came to America in search of adventure. Spaniards in search of gold and the "fountain of youth" established a settlement in present-day Florida in the late sixteenth century.

T.S. Early colonists settled in America for a variety of reasons

| Major Support | Economic Advancement | Escape religious persecution | Adventure |
| Minor Support | Founding of New York | Founding of New England colonies | Founding of 16th-century settlements |

ESL writers will ever completely *master* these intricacies. Therefore, since an attempt to teach all of them, along with the other important processes of writing, would overwhelm and discourage writers, ESL teachers need to emphasize the structures that most affect ESL writers' abilities to communicate effectively in written English.

Researchers have found that for ESL writers there is a crucial difference between "global" errors (those that violate overall sentence organization such as connectors) and "local" errors (minor errors such as articles or agreement).[9] Global, rather than local, errors are shown to have a greater adverse effect on native speakers' comprehension of the ESL writers' efforts.[10] Thus, these writers need to be encouraged to experiment with and thus acquire, if possible, these syntactic forms in the secure setting of the ESL classroom. In confronting global errors, student-writers will concentrate on the "describable relationships [that] may exist between clusters of sentences"[11] which make up the units of discourse. These relationships are signaled by devices that link ideas to one another: connecting words, parallel structures, pronouns, and so on. Acquiring the use of

these devices is particularly important in ESL writers' learning process because they need to know, says Raimes, not only how to put words together but also ideas and propositions (p. 11.). Some of the more important coherence devices are the connectors. We will focus on the ones deemed most crucial for ESL writers.

Connectors

- Coordinating conjunctions—used to create compound sentences

- Subordinating conjunctions—used to create complex sentences

- Transitional devices—used to give information and direct thought

- Parallel structures—used to emphasize ideas of equal importance and provide balance

- Repetition and synonyms—used to emphasize important ideas and enhance tone

- Similes and metaphors—used to clarify and illustrate

All the connectors are used to *emphasize the meaning* of one word, phrase, or proposition *in relation to another.* Further, they allow writers to vary sentence length and structure: the resulting sentence variety lends interest, readability, and sophistication to a piece of writing.

COM + JUNGERE = TO JOIN TOGETHER

Coordinating conjunctions link structures of equal importance and show their relationships to each other. For example,

and
; } show equal emphasis—one thought (in addition to) one thought . . .

yet
but } show equal emphasis of contrary or opposing thoughts

so
for } show equal emphasis of cause and effect

or
nor } show equal emphasis of choices

Correct or incorrect use of these connectors subtly affects the writer's meaning. Notice how the meaning changes in the following sentences.

I live in Thailand, *and* I am a Buddhist.

I live in Thailand, *so* I am a Buddhist.

Subordinating conjunctions link main ideas with less important ideas, or they allow the writer to emphasize one idea more than another. They are words such as

since	while
if	although
when	after
as	because . . .

For example, compare A and B:

A. "*When* Wegener died in 1930 on the Greenland ice cap *while* trying to rescue fellow meteorologists, the concept of continental drift was scorned by all but a few serious scientists."*

B. Wegener died in 1930 on the Greenland ice cap.
Wegener was trying to rescue fellow meteorologists.
The concept of continental drift was scorned by most scientists.

Notice that while both A and B contain explicit and implicit information, the ideas *related* by subordinate connectors in A are more explicit and supply more context than the other set, thus highlighting the main thought the writer wants to convey: "the concept of continental drift . . . ." The other pieces of information, in the form of subordinate structures, cushion the main idea in meaningful background. The meaning of the whole thought depends on the relationship of the main idea to the parts.

These and other connectors link thoughts and groups of thoughts and make them flow. Neglect or misuse of these shaping devices results in run-on sentences, deadwood, comma splices, and illogical connections—any of which may cause the reader to miss the writer's meaning.

Transitional words and phrases also tie sentences and paragraphs together. They signal or give specific information to the reader about the direction a sentence or paragraph is going to take. They show—

1. A shift from one thought pattern to another

2. A change in tone or emphasis

3. Information such as example, addition, concession, sequence, summation, and relationships of comparison/contrast, cause/effect, and condition.

Notice how the writer leads the reader from one point to another in the following editorial about food.

---

*From "The Earth Moves" James Balog for *Pan Am Clipper,* July 1980.

FOOD
The World Is Running Out
Despite Production Increases

by
Jonathan Power

(Transitional signals)

The world is running out of food—<u>or</u> food <u>it</u> can afford to buy. <u>This</u> information is probably a surprise to the farmer of the United States corn belt, the world's most productive granary, <u>as he</u> worries about low prices and piling surpluses.

Coordinate and subordinate connectors

Referential ties

It is probably a surprise to the farmer of the Soviet Union who, although he never seems able to meet the targets of the central planners, has managed to keep his country's deficit within reasonable proportion in the last two years.

information for emphasis

(Ironically,) it will come as the biggest surprise to those who use India as litmus for the Third World. The Indians, thanks to miraculously good weather the last three years but also to hard work and studious inventiveness, appear to be on top of the food problem.

Simile: "India as litmus"

shift: contrast

All this, (however,) is deceptive. Over the last 7 years, in 62 countries representing 43 percent of the developing countries (excluding China), food production has not kept pace with population.

FAMINES RECALLED

emphasis

The food crisis (of course) is no new thing. It has been with us since the days when the serpent tempted Eve to eat the apple. In modern history the Irish famine of 1847 and the Bengali famine of 1943 have carved memories so deep that books are still written about them and plays and films paraphrase the suffering.

shift: time

(More recently,) it was the world's food crisis of 1974 and 1975 that put hunger on the political agenda. At the World Food Conference in Rome in November 1974, all the nations of the world voted unanimously to support Henry A. Kissinger's resolution: "By 1985 no child should go to bed hungry."

additional information

(A word more) about what happened then, for it sets the scene for the situation today.

123

A combination of consecutive bad harvests around the world, massive Russian buying of American food stocks, the disappearance of the Peruvian anchovy, and shortsighted policies in the United States that kept farm land idle created a situation that led to the quadrupling of grain prices.

parallel clauses

Millions of poor people in the Third World found that the prime necessity of life was priced out of reach. Maybe half a million died. The World Food Conference, held fortuitously at the midpoint in the crisis, agreed to a number of remedies: the creation of a new $1 billion fund for agricultural development, a pledge to establish better procedures for emergency food aid, and an internationally coordinated system of food stocks.

SOVIET LIMITS

additional information

The conference (also) shook up the world's largest grain exporter, the United States, and the world's largest grain importer, the Soviet Union, criticizing their shortsighted commercial policies. A year later they responded by signing an agreement setting limits on Soviet freedom to purchase in the United States grain market.

summation

(All this,) together with the return of good growing weather and the seeming Indian breakthrough, took the edge off the international debate. Yet an agreement to establish an internationally coordinated system of nationally held food stocks is still being haggled over.

comparison

The 10 million ton target for international food aid is still unconsummated. (But worse than) this, it has removed the political spotlight from the underlying trends in much of the Third World.

124

This year's cereal imports by the Third World are expected to achieve record levels. The very poor countries, if they are to make ends meet, will have to increase their imports by 16 percent over last year.

shift : time

Today the gross food deficit is 36 million tons of grain. By 1990, based on present trends, it will be 120 to 145 million tons a year.

These figures are the consensus figures of the United National Food and Agricultural Organization, the World Food Council, and the World Bank. The latter in a recent report concludes: "Continual imports of this magnitude cannot be financed." It could be added, neither can charitable exports.

LAND REFORM

summation

comparison and emphasis

There are, in short, only two solutions: either demand is choked off by higher prices—this of course means a sharp increase in malnutrition and mortality—or the world sets about a significant program of investment in Third World agriculture to repeat on a broader scale what has been successfully done in China, Taiwan, Korea, and maybe in India too. This means vigorous land reform and priority for the small farmer, the world's most tested productive unit.

If this is done, and it is backed by a reasonable amount of emergency food aid and evening out of prices through a world stocking system, mass hunger and starvation can become the ghosts of history.

metaphor : "ghosts"

The commitment made for mankind by Kissinger can still be redeemed, but the time left to do it, short enough in 1974, is nearly gone.

Editorial from the *Houston Chronicle*
August 28, 1978

125

Writers should be aware of the types of transitional signals available to them for moving the reader along in the intended direction.

TYPES OF TRANSITIONAL SIGNALS

Transition Type	Word Choices
EXAMPLE	for example, for instance, to illustrate, thus, in this case, in other words, that is
ADDITION	furthermore, in addition, moreover, also, as important as, and, as well as
EMPHASIS	again, indeed, to repeat, in fact, of course, above all
CONCESSION	even though, although, though, in spite of, despite, while
SUMMATION	in sum, in short, all this, finally, briefly
SEQUENCE	
TIME	after, afterward, next, then, now, at last, previously, soon, immediately, when, yesterday, today, tomorrow, in the meantime, meanwhile, subsequently, during, before, eventually
ORDER	first, second, third, secondly, thirdly, in the first place, next, last, finally
SPACE	to the left/right, nearby, above, next to, below, under, beyond, in the foreground/background, opposite to
RELATIONSHIP	
COMPARISON	likewise, in a similar manner, similarly, both . . . and, as . . . as, neither . . . nor, not only . . . but also, as if, as though, like, similar to, more, better, worse
CONTRAST	yet, but, while, however, unlike, though, on the other hand, nevertheless, at the same time, to the contrary, conversely, different from, rather than
CAUSE/EFFECT	because, therefore, thus, since, as a result, hence, due to, consequently, accordingly, so that, in order that, in order to, as, if

---

Sentence variety is an outgrowth of bringing together the various connecting devices into one piece of writing. The following passage from a student journal illustrates the variety of uses and the effectiveness of connectors to convey meaning in a piece of writing.

---

sentence variety:

simple   Religion is the expression of man's belief in God or gods to be worshipped, normally expressed in

complex   conduct and ritual. <u>Since</u> I was born to Buddhist

126

simple

compound

simple

parallel phrases

parents, I became a Buddhist. Lord Buddha was the first person in the world who originated our religion. Though he had enough powers, he was a human being and was born to a royal family. As a Buddhist, I do not believe him to be a god. Lord Buddha understood the instability of human life and he delivered the truth to the people. He told us not to tell lies, not to kill animals, not to steal things from others, and not to misbehave.

complex

compound

simple

Even though I am a Buddhist I usually do not go to the temple very often to pray. I do not believe much about the praying, but I am always prevented from doing any bad things. I always try to do good things.

complex

simple

I trust that if I do good things, always good will come to me. According to our religion we believe in rebirth. So we are compelled to do good things as we expect better lives in our next birth.

Palitha Wickramasinghe,
ESL student

This passage also illustrates uses of parallel structures, repetition, and synonyms, as well as some use of referents as cohesive devices.

Other important devices for achieving global coherence are parallel structures, repetition of key words and phrases, and synonyms, similes, and metaphors. These, too, can all be used with word, phrase, clause, sentence, and paragraph structures. They are internal ties which emphasize equality of ideas, balance expression, and provide a continuous thread throughout a piece of writing.

At the word, phrase, and sentence level, this line from a famous American document illustrates how the writer accomplished his purpose: gaining the attention of and appealing to "the people."

"government of the *people*, by the *people*, for the *people* . . ."

In the following classic passage from Sir Francis Bacon, writers can observe effective use of all these devices throughout the paragraph.

OF STUDIES

types of devices

parallel structures

Studies serve for delight, for ornament, and for ability. Their chief use for delight, is in privateness and retiring; for ornament, is in discourse; and for ability, is in the judgment, and disposition of business. For expert men can execute, and perhaps judge of particulars, one by one;

repetition —
for delight
for ornament
for ability

127

but the general counsels, and the plots and mar-
shalling of affairs, come best, from those that are
learned. To spend too much "time" in studies is sloth;
to use them too much for ornament, is affectation;
to make judgment wholly by their rules, is the
humor of a scholar. They perfect nature, and are
perfected by experience: for natural abilities are
like natural plants, that need proyning, by study;
and studies themselves, do give forth directions too
much at large, except they be bounded in by experience. Crafty men condemn studies, simple men
admire them, and wise men use them; for they
teach not their own use; but that is a wisdom without them, and above them, won by observation.
"Read" not to contradict and confute; nor to believe
and take for granted; nor to find talk and discourse; but to weigh and consider. Some "books" are
to be tasted, others to be swallowed, and some few
to be chewed and digested; that is, some books are
to be read only in parts; others to be read, but not
curiously; and some few to be read wholly, and
with diligence and attention. Some books also may
be read by deputy, and extracts made of them by
others; but that would be only in the less important arguments, and the meaner sort of books, else
distilled books are like common distilled waters,
flashy things. Reading maketh a full man; "conference" a ready man; and "writing" an exact man. And
therefore, if a man write little, he had need have
a great memory; if he confer little, he had need
have a present wit; and if he read little, he had
need have much cunning, to seem to know, that
he doth not. "Histories" make men wise, poets witty; the
mathematics subtile; natural philosophy deep;
moral grave; logic and rhetoric able to contend.
Aneunt studia in mores. Nay, there is no stond or
impediment in the wit, but may be wrought out
by fit studies; like as diseases of the body, may
have appropriate exercises. Bowling is good for
the stone and reins; shooting for the lungs and

simile:
"abilitees like plants"

parallel phrases

simile:
"books like waters"

simile:
"impediment like diseases"

"study"

synonym:
"read"
related word:
"books"

repetition of "books"

related word
"Histories"

128

breast; gentle walking for the stomach; riding for the head; and the like. So if a man's wit be wandering, let him study the mathematics; for in demonstrations, if his wit be called away never so little, he must begin again. If his wit be not apt to distinguish or find differences, let him study the Schoolmen; for they are *cymini sectores*. If he be not apt to beat over matters, and to call up one thing to prove and illustrate another, let him study the lawyers' cases. So every defect of the mind, may have a special receipt.

COHESION

Some of the most important *cohesive* devices writers use or need to know how to use are *referents*: the personal, interrogative, relative, and demonstrative pronouns which semantically relate (1) to words or ideas previously mentioned in the text (cataphoric), (2) to words or ideas which will soon appear in the text (anaphoric) or (3) to persons or ideas outside of the text (exophoric).[12] For readers to understand the writer's meaning, references must be *clear;* the pronouns must specifically relate or point to something else in the text or to a clear reference outside the text. While sentence structure is not affected by failure to use these cohesive devices, meaning definitely is. Further, writers show consideration for readers when they make pronouns agree with their referents.

Personal	—I, you, he, she, it, we, they, me, him, her, them
Demonstrative	—this, that, these, those, them
Interrogative relative	—(person) who, (place) where, (time) when, (thing or idea) which, that, and what

The writer of the passage about food used a number of cohesive referential ties. For example, in the first paragraph are several cataphoric ties.

The world is running out of food—or food *it* can afford to buy.

This information is probably a surprise . . . to the farmer . . . as *he* worries

"It" clearly relates to "food" in the first sentence. "This" clearly relates to the idea that "the world is running out of food." However, the second sentence without the context of the first would have no meaning. In the second paragraph, "*It* is probably no surprise . . ." "It" also relates to the main idea presented in the first paragraph.

In the third paragraph is a good example of exophoric reference to someone outside the text:

Ironically, . . . surprise to *those* who use India as litmus

Based on a reading of this article and an awareness of world events, one might conclude that *it* is no surprise that with food shortages, population booms, and shifts in power great numbers of people are migrating to foreign countries. In the preceding sentence, then, "it" is an anaphoric reference to the "great numbers . . .".

While "local" errors do not cause as much interference for ESL writers as "global" ones, nonetheless they can and do impede communication. As Irmscher notes, "the control that writing represents gives us a way of saying as precisely as possible what we want to say. . . . Writing prods us to be explicit . . . places upon us the ultimate demand for precise and accurate expression" (1979b:244). Certain types of local errors seem to affect precision and accuracy more than others and for various reasons recur frequently in ESL writing. Furthermore, misuse of one structure often appears to be related to the misuse of another such as the writer's inclusion, deletion, or wrong use of specific elements.[13] Although a willing reader may still be able to interpret the writer's meaning, readability is increased—and, consequently, chances for successful communication are improved—as errors are corrected. Further, we have observed that when ESL writers acquire the use of or master one structure, they often master a second one as well.

Among those local errors which recur most often are those related to—

- Articles and number
- Word order and prepositions
- Word form and word choice

Because of the various reasons for these errors—translation patterns, incorrect or insufficient knowledge of the language, or insecurity with mastery of the structure—different learning approaches may be required to master use of these elements of English structure. Teachers need to detect the underlying causes for these communication problems before attempting to help students correct them.[14] Depending on the number of writers making the particular errors and the reasons for the errors, teachers can address some structures with the class as a whole and others with individual assignments.

Articles and number are a problem for many students because some writers' native languages have no English equivalent to articles and others have articles which are used differently. For such students, misuse of articles is a recurring problem. It involves deletion, inclusion, and wrong use, as illustrated in the first example. Notice that misuse of articles also seems to be related to the writer's incorrect use of singulars and plurals in the second passage.

---

1. The Production of Electricity is <u>the</u> simple procedure which includes three main steps. ^ First step is to collect water at ^ high level ~~and~~ *which* then is allowed to fall on the propellor of the turbine. ^ Second step is to produce Electricity*e* and ^ third is to transmit it to different places. This sequence of steps is easy to carry out as compared to ~~the~~ other types of power production ~~like~~ *such as* thermal power and nuclear power. It is known as hydroelectric power production.

While a reader can understand this writer's meaning, reading and thus understanding are made easier when the passage uses articles as follows:

<u>a</u> simple procedure
<u>The</u> first step

<u>a</u> high level
<u>The</u> second step
<u>the</u> third is
~~the~~ other types of power

---

2. Computer <u>are</u> widely used in America and in the developed countries. The computer is an electronic machine used in solving the <u>problem</u> of science, engineering, business, and education. The computer <u>are</u> very useful, because of their ability to operate at a great speed, to produce accurate results, and to carry out a <u>long and complex sequences</u> of operation.

also affects subject-verb agreement

130

The computer is an electronic machine which engineers design and build. The function of the computer is, as its name, to compute. The computer has no brain as ^ human being does, so it can't think. But the computer has the memory which is much better than ours. When we want to use the computer, first of all we must educate it. The computer will memorize

reference? > them all. Then we order it to do what we want. The computer will do it by following what it was educated.

In this passage as well, the reading is easier if the articles and number are clear, such as—

- Computers *are* OR The computer *is* . . .

- the problem OR problems . . .

- a long and complex sequenc*e* OR long and complex sequence*s*

- a human being doe*s* OR human being*s* do

- the memory OR *a* memory (no referent for the)

Word order and prepositions are often (but not always) companion errors. Basic word order and modifier placement differ in other languages from the English patterns such as subject/verb/object and modifier/modifier/noun. Thus the kinds of errors that appear in the following student sentences can occur. Some result from deletion and others from wrong use of the structures.

During this year in Mexico *happened several events* that had effect *in* it. . . (several events happened) (on)

We also have an *exchange in technology.* In the *industry of shoes* they have a good technology that we can take for our industry. (technological exchange, shoe industry)

My car is in the garage. *which he is repairing.*

Working really hard, the dissertation was completed in four years. (Working . . ., *he* completed)

Misuse of these structures results in unclear expression, dangling and squinting modifiers, and misplaced modifiers.

Also important to communication are the *lexical considerations* which affect the accuracy and the tone of a writer's message. Bergan Evans says "words are the tools for the job of saying what you want to say." He adds that "the more words we know, the closer we can come to expressing precisely what we want to" (1974:9). Therefore, reading and word study are key factors in increasing usable word power for the job of writing. Mina Shaughnessy also reminds us that "words, for the most part, must be learned in contexts . . ." (1977: 217). She also states that it is possible to build the students' vocabularies not only by pointing out equivalencies between the words unknown to them and the words they are learning but also by "refining meaning by comparing roots and affixes, looking words up in the dictionary and observing the words in various contexts—all of which tasks serve to fix words in the memory much more efficiently than rote memorization" (p. 219). Thus, when writers encounter words for the first time, one of the ways they can make those words a part of their lexicon is to learn as many facets or uses of the word as possible, thus gaining workable use of that word. One of the ways of doing this is to acquaint them with the various ways words can be used.

WORD FORMS

Roots: are the basis of words
Prefixes: change meaning
Suffixes: determine parts of speech

Pre-fixes	Root	Suffixes			
		Noun	Verb	Adjective	Adverb
mis	+	direc*tor*	to direct	direct	direct*ly*
over	direct	direct*ness*	direc*ted*	direc*tional*	direc*tionally*
under		direc*tion*	modal +		
re			direc*ting*		
in					

131

Misuse of word forms can surely lead to a reader's misunderstanding of the message. For example, does the writer really mean this?

A menu reads— "Our steaks are finely marbled, well-trimmed and broiled to your *likeness.*" (liking?)

A sign on a cash register reads—"No checks *excepted.*" (accepted?)

Word choice involves the writer's consideration of subject and audience. "What is above all needed is to let the meaning choose the word."[15] Which words fit the subject matter, which words convey the idea most accurately, which words will the audience understand and respond to? As Mark Twain said, "The difference between the right word and the almost right word is like the difference between 'lightning' and the 'lightning bug.' " Thus, writers should try out as many words as they can to find those that best fit their needs.

©1981 *New Yorker*

Word choice also involves *word use* or an economy of words. Writers are told to "Be brief," "Be accurate," "Be thorough." These rhetorical rules apply to writers' choice of words as well as to their ideas. The sentence

I know that the house of my father is in Rio.

could just as easily be written

My father's house is in Rio.

or

A group of people dwelling in a domicile of silica combined with oxides to form a substance which is usually transparent should never project small geological specimens.

could just as easily be written

People who live in glass houses should never throw stones.

Neglect of careful consideration of word form, choice and use results in fuzzy or vague expression and deadwood, to say nothing of partial or total communication breakdown.

5.4 Mechanical shaping—editing

The writer's last step in the shaping process is mechanical shaping, which includes meticulous examination of the accuracy of spelling, capitalization, punctuation, paragraphing, handwriting, and overall neatness of the paper, and effective use of illustrations and headings (when applicable). These are perhaps relatively minor points in writing, yet they can affect a reader's understanding and acceptance of a message. Concerning *spelling,* for instance,

U mite asc wy speling is sew mportant-y wun shud knot mak op hiz oan weigh uv speling wurdz. Y ndede?

Ower ansur four ths breef okasion is that standardized spelling—

1. Saves time in reading

2. Helps a writer to convey precise distinctions with accuracy

An unpunctuated or incorrectly *punctuated* sentence can change the entire meaning of a sentence. What does the writer mean, for example, in these sentences?

1. He shouted please don't come in

2. If you are thin don't eat fast if you are fat don't eat fast

Paragraphing, along with transitional words and phrases, signals to a reader that one unit of thought has ended and a new unit of thought has begun. Without benefit of these signals, the reader must work harder to comprehend the writer's logic and the development of his or her presentation. Paragraphing is a writer's courtesy to the reader. Correct punctuation and a division of paragraph four would make the delightful paper below much easier to follow.

STUDENT ESSAY: STAMP COLLECTING

Would you like to travel around the world? Learn about different cultures, languages, money wedges, travel by auto, sailing vessels or steamships, hunt wild animals in the jungle, see strange birds and animals, and learn the costumes of natives all over the world. Begin a stamp collection and all your dreams will come true, one of the most interesting and less expensive hobbies.

First, you have to learn a little bit about stamps, stamps, are usually made of wood, cotton or linen, these fibers are grounded, bleached and then boiled until they become fluid "pulpa." This fluid "pulpa" is then placed in frames to dry, after they dry, they are passed them by heat and pressed them these modifies its appearance and properties. Now they are ready for printing, there are four different kinds of printings: Engraving, typography, photgrovure and lytography, these printings are usually made by big plaques.

The fun of collecting stamps lies partly in finding the stamps you want, and partly in learning more and more about the stamps you have or hope to get, when you want to begin a collection the easiest ways, are: save the stamps you receive in your mail, friends and relatives often will give you stamps if they know you collect, business firms with a large correspondence will give you, if you asked them properly, try to look at your grandmothers attic, you will find a lot of letters there, you can also trade with other collectors. Save duplicates so you will have stamps to trade. Another way is to buy them from advertisements on newspapers or stamp magazines. You must learn to handle your stamps with care too.

After you have get many stamps you should be thinking in getting an album to placed them. There are albums from the United States, United Nations, Europe, and World Wide, all depends on your speciality. You can specialize in collecting only by countries, designs, continents or world wide. When you get your album begin to place them, never use glue or

tape. ⌠For placing a stamp in your album, there are special
little fold papers which are called hinges, these hinges
are folded in two pieces gummed side out. Moisten the
short end and faster the sticky part to the back of the stamp,
then moisten the top of the three quart part of the hinge
to the album page. There are some stamps that still have the
paper to which they were glued, the best way to take off all
bits of paper, is to soak the stamps in a bowl of water,
until the paper floats or can be slid off. Then let the stamp
dry face down on a clean cloth, preferable on a towel.

Stamp collecting is a hobby that you can enjoy as long as you
live. Try to keep your album up to date, because today's stamps
will be the valuable stamps from tomorrow. Do not hesitate,
begin your collection right now.

A final word about shaping: Just as the graphic forms of the rhetorical patterns help ESL students acquire knowledge of those forms so also does working out grammatical-syntactical problems in *context* help students acquire use of these structures. The various pieces of writing included in this chapter illustrate how all forms and structures come together to create the whole. *Recognition* of the forms and structures occurs when writers often read and analyze written work. *Practice* with the forms and structures comes from working cloze exercises, doing sentence combining, expanding kernel sentences, and revising—but as Zamel says, "Students . . . need to be gradually introduced to key concepts relating to the grammar of the sentence which they can use as references in building sentences or analyzing sentences they have built" (1980:84). Further, she advocates introducing "the different types of clauses and conjunctions (and punctuation) that are used to join them by using the students' own writing" or cloze or sentence-combining exercises.

Use of rhetorical patterns found on pages 108–116 is another way of introducing to students some of the coherence devices, in the meaningful context of writing rather than in isolated exercises. *Production* of the forms and structures (the crucial stage of actually using them) comes only when students create. That is, when writers have worked through the processes described to this point, they are ready to read what they have created and if necessary work through that entire process again—until a satisfactory product evolves. (More on revising is found in Chapter 7.) Further, teachers can frame assignments to generate specific rhetorical forms and syntactic structures. A thoughtful combination of the three learning experiences will help developing writers more easily internalize the principles.

How can student-writers identify their successes and failures? Students need specific strategies and workable methods to successfully create a piece of writing that communicates. The ESL COMPOSITION PROFILE, presented in Chapter 6, has proved to be an excellent method for us and our students in identifying accomplishments, teaching principles, learning revision, and evaluating.

The following paper is an example of a student's efforts to address a particular subject, audience, and purpose. Although this paper, like any other piece of writing, might still require fine tuning, it is a fine example of a student working to develop writing skills.

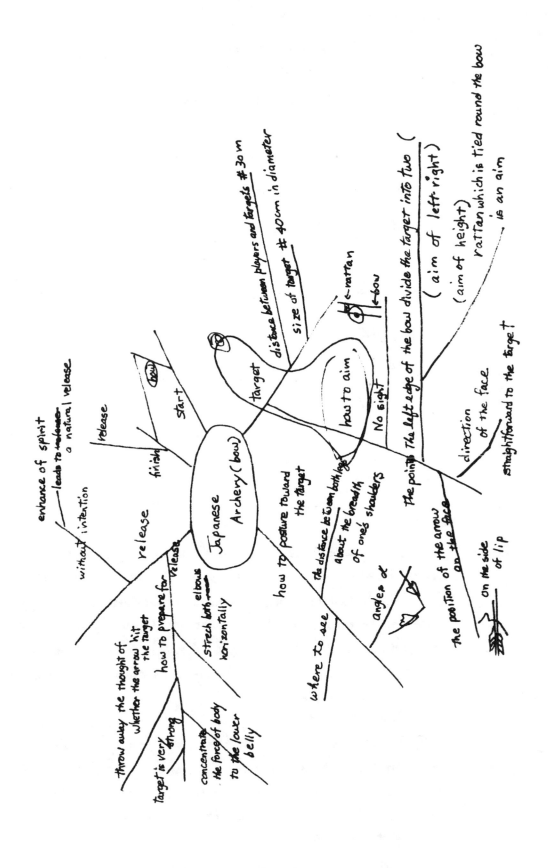

This paper illustrates a student's use of personal experience, knowledge and observation.

135

Japanese Archery
- The Standard Process -

Thesis - Although there are many sects in Japanese archery, the standard process consists of seven steps.

1. Location of the feet

2. Posture

3. Arrow and bow

4. Aim position

5. Aim

6. Vigor

7. Release

Archery is a difficult sport.

Japanese Archery

Japanese Archery is one of the Japanese military arts like ⌈karate⌉ or ⌈Judo⌉. It developed as a kind of sport for the spiritual training of Samurai — warriors in the old time. Japanese Archery is the heritage of the Samurai culture (from the 11th century to the 19th century). Although there are many sects in Japanese Archery, the standard process to do consists of the seven steps.

The first step is the one in which the location of the both feet is determined. At first, you step out your left foot toward a target, and then put your right foot so that the three points — the target, the left foot, the right foot — make a straight line. The left foot makes the angle of 30°, the right foot 150° toward the target.

a target

30°   30°

*wc.
art
prep
red*

136

The second step is ~~the one to make~~ the body (fix) on the floor.   You add the outward force to your ~~both~~ toes and the inward force to your ~~both~~ heds and lower the center of ~~the~~ gravity of your body by making the force concentrate. on your underbelly. At ~~In~~ this step, you form posture. enough to bear the force exerted by a bow.

red.

art

sp

At the third step, you insert a notch of an arrow into a string by which the bow is bent. And you hang the string by the grove. you put on." This grove is

del

← a string

made of deer skin with a wooden part on which there's a notch to hang the string.

a wooden part

grove

we

Tell how you do this here.

The fourth step is ~~the one you~~ hold(ing) the bow up. ~~At~~ In this step, you remove strain and prepare for enhancing your vigor.

prep

The 4th step.

In ~~At~~ the fifth step, you pull the string. you push your left hand toward the target and pull the string in the opposite direction to the target by your right hand at the same time. The force is concentrated on of your ~~both~~ elbows. At this time, you aim at the target. The aim of the left-right is the position where ~~that~~ the left edge of the bow divides the target into two. The aim of the height depends upon the strength of the bow. Each player has its own aim of the height by using a rattan which is bound round the bow as a mark. The action on ∧surface is stopped ~~completed~~ at this step (once.?

good illustrations!

we

The 5th step.

a bow

prep

← rattan

← your left hand

The sixth step is ~~the one you~~ mak(ing) your vigor approach to the maxim state. This step is the most important because this is the time to fight with the target. This step is just the essence of Japanese Archery. The target is so attractive that you will be beaten easily by it if you persist on a hit.

The last step is "release". This step is connected with the previous step. When your vigor reaches the maximum and explodes, "release" is made. "Release" is not an intentional action. "Release" is the phenomenum which occurs when your vigor explodes.

art

The Japanese Archery is the sport that players fight with the invitation from the target. I've never beaten the target

del

although I played it for 7 years. It is very difficult to get rid of worldly thoughts.

Good paper!

Notes

[1]Walker Gibson, "The Writing Teacher as a Dumb Reader," *College Composition and Communication*, 30 (May 1979), 192.

[2]Mike Rose, "Rigid Rules, Inflexible Plans, and the Stifling of Language: A Cognitivist's Analysis of Writer's Block," *College Composition and Communication*, 31 (December 1980), 389.

[3]Robert de Beaugrande, "Linguistic Theory and Composition," *College Composition and Communication*, 29 (May 1978), 134.

[4]Richard L. Larson, "Language Studies and Composing Processes," *Linguistics, Stylistics, and the Teaching of Composition,* ed. Donald McQuade (Ohio: University of Akron, 1979), 188.

[5]Donald Murray, *A Writer Teaches Writing: A Practical Method of Teaching Composition* (Boston: Houghton Mifflin Company, 1968), 5.

[6]Beaugrande, p. 134.

[7]Murray, p. 3.

[8]James Britton, "The Composing Processes and the Function of Writing," *Research on Composing: Points of Departure*, ed. Charles R. Cooper and Lee Odell (Urbana, Ill.: National Council of Teachers of English, 1968), 21.

[9]Ann Raimes, *Language in Education: Theory and Practice* (Arlington: Center for Applied Linguistics, 1979), 9.

[10]Machiko Tomiyana, "Grammatical Errors Communication Breakdown," *TESOL Quarterly*, 14, no. 1 (March 1980).

[11]William Stalter, "A Sense of Structure," *College Composition and Communication*, 9 (December 1978), 343.

[12]M. A. K. Halliday and Ruquaiya Hasan, *Cohesion in English* (London: Longmans Group, Ltd., 1979), 308.

[13]Tomiyana, p. 71.

[14]Raimes, p. 7.

[15]George Orwell, "Politics of the English Language," *Language Awareness*, ed. Paul A. Escholz, Alfred F. Rosa, and Virginia P. Clark (New York: St. Martin's Press, 1974), 33.

CHAPTER SIX

THE ESL COMPOSITION PROFILE—
A GUIDE TO THE PRINCIPLES OF WRITING

---

*Success attained through routes understood all the
way, can be its own best reward. Motivation
coming from increased competence rather than
intrinsic rewards thus becomes a dominant factor in
learning, and leads to further self-learning.*

C. I. C. Estacio

A major goal of all writing instruction is to help students develop the learning strategies, or what can be called the routes, which will enable them to become *independent* of the teacher's guidance as they leave the classroom and continue over their lifetime to grow and mature as writers. Many of the heuristic techniques discussed earlier in this book (in Chapters 4 and 5) will equip ESL learners with permanent, useful strategies for discovering their writing purposes, audiences, and subjects, as well as the shapes of their discourse.

Another important aspect of becoming an independent, lifelong writer is developing the ability to evaluate one's own writing progress and to use feedback from the evaluation as a guide for further growth and improvement. A highly useful heuristic

for teaching and learning this key strategy is the ESL COMPOSITION PROFILE, which draws together in a convenient and capsulized form the essential criteria for effective writing. For teachers, the PROFILE can become an invaluable aid to guide students in recognizing, practicing, and employing the principles of writing. For students, the PROFILE can become an immediate as well as a lifelong learning tool not only for evaluating their own writing progress but for shaping and improving their writing as well. Teachers in particular will find a host of other practical and valuable uses for the PROFILE (not the least of which is *grading* student writing), and many of these potential uses will be discussed later in this and the succeeding chapters.

6.1 Features of the ESL composition profile*

The word "profile," coming from the Latin *pro*, forward + *filare*, to draw a line, and meaning literally "a side view," characterizes the main purpose of the ESL COMPOSITION PROFILE as a teaching-learning-evaluation guide: to provide a side view, an outline, of an ESL writer's success at composing or synthesizing the main elements of writing into a connected, coherent, effective piece of written discourse.

The PROFILE form itself contains *five component scales*, each focusing on an important aspect

of writing and weighted according to its approximate importance for written communication. The *Content* component concerns the *inventio* of writing—having something to say. The *Organization* component addresses *dispositio*, or the rhetorical principles for arrangement. *Vocabulary, Language*

---

*See *Testing ESL Composition: A Practical Approach* for a detailed discussion of the PROFILE's development and the rationale for its design. Newbury House Publishers, Inc. 1981.

139

ESL COMPOSITION PROFILE

STUDENT   DATE   TOPIC

	SCORE	LEVEL	CRITERIA	COMMENTS
CONTENT		30-27	**EXCELLENT TO VERY GOOD:** knowledgeable • substantive • thorough development of thesis • relevant to assigned topic	
		26-22	**GOOD TO AVERAGE:** some knowledge of subject • adequate range • limited development of thesis • mostly relevant to topic, but lacks detail	
		21-17	**FAIR TO POOR:** limited knowledge of subject • little substance • inadequate development of topic	
		16-13	**VERY POOR:** does not show knowledge of subject • non-substantive • not pertinent • OR not enough to evaluate	
ORGANIZATION		20-18	**EXCELLENT TO VERY GOOD:** fluent expression • ideas clearly stated/supported • succinct • well-organized • logical sequencing • cohesive	
		17-14	**GOOD TO AVERAGE:** somewhat choppy • loosely organized but main ideas stand out • limited support • logical but incomplete sequencing	
		13-10	**FAIR TO POOR:** non-fluent • ideas confused or disconnected • lacks logical sequencing and development	
		9-7	**VERY POOR:** does not communicate • no organization • OR not enough to evaluate	
VOCABULARY		20-18	**EXCELLENT TO VERY GOOD:** sophisticated range • effective word/idiom choice and usage • word form mastery • appropriate register	
		17-14	**GOOD TO AVERAGE:** adequate range • occasional errors of word/idiom form, choice, usage *but meaning not obscured*	
		13-10	**FAIR TO POOR:** limited range • frequent errors of word/idiom form, choice, usage • *meaning confused or obscured*	
		9-7	**VERY POOR:** essentially translation • little knowledge of English vocabulary, idioms, word form • OR not enough to evaluate	
LANGUAGE USE		25-22	**EXCELLENT TO VERY GOOD:** effective complex constructions • few errors of agreement, tense, number, word order/function, articles, pronouns, prepositions	
		21-18	**GOOD TO AVERAGE:** effective but simple constructions • minor problems in complex constructions • several errors of agreement, tense, number, word order/function, articles, pronouns, prepositions *but meaning seldom obscured*	
		17-11	**FAIR TO POOR:** major problems in simple/complex constructions • frequent errors of negation, agreement, tense, number, word order/function, articles, pronouns, prepositions and/or fragments, run-ons, deletions • *meaning confused or obscured*	
		10-5	**VERY POOR:** virtually no mastery of sentence construction rules • dominated by errors • does not communicate • OR not enough to evaluate	
MECHANICS		5	**EXCELLENT TO VERY GOOD:** demonstrates mastery of conventions • few errors of spelling, punctuation, capitalization, paragraphing	
		4	**GOOD TO AVERAGE:** occasional errors of spelling, punctuation, capitalization, paragraphing *but meaning not obscured*	
		3	**FAIR TO POOR:** frequent errors of spelling, punctuation, capitalization, paragraphing • poor handwriting • *meaning confused or obscured*	
		2	**VERY POOR:** no mastery of conventions • dominated by errors of spelling, punctuation, capitalization, paragraphing • handwriting illegible • OR not enough to evaluate	

TOTAL SCORE   READER   COMMENTS

Use, and *Mechanics* together deal with *elocutio*—the linguistic and mechanical principles for effective delivery of discourse. The total weight for each component is further broken down into numerical ranges that correspond to *four mastery levels* (Excellent to Very Good, Good to Average, Fair to Poor, and Very Poor) which are characterized and distinguished by *key-word descriptors representing specific criteria* basic to successful written communication. These criteria descriptors function as shorthand "mental hooks" to remind teachers and students of essential concepts and principles in composition, and their differentiation into mastery levels provides a common interpretive framework and standard for determining the degree to which a writer succeeds (or fails) in a communicative effort. For students, then, the criteria function as evaluative heuristics, as a means by which they can evaluate various parts of their writing (during the composing process) as well as the completed piece of work. The specific criteria are described in greater detail on the following pages.

A writer's composition *profile* is indicated in two ways: by the individual scores in each component and by the sum of scores from all five. A *component score* provides information about a writer's mastery of the particular criteria which define that component. The *total score* is a composite profile of the writer's mastery of all the criteria. The separate component scores thus provide specific, diagnostic information about areas of strength and weakness, while the total score provides an index of the writer's overall success at *composing* (from Latin: "to put together") the primary elements of writing into effective discourse.

6.2 The extended profile criteria

Since the criteria descriptors are only shorthand reminders of larger concepts in composition, a clear understanding of them is essential for effective use of the PROFILE. The concepts embody the essential principles of writing—the rules, conventions, and guidelines—that writers must observe to create a successful piece of writing. This section presents a detailed description of the concepts represented by the PROFILE criteria descriptors at the *Excellent to Very Good* mastery level. The other three levels of competence should be thought of as varying degrees of these extended criteria for excellent writing, with the primary distinguishing factor being the degree to which the writer's intended *meaning* is successfully delivered to the reader or is diminished or completely lost by insufficient mastery of the criteria for excellence. The PROFILE's first two mastery levels in each component (*Excellent to Very Good* and *Good to Average*) both indicate that successful communication has occurred (although differing in degree), whereas the two lower levels (*Fair to Poor* and *Very Poor*) suggest there is a communication breakdown of some sort—either partial or complete. *Effect on meaning* thus becomes the chief criterion for distinguishing the degree to which the writer has mastered the criteria for excellent writing.

CONTENT	30-27	**EXCELLENT TO VERY GOOD: knowledgeable • substantive • thorough development of thesis • relevant to assigned topic**
	26-22	**GOOD TO AVERAGE: some knowledge of subject • adequate range • limited development of thesis • mostly relevant to topic, but lacks detail**
	21-17	**FAIR TO POOR: limited knowledge of subject • little substance • inadequate development of topic**
	16-13	**VERY POOR: does not show knowledge of subject • non-substantive • not pertinent • OR not enough to evaluate**

DESCRIPTOR	CRITERIA
Knowledgeable	Is there understanding of the subject?
	Are facts or other pertinent information used?
	Is there recognition of several aspects of the subject?
	Are the interrelationships of these aspects shown?
Substantive	Are several main points discussed?
	Is there sufficient detail?
	Is there originality with concrete details to illustrate, define, compare, or contrast factual information supporting the thesis?
Thorough development of thesis	Is the thesis expanded enough to convey a sense of completeness?
	Is there a specific method of development (such as comparison/contrast, illustration, definition, example, description, fact, or personal experience)?
	Is there an awareness of different points of view?
Relevant to assigned topic	Is all information clearly pertinent to the topic?
	Is extraneous material excluded?

ORGANIZATION

20-18 **EXCELLENT TO VERY GOOD:** fluent expression • ideas clearly stated/supported • succinct • well-organized • logical sequencing • cohesive

17-14 **GOOD TO AVERAGE:** somewhat choppy • loosely organized but main ideas stand out • limited support • logical but incomplete sequencing

13-10 **FAIR TO POOR:** non-fluent • ideas confused or disconnected • lacks logical sequencing and development

9-7 **VERY POOR:** does not communicate • no organization • OR not enough to evaluate

Fluent expression	Do the ideas flow, building on one another?
	Are there introductory and concluding paragraphs?
	Are there effective transition elements—words, phrases, or sentences—which link and move ideas both within and between paragraphs?
Ideas clearly stated/supported	Is there a clearly stated controlling idea or central focus to the paper (a thesis)?
	Do topic sentences in each paragraph support, limit, and direct the thesis?
Succinct	Are all ideas directed concisely to the central focus of the paper, without digressions?

DESCRIPTOR	CRITERIA
Well-organized	Is the overall relationship of ideas within and between paragraphs clearly indicated?
	Is there a beginning, a middle, and an end to the paper?
Logical sequencing	Are the points logically developed, using a particular sequence such as time order, space order, or importance?
	Is this development indicated by appropriate transitional markers?
Cohesive	Does each paragraph reflect a single purpose?
	Do the paragraphs form a unified paper?

VOCABULARY

20-18   **EXCELLENT TO VERY GOOD: sophisticated range • effective word/idiom choice and usage • word form mastery • appropriate register**

17-14   **GOOD TO AVERAGE: adequate range • occasional errors of word/idiom form, choice, usage *but meaning not obscured***

13-10   **FAIR TO POOR: limited range • frequent errors of word/idiom form, choice, usage • *meaning confused or obscured***

9-7   **VERY POOR: essentially translation • little knowledge of English vocabulary, idioms, word form • OR not enough to evaluate**

Sophisticated range	Is there facility with words and idioms: to convey intended information, attitudes, feelings? to distinguish subtleties among ideas and intentions? to convey shades and differences of meaning? to express the logic of ideas?
	Is the arrangement and interrelationship of words sufficiently varied?
Effective word/idiom choice and usage	In the context in which it is used, is the choice of vocabulary accurate? idiomatic? effective? concise?
	Are strong, active verbs and verbals used where possible?
	Are phrasal and prepositional idioms correct? Do they convey the intended meaning?
	Does word placement give the intended message? emphasis?
	Is there an understanding of synonyms? antonyms? homonyms?
	Are denotative and connotative meanings distinguished?
	Is there effective repetition of key words and phrases?
	Do transition elements mark shifts in thought? pace? emphasis? tone?
Word form mastery	Are prefixes, suffixes, roots, and compounds used accurately and effectively?

143

DESCRIPTOR	CRITERIA
	Are words correctly distinguished as to their function (noun, verb, adjective, adverb)?
Appropriate register	Is the vocabulary appropriate to the topic? to the audience? to the tone of the paper? to the method of development?
	Is the vocabulary familiar to the audience?
	Does the vocabulary make the intended impression?

*

LANGUAGE USE

25-22 **EXCELLENT TO VERY GOOD:** effective complex constructions • few errors of agreement, tense, number, word order/function, articles, pronouns, prepositions

21-18 **GOOD TO AVERAGE:** effective but simple constructions • minor problems in complex constructions • several errors of agreement, tense, number, word order/function, articles, pronouns, prepositions *but meaning seldom obscured*

17-11 **FAIR TO POOR:** major problems in simple/complex constructions • frequent errors of negation, agreement, tense, number, word order/function, articles, pronouns, prepositions and/or fragments, run-ons, deletions • *meaning confused or obscured*

10-5 **VERY POOR:** virtually no mastery of sentence construction rules • dominated by errors • does not communicate • OR not enough to evaluate

Effective complex constructions	Are sentences well-formed and complete, with appropriate complements?
	Are single-word modifiers appropriate to function? Are they properly formed, placed, and sequenced?
	Are phrases and clauses appropriate to function? complete? properly placed?
	Are introductory *It* and *There* used correctly to begin sentences and clauses?
	Are main and subordinate ideas carefully distinguished?
	Are coordinate and subordinate elements linked to other elements with appropriate conjunctions, adverbials, relative pronouns, or punctuation?
	Are sentence types and length varied?
	Are elements parallel?
	Are techniques of substitution, repetition, and deletion used effectively?

*If a review of English is necessary, see R. A. Close, *A Reference Grammar for Students of English* (London: Longmans, 1975); M. Frank, *Modern English: A Practical Reference Guide* (Englewood Cliffs, N.J.: Prentice-Hall, Inc., 1972); R. Quirk, S. Greenbaum, G. Leech, and J. Svartvik, *A Grammar of Contemporary English* (London: Longmans, 1975).

DESCRIPTOR	CRITERIA
Agreement	Is there basic agreement between sentence elements: auxiliary and verb? subject and verb? pronoun and antecedent? adjective and noun? nouns and quantifiers?
Tense	Are verb tenses correct? properly sequenced?
	Do modals convey intended meaning? time?
Number	Do nouns, pronouns, and verbs convey intended quality?
Word order/function	Is normal word order followed except for special emphasis?
	Is each word, phrase, and clause suited to its intended function?
Articles	Are *a, an,* and *the* used correctly?
Pronouns	Do pronouns reflect appropriate person? gender? number? function? referent?
Prepositions	Are prepositions chosen carefully to introduce modifying elements?
	Is the intended meaning conveyed?

MECHANICS

5   **EXCELLENT TO VERY GOOD: demonstrates mastery of conventions • few errors of spelling, punctuation, capitalization, paragraphing**

4   **GOOD TO AVERAGE: occasional errors of spelling, punctuation, capitalization, paragraphing *but meaning not obscured***

3   **FAIR TO POOR: frequent errors of spelling, punctuation, capitalization, paragraphing • poor handwriting • *meaning confused or obscured***

2   **VERY POOR: no mastery of conventions • dominated by errors of spelling, punctuation, capitalization, paragraphing • handwriting illegible • OR not enough to evaluate**

Spelling	Are words spelled correctly?
Punctuation	Are periods, commas, semicolons, dashes, and question marks used correctly?
	Are words divided correctly at the end of lines?
Capitalization	Are capital letters used where necessary and appropriate?
Paragraphing	Are paragraphs indented to indicate when one sequence of thought ends and another begins?
Handwriting	Is handwriting easy to read, without impeding communication?

6.3 General procedures for using the profile

Because it has a variety of applications for both students and teachers, procedures for using the PROFILE will vary considerably, depending on its specific purpose in a particular teaching, learning, or evaluation* context. A number of potential applications and recommended procedures for each are discussed in the next chapter. Here we will list some general steps for determining a composition PROFILE; these will, of course, need to be modified as appropriate.

Summary of steps for determining a composition PROFILE

1. In the appropriate space at the top of the PROFILE, write student and paper identification information: student name or code number, topic (if students wrote on more than one topic) and date.

2. Read the composition quickly for an overall first impression, paying particular attention to the *message* which the writer is trying to get across. Trust your judgment.
   KEY QUESTION: *Are the writer's ideas readily apparent, appropriately sequenced, and adequately developed to convey a complete picture?*

3. In the *Content* and *Organization* components of the PROFILE, find the descriptors that best describe the writer's success in delivering a message. Determine a score for each component to reflect these descriptors and record the scores in the spaces provided on the PROFILE.

4. Quickly reread the composition and record scores in the remaining three components after identifying the appropriate criteria descriptors.
   KEY QUESTION: *Is the writer more or less effective than originally thought? Do the syntactical, lexical, and mechanical elements work effectively to convey the*

intended message without distortion or loss of meaning?

5. Sum the five evaluation scores from the components and record under TOTAL.

6. Write reader information (initials or code number). If necessary, make clarifying comments.

In addition to these general steps for obtaining a PROFILE score, it is important that both students and teachers be able to *practice* with the PROFILE on sample papers before actually using it in a particular teaching or learning situation. This practice will acquaint users with the PROFILE's terminology—the criteria descriptors and their associated extended criteria—as well as the numerical values associated with the mastery levels, thus making its use both more efficient and more effective. Some general suggestions for practicing or "training" with the PROFILE follow. The procedures for self-training are suggested for teachers working alone, without the interaction of other teachers, while those for group training are recommended for teachers working together (as in a department-wide system of cooperative grading) or for students who are learning to use the PROFILE (additional practice exercises for familiarizing students with the PROFILE appear in Chapter 7).

Self-training procedures

1. Establish, review, or clarify intended application of the PROFILE and its purpose in this particular use (see pages 147–151).

2. Study the PROFILE and its associated extended criteria (pages 141–145), trying to fix in mind the full meaning of each shorthand descriptor.

3. Study the general steps for determining a PROFILE (this page), adapting them as necessary.

4. Evaluate several sample papers (such as the ones appearing in this book on pages 152–162, those in the Testing book, or others on hand), underlining pertinent descriptors and making clarifying comments as desired.

---

*Complete procedures for evaluating test compositions are described in *Testing ESL Composition: A Practical Approach.*

5. Then, either:
   a. Put those papers aside for a few hours or days and reevaluate them (as above) after the interval. Compare scores on each reading and identify areas of divergence. If there are large differences in either the component or total scores from one reading to the next, review the PROFILE criteria and then try again,

   or

   b. Compare your overall scores and component scores with those given by "expert" readers (for compositions in this book, see pages 153, 156, 163, or if using compositions from the Testing book, see pages 133–139), trying to identify and understand areas of divergence.

6. Evaluate additional samples as necessary, until you can use the PROFILE easily and apply the criteria consistently.

Group-training procedures

1. Discuss and clarify the intended application of the PROFILE for this situation (see Section 6.4).

2. Study and discuss the essential features of the PROFILE until there is a common understanding of the components, descriptors, and associated extended criteria. Try to fix in mind the full meaning of each short-hand descriptor.

3. Review the general steps for determining a PROFILE (page 146), adapting them as necessary.

4. Evaluate the same sample paper (such as the one on page 152), underlining descriptors and writing clarifying comments as necessary.

5. Compare each reader's scores (both component and total), discussing and clarifying points of divergence. If readers differ by more than 10 points in the total PROFILE score, some readers are apparently not interpreting the components or levels accurately. Review criteria and continue discussion until all readers agree on reasons for differences.

6. Evaluate additional samples. After all readers have completed three, stop to compare each reader's scores. Again discuss and clarify areas of divergence until readers reach close agreement on each PROFILE and until they are satisfied that all can use the PROFILE for the particular purpose.

Additional and more detailed procedures for using the PROFILE appear in the Testing book, and we recommend the use of those procedures, composition samples, and "expert" reader scores for the most efficient and accurate use of the PROFILE, especially if the application is for testing.

6.4 Applications of the profile

Although originally developed for use in testing, the PROFILE has important applications for teaching and learning writing as well. Of course, the processes of teaching, learning, and evaluation are frequently so intertwined as to be almost inseparable, but it is possible to distinguish one or another as the primary objective in a particular application of the PROFILE.

TEACHING OBJECTIVES

Teachers will find uses for the PROFILE ranging from the administrative, departmental level to one-on-one communication with individual writers in (or outside) the ESL classroom. Among the potential teaching applications of the PROFILE are these:

Department/program/teacher

The PROFILE might be used within an English/ESL department or program to:

- Clarify and define departmental writing standards

- Establish standards and curricula for levels within a writing program

- Place students in appropriate writing courses

- Determine curricula needs for classroom and

individualized instruction, based on proficiency range and specific writing problems identified by the PROFILE

- Develop appropriate lessons and materials

- (Re)evaluate teaching methods and materials

- Familiarize new instructors with departmental (or program) standards and train them in evaluating compositions according to those standards

- Improve teaching methods by clarifying important foci for instruction

- Report student progress to other teachers, the department, or the school

- Recommend promotion of a student to another level

- Establish guidelines to ensure accurate and uniform grading within a department

Teacher/student

Classroom and individualized instruction can be enhanced by using the PROFILE to

- Establish writing standards within the classroom

- Clarify writing expectations and goals

- Provide a model of writing excellence

- Develop independent learning strategies for self-evaluation

- Report progress, discuss writing problems, and give encouragement to students

- Guide students in developing intuitions about what distinguishes good from poor writing

- Make specific class or individualized assignments for lab work

- Provide specific feedback to students in a nonthreatening manner

- Teach to the "test," such as a proficiency exam, a final exam, or a subject-matter essay exam

- Provide a common focus and terminology for discussing the principles of writing

- Guide students through various phases of the shaping process

The objective teachers have in a particular use of the PROFILE will determine to some extent the exact way in which it should be used, as well as the results that will be obtained from it. For example, teachers who use the PROFILE to define departmental writing standards will probably engage in extended discussion of the criteria inherent in the writing process and how teaching them will affect their program. These teachers will be identifying an acceptable level of writing for the program, the type of course work to be offered, the goals to expect of students, and the meaning of specific PROFILE scores in the context of the program. On the other hand, teachers using the PROFILE to develop appropriate lessons and materials will be focusing not so much on the overall levels of writing proficiency in the class as on the particular problem and needs for each writer as revealed by the PROFILE components. In this case, careful or extensive marking of the criteria descriptors will be essential to provide the information needed for designing appropriate teaching methods and materials.

LEARNING OBJECTIVES

Students will find the PROFILE a valuable heuristic to guide their learning of the writing process. Among the potential learning applications of the PROFILE are these:

Student writer

Student writers (individually and in groups) can foster their understanding and mastery of the writing process by using the PROFILE to

- Monitor their own progress in writing

- Discover which writing principles they have already mastered and which they have yet to master

- Recognize their particular writing strengths and weaknesses

- Formulate their own learning goals

- Focus their learning efforts

- Learn the principles of writing and their importance to effective writing

- Shape a piece of writing through its various stages of development

- Recognize the distinguishing features of

good writing (through evaluating the writing of others)

- Learn the basic terminology necessary for talking *about* the principles of writing

- Evaluate their own writing and that of others

EVALUATION OBJECTIVES

Evaluation of one kind or another is usually an integral component of most teaching and learning, even though it may not be a primary focus. There are, however, several specific evaluation applications of the PROFILE: it might be used by a teacher, department, or school to

- Diagnose student writing needs

- Grade student performance on writing assignments, in a class or in a program

- Determine students' mastery of a particular learning unit

- Judge the effectiveness of certain teaching or curricular emphases

- Determine a student's overall progress in a writing program

- Assess, discuss, and review student progress in a department-wide cooperative evaluation

- Assess a student's level of proficiency for a particular writing course or academic program

The following chapter will describe and illustrate some of the ways we have used the PROFILE in the classroom to guide the teaching and learning of the writing process. Various other teaching applications, as well as some for evauation, will be discussed at length in Chapter 8.

CHAPTER SEVEN

THE PROFILE: A METHOD FOR SHAPING AND EVALUATION

7.1 Introducing students to the profile

When the writing standards for a program have been set, classes assigned, and curriculum determined,* teachers and students are ready to use the PROFILE in the classroom. It is here that the PROFILE becomes an invaluable aid in teaching recognition of, practice with, and production of the writing principles. The PROFILE and the extended criteria upon which it is based reflect the rules, conventions, and guidelines of the writing process, and it therefore becomes a tool for learning and shaping.

In the classroom the PROFILE becomes a silent partner in the teaching-learning process, quietly aiding students and teacher alike as they work toward the common goal of better writing. Once students become familiar with its features and

how to use it, they can profit not only from the feedback of teacher-scored PROFILEs but also from class discussions and their own use of the PROFILE criteria. First, however, students need to have a thorough introduction and considerable practice in using it. If possible, and especially for less proficient students, this introduction should take place in a group session with a number of teachers available to work with students in discussing and practicing with the PROFILE. It can, of course, also be introduced in the classroom, quite efficiently with fairly proficient students in about one class period. Considerably more time may be required (two or perhaps three periods) with a very large class or one at a low to high intermediate proficiency level.

---

*See Appendix A.

7.2 Using the profile in the workshop

We have successfully acquainted student-writers with how the PROFILE can be used by giving them a mini-reader training session at the beginning of the semester. Here is our procedure: first, in an hour to an hour and a half workshop session, 30 to 40 students receive a copy of the PROFILE; at least two teachers team up to discuss with and explain to student-writers the meanings of the terms on the PROFILE with which they may not be familiar. Then teachers distribute to each of the students a set of three ESL student compositions which they will read and evaluate, following the group-training procedures on page 147, giving a first quick reading

for responding to the message, marking descriptors, and scoring content and organization components. A second reading follows to evaluate the effectiveness of vocabulary, language use, and mechanics. When students have finished reading and evaluating, teachers facilitate discussion about each paper, comparing scores from each student and discussing reasons for those scores. The teachers also give their own scores and their reasons as a part of the discussion. Providing this PROFILE introduction early in the school year results in a number of benefits for both teachers and students:

150

1. Students know immediately upon what basis their own work will be evaluated. They gain a bird's-eye view of the expected criteria, and they are able to see the objectivity of the method. Further, they have an opportunity to compare and discuss the criteria and ask for clarification of terms. In addition, they learn from comparing and discussing their results with fellow classmates and with teachers. The focus is on someone else's writing, not their own; so students feel freer to discuss and question.

2. Teachers can pinpoint, by the way individual students score each of the papers, areas of the writing process that students may not know or understand, thus gleaning clues as to where to begin their teaching efforts. It also gives teachers an opportunity at the outset to answer questions about the evaluation procedure and to introduce the idea that the PROFILE may also be used as a guide for shaping a piece of writing.

3. Amazingly enough, of the approximately 200 students who have begun using the PROFILE with this laboratory introduction, some 70 percent arrive at PROFILE scores within a 10–point range of each other and their teachers, a high correlation of scores.

Furthermore, students like the PROFILE's objectivity. Our students have repeatedly told us how fair they find the PROFILE. The number and descriptor system seems to take away the sting of a vague letter grade like A, B, C, D, often given without explanation and often received by the student as a sign of personal failure. The PROFILE signals exactly what successes students have achieved with their writing and exactly what they need to learn.

On the the following pages are the three papers which our classes read and evaluate to train with the PROFILE. Included are the scored and marked PROFILEs indicating the descriptors and thus the criteria which are the basis of discussion about each paper.

The Man in Relation with the Ape.

At the begining of the world, Religion said that man appeared on a paradize without clothe, and unknowing all the things around him. The time passed and some investigations of scientific changed to a new origin that came to be true.

The success of man as a species is the result of the evolutionary development of his brain, which at one time must have resembled the brain of the chimpanzee, also, the ability to solve problems, thoughtfull cooperation and language. The Ability of an animal to use tools to reach objetive, does not make it more intelligent than other animals, which use some members of their family to seach that same good, but man compare's with a chimpanzee in that they made tools to help them reach an objetive. Chimpanzee use this tools for various purposes: for drinking water, for eatin fruits or insects, they also use tools to solve some of their problems. Even though they mad have been taught by human being, However, others chimps must be tested before.

Both chimps and man had seen reassured in stressful situation by physical contact with other individual. I think, this situation probably originated during infancy. Another similarity between them is greeting behavior. My conclusion is that the chimps are unable to perform all this act.

ESL COMPOSITION PROFILE

STUDENT **#1**　　　　　　　　　DATE　　　　　TOPIC *Man and Ape*

	SCORE	LEVEL	CRITERIA	COMMENTS
CONTENT	20	30-27	**EXCELLENT TO VERY GOOD:** knowledgeable • substantive • thorough development of thesis • relevant to assigned topic	
		26-22	**GOOD TO AVERAGE:** some knowledge of subject • adequate range • limited development of thesis • mostly relevant to topic, but lacks detail	
		21-17	**FAIR TO POOR:** limited knowledge of subject • little substance • inadequate development of topic	
		16-13	**VERY POOR:** does not show knowledge of subject • non-substantive • not pertinent • OR not enough to evaluate	
ORGANIZATION	12	20-18	**EXCELLENT TO VERY GOOD:** fluent expression • ideas clearly stated/supported • succinct • well-organized • logical sequencing • cohesive	
		17-14	**GOOD TO AVERAGE:** somewhat choppy • loosely organized but main ideas stand out • limited support • logical but incomplete sequencing	
		13-10	**FAIR TO POOR:** non-fluent • ideas confused or disconnected • lacks logical sequencing and development	
		9-7	**VERY POOR:** does not communicate • no organization • OR not enough to evaluate	
VOCABULARY	14	20-18	**EXCELLENT TO VERY GOOD:** sophisticated range • effective word/idiom choice and usage • word form mastery • appropriate register	
		17-14	**GOOD TO AVERAGE:** adequate range • occasional errors of word/idiom form, choice, usage *but meaning not obscured*	
		13-10	**FAIR TO POOR:** limited range • frequent errors of word/idiom form, choice, usage • *meaning confused or obscured*	
		9-7	**VERY POOR:** essentially translation • little knowledge of English vocabulary, idioms, word form • OR not enough to evaluate	
LANGUAGE USE	17	25-22	**EXCELLENT TO VERY GOOD:** effective complex constructions • few errors of agreement, tense, number, word order/function, articles, pronouns, prepositions	
		21-18	**GOOD TO AVERAGE:** effective but simple constructions • minor problems in complex constructions • several errors of agreement, tense, number, word order/function, articles, pronouns, prepositions *but meaning seldom obscured*	
		17-11	**FAIR TO POOR:** major problems in simple/complex constructions • frequent errors of negation, agreement, tense, number, word order/function, articles, pronouns, prepositions and/or fragments, run-ons, deletions • *meaning confused or obscured*	
		10-5	**VERY POOR:** virtually no mastery of sentence construction rules • dominated by errors • does not communicate • OR not enough to evaluate	
MECHANICS	3	5	**EXCELLENT TO VERY GOOD:** demonstrates mastery of conventions • few errors of spelling, punctuation, capitalization, paragraphing	
		4	**GOOD TO AVERAGE:** occasional errors of spelling, punctuation, capitalization, paragraphing *but meaning not obscured*	
		3	**FAIR TO POOR:** frequent errors of spelling, punctuation, capitalization, paragraphing • poor handwriting • *meaning confused or obscured*	
		2	**VERY POOR:** no mastery of conventions • dominated by errors of spelling, punctuation, capitalization, paragraphing • handwriting illegible • OR not enough to evaluate	

TOTAL SCORE　　READER　　COMMENTS

66

Penaeus monodon, *Penaeus japonicus*, and *Penaeus indicus* are the three most commonly cultured marine shrimp in Taiwan. Many factors must be considered when a farmer is deciding which species he should culture. As an aid in choosing which species to culture, some advantages and disadvantages of the three species will be compared.

P. monodon attains a large size. This species with a size of 10 to 12 pieces/kg are common, and sizes of 5 to 7 pieces/kg have been grown in ponds. It's the fastest growing of all shrimp tested for culture. In ponds fry of 3 cm in length have been grown to a size of 75 to 100 g in only five to six months. Due to its large size, it brings a high price to the farmer. Over US$ 7 per kg of shrimp weighing 15 pieces/kg has been kept in market. Besides, it can tolerate a wide range of environmental changes. For examples, it can tolerate salinity from 2 to 70 ppm, salinity within 10 to 25 ppm has no significant effect on growth, and it can tolerate temperatures from 15°c to 38°c. The most favorable factor for the farmer to culture this species is that it grows rapidly whatever we feed it, animal or vegetable diet. And food conversion rate is favorable too. It seems the most promising species to culture in Taiwan. Yet there still have some disadvantages about this species. The first one is that there is a sparse supply of wild fry so that the wild fry are usually insufficient and expensive. Secondarily, the exoskeleton of this species is rather thick so that processors find it harder to remove than that of other species.

P. japonicus also can grow to a fairly large size like P. monodon and brings a good market price, especially the price of live edible size shrimp exported to Japan is twice higher than that of P. monodon. Gravid females of this species are relatively ease to obtain from the wild and it's much easier to artificially propagate them than other species. From each female, more than 500,000 fry can be got by artificial propagation, so the price of the fry is comparably cheap. Though this species get many favorable conditions it still has some problems we cannot overcome up to now. First of all, this species spends a great part of its life embedded in

154

the bottom soil. Experiences have shown that the growth of this species is greatly retarded by a filthy bottom layer. We must keep the bottom sand clean enough to get a good growth rate but in fact, it's still very difficult to control so. The second disadvantage is that it has less tolerance to low salinity than other species. 15-30 ppt is optimum. So it cannot be cultured in a rainy area. After a sudden downpour, the shrimp we'll die because the water salinity will be diluted below the optimal level. The last problems is that high protein (about 60%) feed is required for best growth, it means that cost of feed is higher

P. indicus can grow to a fairly large size and also demand a good market price. Its fry are usually abundant in estuaries and cheap. Its fairly fast growing, especially when young. It was reported that cultured in tanks at a high stocking density of 15 pieces/m². it reached a size of 14 g in 16 weeks and survival rate is high and good growths had been obtained in intensive culture with a feed having 40% protein content, which is lower than that required for some other species. Besides, the exoskeleton is relatively thin, giving greater portion of edible meat to total weight. The big problem of this species is that relatively high salinity (20-30 ppt) is required for best growth so that the pond must be located by the shoreline. And it cannot tolerate high temperature. it means that it cannot be cultured in tropical area. The last one, also the biggest disadvantage of this species is that with present technology, great difficulty has been encountered in culturing this species for longer than three months without heavy mortality.

Now. from the information given above, farmers can choose the most desirable species to culture according to their own situations. which include different seasons and different areas. For example, due to its large size and high price, P. monodon is generally considered the most desirable, but if fry are not available or too expensive in that area where the pond is located, it might be worthwhile to grow another species.

ESL COMPOSITION PROFILE

STUDENT #2   DATE   TOPIC *shrimp*

	SCORE	LEVEL	CRITERIA	COMMENTS
CONTENT	27	30-27	**EXCELLENT TO VERY GOOD:** knowledgeable • substantive • <u>thorough development of thesis</u> • relevant to assigned topic	
		26-22	**GOOD TO AVERAGE:** some knowledge of subject • adequate range • limited development of thesis • mostly relevant to topic, but lacks detail	
		21-17	**FAIR TO POOR:** limited knowledge of subject • little substance • inadequate development of topic	
		16-13	**VERY POOR:** does not show knowledge of subject • non-substantive • not pertinent • OR not enough to evaluate	
ORGANIZATION	18	20-18	**EXCELLENT TO VERY GOOD:** fluent expression • ideas clearly stated/supported • succinct • <u>well-organized</u> • <u>logical sequencing</u> • cohesive	
		17-14	**GOOD TO AVERAGE:** somewhat choppy • loosely organized but main ideas stand out • limited support • logical but incomplete sequencing	
		13-10	**FAIR TO POOR:** non-fluent • ideas confused or disconnected • lacks logical sequencing and development	
		9-7	**VERY POOR:** does not communicate • no organization • OR not enough to evaluate	
VOCABULARY	15	20-18	**EXCELLENT TO VERY GOOD:** sophisticated range • effective word/idiom choice and usage • word form mastery • appropriate register	
		17-14	**GOOD TO AVERAGE:** adequate range • <u>occasional errors of word/idiom form, choice, usage</u> *but meaning not obscured*	*"fries"*
		13-10	**FAIR TO POOR:** limited range • frequent errors of word/idiom form, choice, usage • *meaning confused or obscured*	
		9-7	**VERY POOR:** essentially translation • little knowledge of English vocabulary, idioms, word form • OR not enough to evaluate	
LANGUAGE USE	18	25-22	**EXCELLENT TO VERY GOOD:** effective complex constructions • few errors of agreement, tense, number, word order/function, articles, pronouns, prepositions	
		21-18	**GOOD TO AVERAGE:** effective but simple constructions • minor problems in complex constructions • several errors of agreement, tense, <u>number</u>, word order/function, articles, pronouns, prepositions *but meaning seldom obscured*	
		17-11	**FAIR TO POOR:** major problems in simple/complex constructions • frequent errors of negation, agreement, tense, number, word order/function, articles, pronouns, prepositions and/or fragments, <u>run-ons, deletions</u> • *meaning confused or obscured*	
		10-5	**VERY POOR:** virtually no mastery of sentence construction rules • dominated by errors • does not communicate • OR not enough to evaluate	
MECHANICS	4	5	**EXCELLENT TO VERY GOOD:** demonstrates mastery of conventions • few errors of spelling, punctuation, capitalization, paragraphing	
		4	**GOOD TO AVERAGE:** occasional errors of spelling, punctuation, capitalization, <u>paragraphing</u> *but meaning not obscured*	
		3	**FAIR TO POOR:** frequent errors of spelling, punctuation, capitalization, paragraphing • poor handwriting • *meaning confused or obscured*	
		2	**VERY POOR:** no mastery of conventions • dominated by errors of spelling, punctuation, capitalization, paragraphing • handwriting illegible • OR not enough to evaluate	

TOTAL SCORE   READER   COMMENTS

82

The Ancient Egyptian Settlements

The Egyptian civilization had a dominant position among the various nations of the ancient world for about 3,000 years, between the fourth and the first millennium before Christ.

As human settlements are one of the major impacts of civilization, their study will reflect some characteristic elements of ancient Egypt. The various types of settlements during this period are: the Royal Town, the Necropolis, the Fortress, the Workmen's Village, and the Agricultural Village. Each type demonstrated a particular side of the Egyptian civilization.

The Royal Town was the capital and the largest town of the empire. The most famous were Thebes ('the hundred-gated' as known to the Greeks), Memphis, and Akhetaten (the first New Town ever experienced by man, known also as Tel-el-Amarna). The only remaining parts of the two former towns are the temples. According to Akhetaten remains one could tell that it was composed of three longitudinal thoroughfares parallel to the river Nile and few transversal streets.

In general, the Royal Town contained the Pharaoh's palace, the nobles' and the courtiers' mansions, the priests', the scribes', and the artisans' dwellings. A social stratification was clearly expressed in the dwelling size and location. The higher the rank of the dweller, the larger the dwelling size and the nearer to the Pharaoh's palace it was. One or more huge stone temples were centrally located in the town.

As the Egyptians believed in a second physical life after death, they considered the Necropolis, or the "City of the Dead", as important as the Royal Town, if not more so. Zoser Complex at Sakkara and Guiza Pyramids are the most ancient and the most significant Necropolises.

The penetration within the "City of the Dead" was restricted to certain officials. A masonry wall surrounded the tombs. The causeway formed the major circulation artery during the funeral ceremonies. It consisted of a long axial path bordered by two rows of sphinx or ram statues. Cheops causeway was about 2,000 feet long and 60 feet wide.

The Pharaoh's tomb was as rich and as big as his palace. The tomb, or the "house of eternity", contained besides the statues of the buried person, his mummy and the mummy of his beloved animals as well as his preferred jewelry and furniture.

Mystery and monumentality were the tomb main design objectives. The former was aiming at preserving its precious contents, while the latter was to illustrate how important the buried person was. For example, in Cheops Pyramid (B.C. 2570), the highest stone construction in the world (481 feet high), the Pharaoh's Chamber remained undiscovered for about forty-four centuries.

The ~~necropolis~~ 'City of the Dead' plan followed a concentric pattern. All the tombs were located around the Pharaoh's tomb in the same hierarchy of their dwellings' location in the Royal Town. The entire ~~settlement~~ necropolis was built with unperishable material such as stone, while all other settlements ≠ ~~including the Royal Town,~~ were built with sun-dried mud-bricks.

The geographic position of the Necropolis was symbolically selected. It was located on the western bank of the river Nile where the sun sets; as death was thought of as a temporary 'sunset'. On the other hand, all other 'living' settlements were constructed on the eastern bank — the sunrise side. The only exception was the Fortress. Its site location was chosen according to strategic considerations rather than symbolic ones.

The Fortress was a defensive frontier settlement of a smaller size than the Royal Town and the Necropolis. It was only erected on the Nile bank, in the south, near the Sudanese borders.

These river forts were generally surrounded by a deep ditch and an adobe wall, 15-25 feet thick and more than thirty feet high. While shaped with respect to the typography to take full advantage of the terrain potentiality, both the defensive wall and the settlement had clear and definite geometric forms. Although the early Egyptian Fortresses were generally rectangular, Uronarti with its triangular plan and the L-shaped Semna are the most characteristic ones. The street pattern is formed by two or more main perpendicular roads and an internal circumferential one.

The fourth type of settlements was the Workmen's Village. It was a work camp built to house the artisans and the builders involved in the construction of either a Royal Town or a Neorpolis. Its size was small (by) but proportionate to the major settlement under construction. The best examples are Kahun (or El-Lahun) and Tel-el-Amarna Workmen's Villages.

The street pattern is composed of either parallel streets or a grid iron system forming oblong street blocks. The settlements were either square or rectangular and surrounded by a wall for control. The extension of the settlement size caused a wall extension. Tel-el-Amarna plan was entirely homogeneous; with the exception of the overseer's house, one housing type was stereotyped. On the other hand, Kahun was subdivided into several homogeneous areas, each having a certain housing type.

Social stratification was generally based on the degree of knowledge, skill, and talent. This was clearly illustrated through an extremely large variety of dwelling sizes and designs, ranging from the workmen's tenement house (3 or 4 small rooms) to the high officials' mansions (50 rooms and large halls with private open space). A modular system guided both the settlement plans.

Last, the most widespread settlement was the Agricultural Village, as Egypt's economy was predominantly based on agriculture. No particular example is remaining. When destroyed by river floods or fire hazards, they were rebuilt on the same site. According to the agricultural villages existing nowadays, one can expect that the precedent settlements were compact, densely populated, and very poorly organized. The streets were very narrow and winding. The peasants' houses were small and had an introverted design.

The main design aims were symbolism, functional arrangement, and the honest creation of a total coherent whole. An orthogonal conception dominated the city planning creativity. The major cornerstones of this local creativity were the methodical design, the modular and predetermined plans, the restricted and controlled growth, as well as accuracy and organization. The use of the straight line, axiality, grandiose vista, and geometric forms were also clearly emphasized in the Egyptian settlements.

Other than the achievements illustrated in this paper, the Pharaohs' civilization played a pioneer role in various fields of specialization, such as medicine, magic, legislation, management, astronomy, calculus, geometry, engineering, and art.

ESL COMPOSITION PROFILE

STUDENT **#3**   DATE   TOPIC *Egyptian Settlements*

	SCORE	LEVEL	CRITERIA	COMMENTS
CONTENT	30	30-27	**EXCELLENT TO VERY GOOD:** <u>knowledgeable</u> • substantive • thorough development of thesis • <u>relevant to assigned topic</u>	
		26-22	**GOOD TO AVERAGE:** some knowledge of subject • adequate range • limited development of thesis • mostly relevant to topic, but lacks detail	
		21-17	**FAIR TO POOR:** limited knowledge of subject • little substance • inadequate development of topic	
		16-13	**VERY POOR:** does not show knowledge of subject • non-substantive • not pertinent • OR not enough to evaluate	
ORGANIZATION	20	20-18	**EXCELLENT TO VERY GOOD:** <u>fluent expression</u> • <u>ideas clearly stated/supported</u> • succinct • <u>well-organized</u> • <u>logical sequencing</u> • <u>cohesive</u>	
		17-14	**GOOD TO AVERAGE:** somewhat choppy • loosely organized but main ideas stand out • limited support • logical but incomplete sequencing	
		13-10	**FAIR TO POOR:** non-fluent • ideas confused or disconnected • lacks logical sequencing and development	
		9-7	**VERY POOR:** does not communicate • no organization • OR not enough to evaluate	
VOCABULARY	15	20-18	**EXCELLENT TO VERY GOOD:** <u>sophisticated range</u> • effective word/idiom choice and usage • word form mastery • <u>appropriate register</u>	
		17-14	**GOOD TO AVERAGE:** adequate range • <u>occasional errors of word/idiom form, choice, usage</u> *but meaning not obscured*	
		13-10	**FAIR TO POOR:** limited range • frequent errors of word/idiom form, choice, usage • *meaning confused or obscured*	
		9-7	**VERY POOR:** essentially translation • little knowledge of English vocabulary, idioms, word form • OR not enough to evaluate	
LANGUAGE USE	23	25-22	**EXCELLENT TO VERY GOOD:** effective complex constructions • <u>few errors of agreement, tense, number, word order/function, articles, pronouns, prepositions</u>	
		21-18	**GOOD TO AVERAGE:** effective but simple constructions • minor problems in complex constructions • several errors of agreement, tense, number, word order/function, articles, pronouns, prepositions *but meaning seldom obscured*	
		17-11	**FAIR TO POOR:** major problems in simple/complex constructions • frequent errors of negation, agreement, tense, number, word order/function, articles, pronouns, prepositions and/or fragments, run-ons, deletions • *meaning confused or obscured*	
		10-5	**VERY POOR:** virtually no mastery of sentence construction rules • dominated by errors • does not communicate • OR not enough to evaluate	
MECHANICS	4	5	**EXCELLENT TO VERY GOOD:** demonstrates mastery of conventions • few errors of spelling, punctuation, capitalization, paragraphing	
		4	**GOOD TO AVERAGE:** <u>occasional errors</u> of spelling, punctuation, capitalization, paragraphing *but meaning not obscured*	
		3	**FAIR TO POOR:** frequent errors of spelling, punctuation, capitalization, paragraphing • poor handwriting • *meaning confused or obscured*	
		2	**VERY POOR:** no mastery of conventions • dominated by errors of spelling, punctuation, capitalization, paragraphing • handwriting illegible • OR not enough to evaluate	

TOTAL SCORE   READER   COMMENTS

92

7.3 Using the profile in the classroom

After student-writers have practiced with the PROFILE in the lab session and are familiar with its criteria, they can use it in the classroom to focus on single parts of the process of forming and shaping writing. Of course, it is essential that writers first work through the invention process and have a body of content with which to work. But when this has been done, writers can apply the descriptors and criteria as a guide for analysis of their work and revision. In other words, the PROFILE becomes an aid to their language monitors.

In the classroom, our students often use the PROFILE to examine other pieces of writing to determine how they were developed and what makes them effective or ineffective pieces of writing. In fact, we sometimes have them look again at the third paper in the lab series in order to analyze closely why they scored it as they did.

Invention materials, an annotated paper, and a set of questions for an ESL student's paper which focuses on one component of the PROFILE at a time are included here as an example of how we have carried out such an analysis with a class.

The following paper, which is presented for analysis, is a revision of the student's original draft. It illustrates the excellent writing students can generate when they are made aware of and learn to apply the principles of composition.

The paper was written by Sami Shaker, an Egyptian student studying urban planning at Texas A&M University. The process for developing this paper included: (1) using brain patterns and the pyramid diagram, (2) limiting and outlining his ideas, (3) submitting a rough draft of the paper for an initial analysis and marking with the PROFILE (no score was assigned at this time), (4) revising the paper based on the results of the analysis and suggestions made by the instructor, and (5) re-submitting the paper for a score.

The purpose of the paper was to inform his audience about the impact of ancient Egyptian settlements on civilization. The audience was a class of university graduate students working in various fields of study. Using the invention process, Mr. Shaker worked from the general idea of dwelling places to dwelling places in his home region during a particular time period. To convey his information in the best way, he chose the overall method of classification for his paper. His principle for classification is the structure of each kind of community. By careful selection of facts and examples, showing the most famous representatives of each group, and by making point-by-point comparisons of each, Mr. Shaker developed substantial content for his thesis. His diction and syntax are, on the whole, quite appropriate to both his subject and his audience. He has achieved clear communication of his message to his readers.

For an objective in-class teaching unit on the creative and analytic process we have had students read through the diagram, the outline, and the paper and answer the questions which follow it.

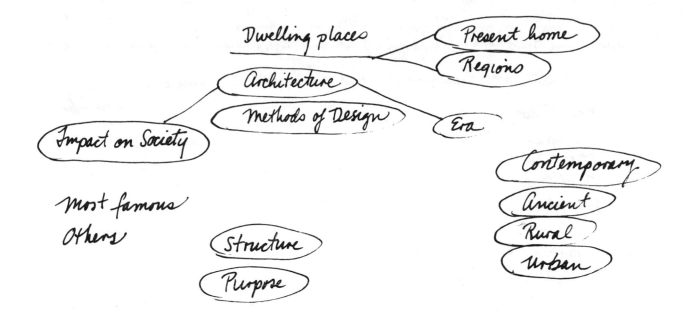

Dwelling places — Present home, Regions

Architecture
Methods of Design — Era

Impact on Society

Most famous
Others

Structure
Purpose

Contemporary
Ancient
Rural
Urban

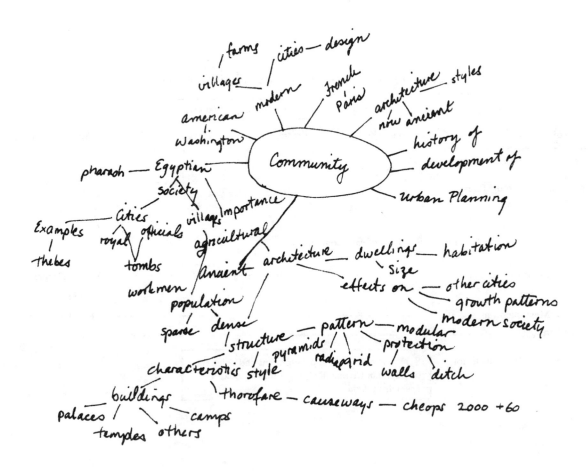

farms / cities — design
villages
modern French
Paris
american architecture styles
Washington now ancient
pharaoh — Egyptian history of
society development of
Community Urban Planning
Examples cities village Importance
Thebes royal officials agricultural
tombs Ancient architecture — dwellings — habitation
workmen effects on size
population other cities
sparse dense growth patterns
structure — pattern — modular modern society
pyramids protection
characteristics style radial grid walls ditch
buildings thorofare — causeways — cheops 2000 +60
palaces camps
temples others

Thesis: The methodical Design of Ancient Egyptian Settlements — architectural development — had an impact on many areas of modern day life

I. Royal Town
   Example
   Street design
   Dwellings
II. Necropolis
III. Fortress
IV. Workman's Village
V. Agricultural Village

CLASSIFICATION: THE ANCIENT EGYPTIAN SETTLEMENTS

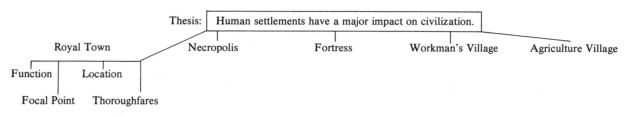

Thesis: Human settlements have a major impact on civilization.

Royal Town   Necropolis   Fortress   Workman's Village   Agriculture Village

Function   Location

Focal Point   Thoroughfares

PRINCIPLE OF CLASSIFICATION: Structure of each community

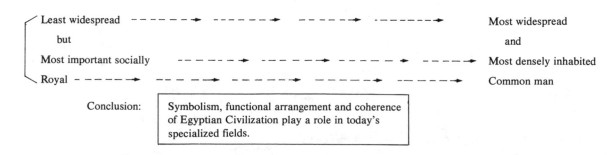

Least widespread - - - - → - - - - → - - - - → - - - - →   Most widespread

but   and

Most important socially - - - - → - - - - → - - - - → - - - →   Most densely inhabited

Royal - - - → - - - → - - - → - - - → - - - →   Common man

Conclusion: Symbolism, functional arrangement and coherence of Egyptian Civilization play a role in today's specialized fields.

166

THE ANCIENT EGYPTIAN SETTLEMENTS

Thesis: As human settlements are one of the major impacts of civilization, their study will reflect some characteristic elements of ancient Egypt.

I. The Royal Town was the capital and the largest town of the empire.

    A. The most famous towns were:
       1. Thebes
       2. Memphis
       3. Akhetaton (Tel-el-Amarna)

    B. Thoroughfares were parallel to the Nile.

    C. Dwellings showed social stratification.
       1. Pharoah's Palace was the hub of the society.
       2. Mansions of the courtiers were nearest the Pharoah's Palace.
       3. Other dwellings were arranged in descending order.

    D. The temples were the focal point of the town.

II. As the Egyptians believed in a second physical life after death, they considered the Necropolis, or the "City of the Dead," as important as Royal Town, if not more so.

    A. The most ancient and significant were:
       1. Foser Complex at Sakkara
       2. Guiza Pyramids

    B. Only certain officials were allowed to enter the city.

    C. The city was surrounded by a wall.

    D. The Causeway was the major circulation artery during funerals.
       1. It was bordered by two rows of the sphinx.
       2. Cheops was 2,000 feet long and 60 feet wide.

    E. The design objectives of Pharoah's tomb were mystery and monumentality.

    F. Pharoah's tomb was the center of a concentric pattern of other tombs.

    G. Building materials were imperishable.

    H. The "City of the Dead" was located on the west bank of the Nile.

III. The Fortress was a defensive frontier settlement of a smaller size than the Royal Town and the Necropolis.

    A. It was located on the west bank.

    B. It was surrounded by protective devices which included:
       1. a ditch
       2. a wall

    C. Most characteristic examples were:
       1. Unonarti
       2. Semna

    D. Street patterns were:
       1. main perpendicular roads
       2. internal circumferential ones

IV. The fourth type of settlement was the Workman's Village.

    A. They were work camps built to house:
        1. artisans
        2. builders

    B. The best examples were:
        1. Kahun
        2. Tel-el-Amarna

    C. Street patterns were:
        1. parallel
        2. grid iron

    D. Characteristics of the settlement included:
        1. the shape—which was either square or rectangular
        2. the wall—which surrounded the village
        3. the housing—which was mostly homogeneous
        4. social stratification based on:
            a. knowledge
            b. skill
            c. talent
        5. a modular system—which guided the settlement plans.

V. Last, the most widespread settlement was the Agricultural Village since Egypt's economy was predominantly based on agriculture.

    A. No particular example remains because of natural hazards such as:
        1. floods
        2. fire

    B. Rebuilt villages suggest that villages were characterized by:
        1. compactness
        2. dense population
        3. poor organization
        4. narrow, winding streets
        5. small houses

VI. Main design aims—symbolism, functional arrangement, coherence of methodological design, modular design, controlled growth and geometric forms played a pioneer role in various fields of specialization to the present time.

The Ancient Egyptian Settlements

Introduction (1) The Egyptian civilization had a dominant position among the various nations of the ancient world for about 3,000 years, between the fourth and the first millennium before Christ.

Thesis Statement (2) As human settlements are one of the major impacts of civilization, their study will reflect some characteristic elements of ancient Egypt. The various types of settlements during this period are: the Royal Town, the Necropolis,

Enumeration the Fortress, the Workman's Village, and the Agricultural Village. Each type demonstrated a particular side of the Egyptian civilization.

Topic Sentence (3) The Royal Town was the capital and the largest town of the empire. The most famous were Thebes ('the hundred-gated' as known to the Greeks), Memphis,

Example and Akhetaten (the first New Town ever experienced by man, known also as Tel-el-Amarna). The only remaining parts of the two former towns are the temples. According to Akhetaten remains one could tell that

Facts it was composed of three longitudinal thoroughfares parallel to the river Nile and few transversal streets.

(4) In general, the Royal Town contained the Pharaoh's palace, the nobles' and the courtiers' mansions; the priests',

Paragraph pattern circles in to focal point the scribes', and the artisans' dwellings. A social stratification was clearly expressed in the dwelling size and location. The higher the rank of the dweller,

169

Facts the larger the dwelling size and the nearer to the Pharaoh's palace it was. One or more huge stone temples were centrally located in the town.

good transition using repetition

Topic Sentence (5) <u>As the Egyptians believed in a second physical life after death, they considered the Necropolis, or the 'City of the Dead', as important as the Royal Town, if not more so.</u> Zoser Complex at Sakkara and Guiza Pyramids are the most ancient and the most

Example significant Necropolises.

(6) The penetration within the 'City of the Dead' was restricted to certain officials. A masonry wall sur-rounded the tombs. The causeway formed the major circulation artery during the funeral ceremonies. It

Facts consisted of a long axial path bordered by two rows of sphinx or ram statues. Cheops causeway was about 2,000 feet long and 60 feet wide.

extraneous?

(7) The Pharaoh's tomb was as rich and as big as his palace. The tomb, or the 'house of eternity', contained besides the statues of the buried person, his mummy and the mummy of his beloved animals & his preferred *as well as* jewelry and furniture.

extraneous — could be deleted

(8) Mystery and monumentality were the tomb main design objectives. The former was aiming at preserving

Example its precious contents, while the latter was to illustrate how important the buried person was. For example, in Cheops Pyramid (B.C. 2570), the highest stone

Facts construction in the world (481 feet high), the Pharaoh's Chamber remained undiscovered for about forty-four centuries.

(9) The 'City of the Dead' plan followed a concentric pattern. All the tombs were located around the Pharaoh's tomb in the same hierarchy of their dwellings' location in the Royal Town. The entire Necropolis was built with unperishable material such as stone, while all other settlements, were built with sun-dried mud-bricks.

Facts

(10) The geographic position of the Necropolis was symbolically selected. It was located on the western bank of the river Nile where the sun sets; as death was thought of as a temporary "sunset". On the other hand, all other 'living' settlements were constructed on the eastern bank — the sunrise side. The only exception was the Fortress. Its site location was chosen according to strategic considerations rather than symbolic ones.

Contrast

good transition using repetition of key words

Topic Sentence

(11) The Fortress was a defensive frontier settlement of a smaller size than the Royal Town and the Necropolis. It was only erected on the Nile bank, in the south, near the Sudanese borders.

Facts

(12) These river forts were generally surrounded by a deep ditch and an adobe wall, 15-25 feet thick and more than thirty feet high. While shaped with respect to the topography to take full advantage of the terrain potentiality, both the defensive wall and the settlement had clear and definite geometric forms. Although the early Egyptian Fortresses were generally rectangular, Uronarti with its triangular plan and the L-shaped Semna are the most characteristic ones. The street pattern is formed by two or more main perpendicular roads and an internal circumferential one.

Example

171

Topic Sentence (13) The fourth type of settlements was the Workmen's Village. It was a work camp built to house the artisans and the builders involved in the construction of either a Royal Town or a Necropolis. Its size was small (by) but proportionate to the major settlement under construction. The best examples are Kahun (or El-Lahun) and Tel-el-Amarna Workmen's **Example** Villages.

Facts (14) The street pattern is composed of either parallel streets or a grid iron system forming oblong street blocks. The settlements were either square or rectangular and surrounded by a wall for control. The extension of the settlement size caused a wall extension. Tel-el-Amarna plan was **Example** entirely homogeneous; with the exception of the overseer's shows contrast house, one housing type was stereotyped. On the other hand, Kahun was subdivided into several homogeneous areas, each having a certain housing type.

Facts (15) Social stratification was generally based on the degree of knowledge, skill, and talent. This was clearly illustrated through an extremely large variety of dwelling sizes and designs, ranging from the workmen's tenement **Examples** house (3 or 4 small rooms) to the high officials' mansions (50 rooms and large halls with private open space). A modular system guided both settlement plans.

Topic Sentence (16) Last, the most widespread settlement was the Agricultural Village, as Egypt's economy was predominantly based on agriculture. No particular example is remaining. When destroyed by river floods or fire hazards, they were rebuilt on the same site. According to the agricultural villages existing nowadays, one can expect that the precedent settlements were

Opinion compact, densely populated, and very poorly organized. The streets were very narrow and winding. The peasants' houses were small and had an introverted design.

Conclusion (17) The main design aims were symbolism, functional arrangement, and the honest creation of a bold coherent

(Summary) whole. An orthogonal conception dominated the city planning creativity. The major cornerstones of this local creativity were the methodical design, the modular and predetermined plans, the restricted and controlled growth, as well as accuracy and organization. The use of the straight line, axiality, grandiose vista, and geometric forms were also

Extension clearly emphasized in the Egyptian settlements.

(18) Other than the achievements illustrated in this paper,

Confirms the Pharaohs' civilization played a pioneer role in various

Expands
Thesis fields of specialization, such as medicine, magic, legislation, management, astronomy, calculus, geometry, engineering, and art.

PROFILE QUESTIONS (class exercise)

A. 1. Evaluate Mr. Shaker's paper with the PROFILE, referring to the criteria if necessary.

   2. What was your score?

B. Now to gauge how accurately you used the PROFILE, answer the following questions related to the *Organization* component.

   *1. What is his stated purpose (thesis)? Is it fully developed?

   2. List the topic sentences that support it.
       a. _____
       b. _____
       c. _____
       d. _____

   *3. Is the paper interesting? What makes it so?

   *4. What overall method of development does the author use?

   *5. Is the method logically developed?

   6. What technique does the author use in the introduction to catch the reader's interest?

   7. What device does the author use to signal the method of organization?

   *8. Does the introduction succeed?

   9. Does the conclusion reemphasize and/or expand the introduction? How? Could it be improved? How?

C. Answer the following questions using the *Content* component.

   1. Does the writer appear to know much about his subject?

   *2. Is all the information in the paper pertinent to the thesis statement? to the topic sentences? in each classification?

   3. Look at paragraphs 3 and 4. Is there a strong topic sentence? What is it? How could it be improved?

   4. Is there "thorough," "adequate," or "limited" content development? Give reasons for your choice.

5. What methods does he use to develop the content? Are they balanced?

6. How does the author conclude his paper? Is it strong or weak? How could it be improved?

7. Does the conclusion reemphasize the introduction?

D. Answer the following questions using the *Vocabulary* component.

   1. What is the overall tone of the paper?
       a. What is the range of the vocabulary? the register?
       b. Is is appropriate to the topic?
       c. Is it appropriate to the audience?

   2. What sophisticated word choices are included in paragraphs 3 and 4? 9 and 10?

   3. What expressions has the author used to show degrees of importance? Does he use them correctly?

   *4. What methods of transition are used in the paper?
       a. within paragraphs?
       b. between paragraphs?
       Note: paragraphs 4, 5, 10, 11, 13, 16.

E. Answer the following questions using the *Language use* component.

   *1. Find an example of sentence subordination in paragraph 12.

   *2. Find evidence of parallel verb forms.

F. 1. Rate the paper with the PROFILE again. What is your score this time?

   2. Did it change from your first score? in which component(s)? Do you understand the reason for the change?

---

*Class discussion questions.

174

7.4 The final shaping—revision

By beginning with a representative sample, moving to a class effort, and working carefully through each component in the PROFILE, students should now have the confidence to utilize the PROFILE as a checklist and revision guide for shaping their own work. Teachers, in turn, can now use the PROFILE to measure the student's progress in all five components. Until the final revision of a paper is submitted, however, students feel freer to continue writing and rewriting if teachers mark descriptors only and refrain from assigning numerical scores until the final paper is submitted.

Therefore, we suggest that when teachers receive and read sets of papers, they just mark descriptors on the PROFILE and leave the papers unscored. Then they can return the papers to the class for revision, thus encouraging the students to apply the writing criteria for shaping their own compositions as well as for finding and correcting their own errors. Depending upon time constraints and numbers of papers, teachers may choose to score the papers after the first revision, or they may return the papers for further revision before scoring.

The next paper was revised several times before the final draft was scored. Junton, an ESL student, used mechanical devices quite well, and vocabulary and grammar satisfactorily. Further, he had a number of strong major points; yet his paper lacked organization, logical sequencing, and specific content to develop the major points. The first revision illustrates how he was able to focus on those two components in reshaping his work.

One technique the teacher used to help Junton with this revision was to encourage him to "cut and paste" his work rather than engage in a complete rewriting. His major points were firm and relevant to his thesis; they only needed reordering and expanding. Thus, the teacher sat down with him in an individual conference, and as he cut his paper apart, they talked over what points he wanted to emphasize and where they should be placed in the overall design. Then, as he began to reorder them, the teacher asked Junton questions about each point to help him find out what kinds of information he wanted to use in developing the rest of the paper. As Junton talked, the teacher jotted notes to show him how he could develop each paragraph more fully and to illustrate to him that he did, indeed, have something more to say. The following samples include Junton's rough draft, brain pattern, two revisions, and a final draft. With each successive revision he concentrated on meeting the criteria of the various PROFILE components, first organization and content and later vocabulary, language use, and mechanics.

175

The laws of forests are both
useful and beautiful

Forests are useful because they can provide wood and its products. However, when you clear away the forests, the beautiful of forests will be destroyed too. So the forests utilized by man we need them both useful and beautiful.

Paper is one of the products of forests. paper is essential in the society of civilization. Also, the furniture, boxes, and plywood, and soon are made of wood which to which are related with people daily living.

However, forests are vital to us in many other ways another than timber. They can protect the soil from erosion. They supply the beautiful places for people's recreation and for wildlife. If the forests are destroyed, the beautiful of forests will not exist any more.

So there are two attitudes toward the forests. The first attitude is represented by who people whose interests toward the forests lies in its economic value. The other attitude

176

toward forests is represented by people who are interested in its aesthetic enjoyment in which forests can provide people with study, recreation, and the protection of watershed.

Both attitudes are indispensible for people. So the only is to compromise. But how?
way

I think that the harvest of forests should be on a sustained yield basis. My country for example, Taiwan is covered by 60% of forest land. To deal with the reverse question between the useful and the beautiful of forests, my goverment regulated that the quantity ~~futility~~ of timber harvest could not over one million m³ per year. Moreover reforestation is over 60,000 acres each year which is four times of the log-cutting. Also, many places are protected as a conservation areas in which harvesting is not allowable. The results are appraiseable.

The stately forests are our national treasure. They deserve our soliciteous preservation and management. So it is our responsibility to make the forests both beautiful and useful.

177

Revision #1

Laws Of Forests Are Useful And Beautiful
****

good

Laws of forests are the policies or attitudes toward the utilization of forests. Forests are useful to us because they can provide wood and its products.* However,

wf

when man clears away the forests, the beaut*iful* of forests will be destroyed too. So the laws of forests utilized by man should be both useful and beautiful.

* this would be better placed in first paragraph

From the forests we get the wood to make paper. Paper is one of the greatest needs of civilized people. We also get the wood for furniture, boxes, plywood, and many arti-cles of great importance in our daily lives.

~~However~~, There are many reasons for us to keep the forests intact. They protect the watersheds and give us clean, sweet streams to provide us with water and many forms of recreation. They control temperatures, rainful, and to a large degree, the climate of an area. They harbor many forms of wild-life. They provide windbreaks and shel-

Is this a law? state the policy and use this informa-tion to justify it.

del.

ter and, *they* beautify the countryside.

When man cut away the forests, the land was left uncovered, and, as a result, water ran off quickly and carried soil with it which led to the loss of soil and

del.

water, and to the destruction of the beautiful *? what*.

So, there are two different attitudes toward the fores*t*:

P, wf.

~~the~~ the one identified with the beaut*iful*, the other with

wf

the useful. The first attitude is held by people *who* main interest in the forest lies in its value as a place for recreation, study, protection of the watersheds, and the enjoyment of the beauty of nature. Another attitude is found among those who think of the forest as primarily an economic resource the function of which, above all, is to provide timber.

use one para-graph to dis-cuss the first law and a second ¶ to discuss the 2nd

wf

A day is coming when th*ese* will be so many people in the country that we shall have to use all of the

n

forest to accommodate everybody who wants to go to in

R-O

for esthetic enjoyment, and when, at the same time, we shall have to use all of the forest to grow the timber

178

wf.
needed to meet the demand for wood; that is, the same
forest will have to do for the useful and the beautiful.

To deal with these two contrary problems which are
both indispensable to human life, I think we have to
manage and harvest timbers on a sustained yield basis

wc
which means that wherever the trees are planningly cut,
reforestation must be done right away, and the special
areas like watersheds should be kept intact.

del
For instance, we spent billion of dollars in setting
up a reservoir for hydraulic power generation before
in central Taiwan. But the reservoir has almost lost

wc, wf
it
its function for because the sudden short of water volume which
was resulting ed from the excessive felling of trees in the
upper course of watersheds.

Therefore, a special organization was formed to
make the policies of the development of forests, and
a certain actions had been taken. For example, we
divided many places as conservation areas where the
forest could not be harvested. We also regulated that

t
the total quantity of timber harvest could not be over
one million M3 per year. Furthermore, reforestation is
proceeding at a rate of more than 60,000 acres each year,
about four times the cut-over areas.

In conclusion, the stately forests are a national
treasure deserving the solicitous care of people.
Therefore, the laws of forests are the forests utilized
by man should be both useful and beautiful.

√+

water
recreation
study   beautiful ← ① Laws of Forests ② → useful
beauty   (products)
temperature

attitude   relation   attitude

paper
furniture
plywood
others

Useful & Beautiful

How?
(example)

You also need a formal
outline to help you organize your
major points and their support.

Revision #2

Junton Ho

LAWS OF FORESTS ARE USEFUL~~NESS~~ *to Protect* AND BEAUT~~IFUL~~

Laws of forests are the policies or attitudes toward the utilization of forests. Forests are useful to us because they can provide ~~wood and its products~~ *products which stimulate our economy; they can serve as means of conservation; and they can provide a place of beauty and recreation for us. Therefore, laws need to be created and enforced to protect this valuable resource.*

First, From the forests we get the wood to make paper. Paper is one of the greatest needs of civilized people. We also get the wood for furniture, boxes, plywood, and many articles of great importance in our daily lives.

Secondly, since the forest provides. Conservation of the land, laws especially need enforcement.

~~However~~, There are many reasons for us to keep the forests intact. They protect the watersheds and give us clean, sweet streams to provide us with water and many forms of recreation. They control temperatures, rainful, and to a large degree, the climate of an area. They harbor many forms of wild-life. They provide windbreaks and shelter and they beautify the countryside.

When man cut away the forests, the land was left uncovered, and, as a result, water ran off quickly and carried soil with it which led to the loss of soil and water, and to the desctuction of the beautiful _____. *what?*

180

For instance, we spent billions of dollars in setting up a reservoir for hydraulic power generation ~~before~~ in central Taiwan. But the reservoir has almost lost its function ~~for~~ because the sudden shortage of water ~~volume~~ which ~~was~~ resulted from the excessive felling of trees in the upper course of watersheds. By applying the laws of conservation, we can prevent this kind of disaster and also beautify our land.

So, there are two different attitudes toward the forest; the one identified with the beautiful, the other with the useful. The first attitude is held by people whose main interest in the forest lies in its value as a place for recreation, study, protection of the watersheds, and the enjoyment of the beauty of nature. The other attitude is found among those who think of the forest as primarily an economic resource the function of which, above all, is to provide timber. The important view, for me, is the concern with recreation and beauty.

A day is coming when there will be so many people in the country that we shall have to use all of the forest to accommodate everybody who wants to go to in for esthetic enjoyment. How do people use the forest? Why is it important that they be able to use the forest? and when, at the same time, we shall have to use all of the forest to grow the timber needed to meet the demand for wood; that is, the same forest will have to do for the useful and the beautiful.

To deal with these two contrary problems which are both indispensable to human life, ~~I think~~ we have to manage and harvest timbers on a sustained yield basis which means that wherever the trees are ~~planningly~~ *purposefully* cut, reforestation must be done right away, and the special areas like watersheds should be kept intact.

Therefore, a special organization was formed to make the policies of the development of forests, and a certain actions had been taken. For example, we divided amny places as conservation areas where the forest could not be harvested. We also regulated that the total quantity of timber harvest could not be over one million M3 per year. Furthermore, reforestation is proceeding at a rate of more than 60,000 acres each year, about four times the cut-over areas.

In conclusion, the stately forests are a national treasure deservng the solicitous care of people. Therefore, the laws of forests are the forests utilized by man should be both useful and beautiful. However, when man clears away the forests, the beautiful of forests will be destroyed too. So the laws of forests utilized by man should be both useful and beautiful.

Junton Ho

Laws of Forests Are to Protect Usefulness and Beauty

Laws of forests are the policies or attitudes toward the utilization of forests. Forests are useful to us because they can provide products which stimulate our economy; they can serve as means of conservation; and they can provide a place of beauty and recreation for us. Therefore, laws need to be created and enforced to protect this valuable resource.

From the forests we get the wood to make paper. Paper is one of the greatest needs of civilized people. We also get the wood for furniture, boxes, plywood, and many articles of great importance in our daily lives. The employment, payrolls, and value added which are significant to our economy ~~that~~ can be attributed to timber and the timber based industries. For instance, plywood, wood products and furniture are the leading industries in Taiwan, and these are exported with sales of more than US$2.5 billion, over 20 percent of the nation's total exports in 1980.

Since the forest provides conservation of the lands, laws especially need to be enforced to keep the forest intact. They protect the watersheds and give us clean, sweet streams to provide us with water and many forms of recreation. They control temperatures, rainful, and to a large degree, the climate of an area. They harbor many forms of wild-life. They provide windbreaks and shelter and they beautify the countryside.

When man cut away the forests, the land was left uncover-ed, and, as a result, water ran off quickly and carried soil and water, ~~and~~ to the destruction of the beauty of forest. For instance, we spent billion of dollars in setting up a reservoir for hydraulic power generation in central Taiwan. But the reservoir has almost lost its function because the sudden shortage of water volume which resulted from the excessive felling of trees in the upper course of watersheds. By applying the laws of conservation, we can prevent this kind of disaster and ~~also~~ beautify our land as well.

There are two different attitudes toward the forest: the one identified with the beautifying, the other with the usefulness. The first attitude is held by people whose main interest in the forest lies in its value as a place for recreation, study, protection of the watersheds, and the enjoyment of the beauty of nature. The other attitude is found among those who think of the forest as primarily an economic resource the function of which, above all, is to provide timber.

183

The important view, for me, is the concern with recreation and beauty. A day is coming when there will be so many people in the country that we shall have to use all the forests to accommodate everybody who wants to go to in for esthetic enjoyment. People use forest for sight-seeing, picniking, boating, camping, nature walks, hiking and so on. These activities provided by ^forest can restore a person's vitality, initiative, and perspective of life, thereby preparing the individual to return to his toil.

To deal with these two contrary problems which are both indispensable to human life, ~~I think~~ we have to manage and harvest timbers on a sustained yield basis which means that wherever the trees are schemely cut, reforestation must be done right away. ~~and~~ the special _Furthermore,_ areas like watersheds should be kept intact.

~~Therefore,~~ A special organization was formed to make the policies of the development of forests, and ~~ec~~certain actions had been taken in Taiwan. For example, we divided many places as conservation areas where the forest could not be harvested. We also _ruled_ regulated that the total quantity of timber harvest could not be over one million M3 per year. Furthermore, ʌeforestation is proceeding at a rate of more than 60,000 acres each year, about four times the cut-over areas.

In conclusion, the stately forests are a national treasure deserving the solicitous care of people. When man clears away the forests, the beauty of forests will be destroyed too. Therefore, the laws of forests utilized by man should be both useful and beautiful.

ESL COMPOSITION PROFILE

STUDENT _Junton Ho_   DATE _2/16/81_   TOPIC _Laws_

	SCORE	LEVEL	CRITERIA	COMMENTS
CONTENT	1st Scoring / 2nd Scoring **26/28**	30-27	EXCELLENT TO VERY GOOD: knowledgeable • substantive • thorough development of thesis • relevant to assigned topic	Good definition of laws. Your major points are strong. Please continue to develop them in your revision.
		26-22	GOOD TO AVERAGE: some knowledge of subject • adequate range • limited development of thesis • mostly relevant to topic, but lacks detail	
		21-17	FAIR TO POOR: limited knowledge of subject • little substance • inadequate development of topic	
		16-13	VERY POOR: does not show knowledge of subject • non-substantive • not pertinent • OR not enough to evaluate	
ORGANIZATION	**14/19**	20-18	EXCELLENT TO VERY GOOD: fluent expression • ideas clearly stated/supported • succinct • well-organized • logical sequencing • cohesive	You convey clear concerns about the forest. Reexamine what you want to emphasize and try using an outline to help with reorganization.
		17-14	GOOD TO AVERAGE: somewhat choppy • loosely organized but main ideas stand out • limited support • logical but incomplete sequencing	
		13-10	FAIR TO POOR: non-fluent • ideas confused or disconnected • lacks logical sequencing and development	
		9-7	VERY POOR: does not communicate • no organization • OR not enough to evaluate	
VOCABULARY	**14/18**	20-18	EXCELLENT TO VERY GOOD: sophisticated range • effective word/idiom choice and usage • word form mastery • appropriate register	
		17-14	GOOD TO AVERAGE: adequate range • occasional errors of word/idiom form, choice, usage but meaning not obscured	
		13-10	FAIR TO POOR: limited range • frequent errors of word/idiom form, choice, usage • meaning confused or obscured	
		9-7	VERY POOR: essentially translation • little knowledge of English vocabulary, idioms, word form • OR not enough to evaluate	
LANGUAGE USE	**18/21**	25-22	EXCELLENT TO VERY GOOD: effective complex constructions • few errors of agreement, tense, number, word order/function, articles, pronouns, prepositions	
		21-18	GOOD TO AVERAGE: effective but simple constructions • minor problems in complex constructions • several errors of agreement, tense, number, word order/function, articles, pronouns, prepositions but meaning seldom obscured	
		17-11	FAIR TO POOR: major problems in simple/complex constructions • frequent errors of negation, agreement, tense, number, word order/function, articles, pronouns, prepositions and/or fragments, run-ons, deletions • meaning confused or obscured	
		10-5	VERY POOR: virtually no mastery of sentence construction rules • dominated by errors • does not communicate • OR not enough to evaluate	
MECHANICS	**5/5**	5	EXCELLENT TO VERY GOOD: demonstrates mastery of conventions • few errors of spelling, punctuation, capitalization, paragraphing	Great! The appearance of your paper is very neat, and it is easy to read.
		4	GOOD TO AVERAGE: occasional errors of spelling, punctuation, capitalization, paragraphing but meaning not obscured	
		3	FAIR TO POOR: frequent errors of spelling, punctuation, capitalization, paragraphing • poor handwriting • meaning confused or obscured	
		2	VERY POOR: no mastery of conventions • dominated by errors of spelling, punctuation, capitalization, paragraphing • handwriting illegible • OR not enough to evaluate	

TOTAL SCORE   READER   COMMENTS

77/91   _JBH_

Please Revise

1st Scoring — This is a neat and interesting presentation, but your paper needs reorganization and further development.

2nd scoring — This is terrific. Congratulations!

185

On pages 187–196 are three samples by a single student who revised major errors in his own paper. Sample A was the first paper submitted. The instructor made notations on the paper and marked the PROFILE, but left the paper unscored. (The score appearing on the PROFILE, page 192, was assigned after the first revision.) The paper was then returned to the student with a request that he develop a thesis statement and an outline making more complete comparisons. Notice that even though there are many needed corrections, only one or two are requested by the instructor for each revision, thus making the revision a manageable task for the student. Organization and content are the first areas focused on for revision by the instructor, since grammar problems can be referred to lab work if necessary.

Sample C (pages 193–195) is not yet a perfect paper; for instance, only the word "conclusion" rather than the concluding idea is added to the outline. There are still uncorrected language use and vocabulary errors, and the introductory paragraph has not been revised as requested. However, the student *has* made definite progress. When the student was provided with specific suggestions on the PROFILE, he was able to make the following revisions. He has corrected the outline form, provided specific examples, made a clear comparison, improved some word choices, added a concluding paragraph and (*notice!!*) improved the appearance of the paper. This revision process was successful in several areas. Notice, too, that only one or two comments were emphasized for correction in each revision: content and organization in Samples A and B and vocabulary and language use in Sample C.

Using the PROFILE enables teachers to emphasize students' strengths as well as to illustrate weaknesses. Furthermore, students can easily see the progress they have made in any or all components.

Further discussion of monitoring progress—progress for a whole semester as well as progress on one paper—appears in Section 7.5.

Compare the use of mass media such as radio television, and newspapers in the U.S. and in my country.

wo   When we saw "mass media" these words, we thought about radio, television and newspapers

t?   because they were the tools of mass media. In Taiwan, We also have radio, television and newspapers. The role which they play in the mass media is just the same as they are in

cap   the U.S. ; However, there are some difference in the policy and programs.

     →   In Taiwan. Government used the mass media as a tool to teach her people. You can

agr   see some TV programs which is provided by Government to let people know what the

del   world is ^; when, where and how they can get

del   help from the Government if they need^. In the U.S., you can hardly see such programs.

art   ^ Press in Taiwan has the same power as it

p,wc   has in America. but the farmer is more tend to support the Government and not controls by some

noR   large Company as the later in the U.S. ←

← ——————————————— You can even see novels
and histories from the Press in Taiwan. People
in Taiwan see the newspaper not only for its
news but also for its entertainment. In my
point of view, I think the press of Taiwan
is more readble than the press of America.

Note: The paper needs a clear
comparison. Extend paragraph 2
to tell what you do see on television
in the U.S. Extend the last
paragraph to tell what is found
in the U.S. press. Make a comparison.

Sample B, which follows, is the first revision of this paper. The student has added an outline and a thesis statement which give needed direction to his paper. He has completed the comparison; however, a conclusion is still missing and grammatical errors abound. The first paragraph is somewhat weak because the introductory sentences do not emphasize or strengthen the thesis. At this point, the paper is scored and again returned for further revision with a request for the addition of a conclusion, a revision of the first paragraph, and corrections in language use.

Outline

Mass Media in America and Free China

I. Mass Media is different between America and Taiwan

age II difference ~~exsist~~ in policy and Program ~~between~~ the two country's TV.

   A. Taiwan's TV

If you have (1) — (1) The Government provided some program for helping *you must also have* her people.

(2).   B. America's TV

It is better to make A. and B. topic sentences   (U) ~~Programs are about~~ most of *the* programs are commercial charaters.

III ~~Difference in Tai~~ There are differences between Taiwan's press and America's.

   A. ~~The~~ *The* Press in Taiwan.

age   (1) The Press ~~are~~ ~~it~~ *the* supporter of our Government

  (2) It contains some entertaining articles.

  B. The press in America.

\#   (1) It has different viewpoint.

t   (2) too much Advertisement ~~could~~ ~~be~~ seen.

189

Mass Media in America and Free China

\# Theses statement — Difference in the policy and the programs makes the major difference of mass media in America and Free China.

Mass media is different from time to time and place to
P place. When we saw these words ∧ "mass media", we thought about television and newspapers because they are the tools of the mass media. They both have great power, not only in America but also in Taiwan; however, they also have differences in their policies and
P C/C programs.

In Taiwan, besides the commercial purpose
Art of ∧ TV company itself, the Government used it as a tool to teach her people. You can see
Prep (wc) no programs in TV. It is provided by the Government. Its purpose is to broad people's knowledge such as: a program for farmers telling them
\#, wc about new method and in improving their ∧griculture,
wo and programs about telling people which where and how they can get help from the Government of when they need help. In America, you can hardly see a
t, prep (wc) program like that. The TV programs was full with

190

Commericalism. Old moves and ~~two~~ different kinds of entertainment shows ~~take~~ Almost the whole TV programs. Even the

age news withdraw to the ~~almost~~ second role.

NI   The Press in Taiwan has the same power as it
             has in America, but the farmer ~~is more toward to~~
//   support the Government and ∧ not controled by some
             large Company. You can even see novels and historical

#,wc   story on the ~~taiwan's~~ press. People in Taiwan see
             the press not only for its news but also for its
             entertainment.   America's press has more

viewpoint than Taiwan's; however, when it ~~is~~
             conflict ~~s~~ with its owner's benifits, it ~~will~~ always

~~its~~ follows the owner's will. You can't see any novel
             OK
#,wc   or story on America's press. You ~~can~~ could notice
             OK
wo/#   that ~~there are~~ Advertisement is more than other
             categories. A lot of people ~~its~~ ordered the press
             just because they wanted to know when and where
             there is a white sale.

Conclusion is lacking. Please add
one, and rewrite the introductory
paragraph. Also please correct
the number problems.

ESL COMPOSITION PROFILE

STUDENT _Sample A marked_   DATE   TOPIC _Media comparison paper_
Sample B scored

SCORE	LEVEL	CRITERIA	COMMENTS

CONTENT — **24**

30-27	**EXCELLENT TO VERY GOOD:** knowledgeable • substantive • thorough development of thesis • relevant to assigned topic
26-22	**GOOD TO AVERAGE:** some knowledge of subject • adequate range • (limited development of thesis) mostly relevant to topic, but lacks detail
21-17	**FAIR TO POOR:** limited knowledge of subject • little substance • inadequate development of topic
16-13	**VERY POOR:** does not show knowledge of subject • non-substantive • not pertinent • OR not enough to evaluate

ORGANIZATION — **14**

1. What is the thesis statement?
2. Good! Organization improved — add a conclusion

20-18	**EXCELLENT TO VERY GOOD:** fluent expression • ideas clearly stated/supported • succinct • well-organized • logical sequencing • cohesive
17-14	**GOOD TO AVERAGE:** somewhat choppy • loosely organized but main ideas stand out (limited support) logical but incomplete sequencing
13-10	**FAIR TO POOR:** non-fluent • (ideas confused) or disconnected • lacks logical sequencing and development
9-7	**VERY POOR:** does not communicate • no organization • OR not enough to evaluate

VOCABULARY — **14**

20-18	**EXCELLENT TO VERY GOOD:** sophisticated range • effective word/idiom choice and usage • word form mastery • appropriate register
17-14	**GOOD TO AVERAGE:** adequate range • occasional errors of (word/idiom form, choice, usage) but meaning not obscured
13-10	**FAIR TO POOR:** limited range • frequent errors of word/idiom form, choice, usage • meaning confused or obscured
9-7	**VERY POOR:** essentially translation • little knowledge of English vocabulary, idioms, word form • OR not enough to evaluate

LANGUAGE USE — **11**

25-22	**EXCELLENT TO VERY GOOD:** effective complex constructions • few errors of agreement, tense, number, word order/function, articles, pronouns, prepositions
21-18	**GOOD TO AVERAGE:** effective but simple constructions • minor problems in complex constructions • several errors of (agreement, tense, number, word order/function, (articles) pronouns, (prepositions) but meaning seldom obscured **11**
17-11	**FAIR TO POOR:** major problems in simple/complex constructions • frequent errors of negation, agreement, tense, number, word order/function, articles, pronouns, prepositions and/or fragments, run-ons (deletions) • meaning confused or obscured
10-5	**VERY POOR:** virtually no mastery of sentence construction rules • dominated by errors • does not communicate • OR not enough to evaluate

MECHANICS — **4**

5	**EXCELLENT TO VERY GOOD:** demonstrates mastery of conventions • few errors of spelling, punctuation, (capitalization) paragraphing
4	**GOOD TO AVERAGE:** occasional errors of spelling, (punctuation) capitalization, paragraphing but meaning not obscured
3	**FAIR TO POOR:** frequent errors of spelling, punctuation, capitalization, paragraphing • poor handwriting • meaning confused or obscured
2	**VERY POOR:** no mastery of conventions • dominated by errors of spelling, punctuation, capitalization, paragraphing • handwriting illegible • OR not enough to evaluate

TOTAL SCORE   READER   COMMENTS   _You have done a good job improving the content — let's work on correcting the grammar errors in the paper._

67

Outline
Mass Media in America and Free China

I Mass media is different between America and Taiwan

II Differences exist in Policy and Program between the two country's TV.
    A. Taiwan's TV — The Government provided some Programs for helping her people.

    B. America's TV — Most of the programs are Commerical ∧ character.

trepdel

III There are differences between Taiwan's Press and America's.
    A. The Press in Taiwan
      (1) The press is the supporter of our Government.
      (2) It contains some entertaining articles.
    B. The Press in America.
      (1) It has different viewpoints.
      (2) too much advertisements can be seen.

IV Conclusion — make a complete statement.

Mass Media in America and Free China

Thesis Statement — Differences in the policy and the program make the major difference of mass media in America and Free China.

Mass Media is different from time to time and place to place. When we saw these words, "Mass Media" we thought about television and newspapers because they are the tools of the mass media. They both have great power not only in America but also in Taiwan; however, they also have differences in their policies and programs.

In Taiwan, besides the commercial purpose of the TV Company itself, the Government uses it as a tool to teach her people. You can see some programs on TV. It is provided by the Government. Its purpose is to broaden people's knowledge—such as: a program for farmers telling them about new methods about improving their Agriculture, and Programs telling people about where and how they can get help from the Government. In America, you can hardly see a program like that. The TV Programs are full of Commercialism. Old moves and

be specific: what kind of programs?

agr.

prep

NI   different kind of entertainment shows take ^ almost the whole TV programs. Even the news withdraws to the second role.

The press in Taiwan has the same power as it has in America but the former (supports) ___?___ the Government and is not controlled by some large company. You can even see novels and historical

art   stories in the Taiwan's Press. People in Taiwan see the Press not only for its news but also for its entertainment. America's Press has more viewpoints than Taiwan's;

age   however, when it conflict with its owner's benefits, it always follows the owner's will. You can't see any novels or stories in America's Press. You can notice that there are more advertisements than other categories. A lot of people ordered the press

t   just because they wanted to know when and where there is a white sale.

art   Following the Time flow, ^ Mass media becomes
NI, age more sticked with people's life. Men are impressed with what the TV and Press say. Day after day, men lost their own observations and judgements. It is time for people to express their opinions to the TV Companies and Press Companies. They have rights to

t   know what they should know not what they were told.

You have shown great improvement. Thank you.

ESL COMPOSITION PROFILE

STUDENT *Sample C*   DATE   TOPIC *Media comparison - Revision*

	SCORE	LEVEL	CRITERIA	COMMENTS
CONTENT	25	30-27	**EXCELLENT TO VERY GOOD:** knowledgeable • substantive • thorough development of thesis • relevant to assigned topic	*Good addition of specific information to support your comparison.*
		26-22	**GOOD TO AVERAGE:** some knowledge of subject • adequate range • limited development of thesis • mostly relevant to topic, but lacks detail	
		21-17	**FAIR TO POOR:** limited knowledge of subject • little substance • inadequate development of topic	
		16-13	**VERY POOR:** does not show knowledge of subject • non-substantive • not pertinent • OR not enough to evaluate	
ORGANIZATION	17	20-18	**EXCELLENT TO VERY GOOD:** fluent expression • ideas clearly stated/supported • succinct • well-organized • logical sequencing • cohesive	*Concluding paragraph helps complete the paper.*
		17-14	**GOOD TO AVERAGE:** somewhat choppy • loosely organized but main ideas stand out • limited support • logical but incomplete sequencing	
		13-10	**FAIR TO POOR:** non-fluent • ideas confused or disconnected • lacks logical sequencing and development	
		9-7	**VERY POOR:** does not communicate • no organization • OR not enough to evaluate	
VOCABULARY	16	20-18	**EXCELLENT TO VERY GOOD:** sophisticated range • effective word/idiom choice and usage • word form mastery • appropriate register	*Word choice and word form are improved — good!*
		17-14	**GOOD TO AVERAGE:** adequate range • occasional errors of word/idiom form, choice, usage *but meaning not obscured*	
		13-10	**FAIR TO POOR:** limited range • frequent errors of word/idiom form, choice, usage • *meaning confused or obscured*	
		9-7	**VERY POOR:** essentially translation • little knowledge of English vocabulary, idioms, word form • OR not enough to evaluate	
LANGUAGE USE	18	25-22	**EXCELLENT TO VERY GOOD:** effective complex constructions • few errors of agreement, tense, number, word order/function, articles, pronouns, prepositions	
		21-18	**GOOD TO AVERAGE:** effective but simple constructions • minor problems in complex constructions • several errors of agreement, tense, number word order/function, articles pronouns, prepositions *but meaning seldom obscured*	
		17-11	**FAIR TO POOR:** major problems in simple/complex constructions • frequent errors of negation, agreement, tense, number, word order/function, articles, pronouns, prepositions and/or fragments, run-ons, deletions • *meaning confused or obscured*	
		10-5	**VERY POOR:** virtually no mastery of sentence construction rules • dominated by errors • does not communicate • OR not enough to evaluate	
MECHANICS	4	5	**EXCELLENT TO VERY GOOD:** demonstrates mastery of conventions • few errors of spelling, punctuation, capitalization, paragraphing	
		4	**GOOD TO AVERAGE:** occasional errors of spelling, punctuation, capitalization, paragraphing *but meaning not obscured*	
		3	**FAIR TO POOR:** frequent errors of spelling, punctuation, capitalization, paragraphing • poor handwriting • *meaning confused or obscured*	
		2	**VERY POOR:** no mastery of conventions • dominated by errors of spelling, punctuation, capitalization, paragraphing • handwriting illegible • OR not enough to evaluate	

TOTAL SCORE   READER   COMMENTS   *You have worked hard on these papers*

80   *and your efforts show!*

THE PROGRESS TALLY

Teachers using the PROFILE to score student compositions throughout a semester can easily keep a continuous record of student progress. In addition, from the corrections and notations made on each PROFILE, they can keep a Progress Tally (shown below) for each student. The Tally is essentially a long-range chart developed from the descriptors of the PROFILE. The abbreviations in the Tally taken from the PROFILE are those used in marking students' papers and, therefore, are familiar symbols to them. The Tally provides space for notations on up to five consecutive papers so that both teachers and students are able to see, in brief, a pattern of the student's progress during a marking period.

Most teachers probably assign at least 5, and often as many as 10, papers per student per semester, and with as many as 30 or more students, few of us can readily remember specific information about so many students and their progress. A simple number in a grade book gives only a general indication of the student's progress: we may know that the grades have remained stable or improved, but we may not always remember why, that is, which composition principles a student has mastered and which particular problems are persistent. Of course, it is possible to keep a set of PROFILES for each student; however, it would be necessary to examine each one to provide feedback or make assignments to a student. Further, much more is accomplished by returning PROFILES to students so that they know the areas in which they are improving or not improving. Therefore, we suggest that a Progress Tally be marked for each student at the same time a PROFILE is marked. The few seconds that it takes to code a Tally is efficient use of time for obtaining a constant and specific record of each student's progress which *both* student and teacher can see at a glance. Such a record also allows both to discuss problems more accurately and quickly and see progress.

By having this information constantly available, a teacher is further aided in:

1. Making assignments promptly when problem areas persist.

2. Being specific in extra assignments to labs, grammar, and/or vocabulary classes.

3. Consulting meaningfully with each student.

4. Determining accurate referral: for promotion or to other English courses.

To use the Progress Tally:

1. Provide, or ask the student to provide, a manila folder in which each assignment is submitted.

2. Attach a Tally to the inside of each folder.

3. Code the information from each marked PROFILE simply and quickly onto the Tally with a plus $(+)$, a minus $(-)$, a check $(\checkmark)$, or key words describing progress or problems.

   Also note, if desired,
   a. In-class or out-of-class papers
   b. Revisions
   c. Specific complex construction problems, such as redundancies and deadwood.

MEASUREMENT AND FEEDBACK

As is apparent on the Progress Tally, the teacher has numbered the papers and made notations as to methods used to develop each paper. The (R) in the right-hand margin indicates that the paper was revised. (I-C), (O-C) tell that the paper was written either in-class or out-of-class, important information for recognizing what basic information the student has without outside assistance or revision. The teacher used $(+)$ marks to tell the student what areas of the paper were strong, $(-)$ marks to indicate what areas presented problems, and $(\checkmark)$ marks to show what particular skills were adequate. Notice also the brief comments that indicate more specific problems. *Caution:* pluses are as important as minuses in that they convey success in some areas, thus giving encouragement to students. All minuses would tend to discourage students so that they might lose their enthusiasm for the next assignment.

This example shows that the student wrote five papers in this marking period. This was actually a record of progress from the beginning of the semester to the mid-term. The first paper was a general assignment about "a recent world event." It was written in class (I-C) so the teacher could gain information about the student's strengths and

PROGRESS TALLY FOR ESL COMPOSITION PROFILE

STUDENT _____

CONTENT

	PAPER	SUBSTANTIVE	DEVELOPMENT OF THESIS	RELEVANT TO TOPIC	
Event (1-c)	1	Adequate	✓	✓	R
classif.	2	Limited	General	✓	R+
comp.	3	Limited	General	+ (good)	
defin.	4	Shows considerable improvement			
process	5	+	+	+ !	R

ORGANIZATION

PAPER	FLUENT	CLEAR	SUCCINCT	ORGANIZED	LOGICAL	COHESIVE
1	choppy					
2				Loose — Limited		
3		+	Limited	✓	✓	try opposing pattern
4	—	+	___	+	+	___
5	+	+	+	+	+	+

VOCABULARY

PAPER	RANGE	W/I CHOICE	W/I FORM	W/I USE	REGISTER
1		—	—		
2		—	—	—	
3		—	=		
4		+	+	+	+ !
5	✓	—	—		

LANGUAGE USE

PAPER	CX CON	NEG	AGR	T	#	WO/F	ART	PRO	PREP	FRAG	R-O	DEL
1	conj. - //			—	—		—		—			
2	redundant		—	—	✓		—					—
3				—			—					
4				—								—
5					—	—	—	del				

MECHANICS

PAPER	SPELLING	PUNCTUATION	CAPITALIZATION	PARAGRAPHING	HANDWRITING
1	—				
2		—			
3	—				
4	+	_____			→
5	—	—			

weaknesses and decide how best to work with this student. The next papers developed expository methods and were written outside of class. Some were revised (R).* As well as using (+), (−), and (✓), the instructor used particular key words to tell the student what needed attention ("choppy," "try opposing pattern") or to give encouragement ("shows considerable improvement"). When this student and teacher met for conference after the fifth paper, the teacher was able to tell him, "You now seem to have a firm grasp of organization methods and you develop content well. Word choice and form have improved. Now we must concentrate our efforts on correcting number and article problems by continuing to use the worksheets and tapes in the lab."

SAMPLE PAPERS

Samples (IA, B, C and IIA, B) further demonstrate how one teacher used the PROFILE to score student papers. The teacher used the Progress Tally to monitor continuous progress of the students.

The papers exhibit how the PROFILE was used in reading the papers, while the Tally for each set shows the progress two students made during a semester. The first papers for each student were written near the beginning of the semester. The last two were written near the end of that semester. Notice that one student progressed to an acceptable level of proficiency according to the established standards of this program. While the other student made progress, he will probably require further language study. In the Progress Tally accompanying Samples I and II, both students show improvement in content and organization. Sample II also shows progress in language use and vocabulary by the absence of run-on sentences and improvement in the use of articles, word choice, and word form. He clearly has progressed to a point where he can compete effectively in an academic system. Along with progress, however, the Tally clearly points up persistent problems. Sample I, for instance, still has problems with punctuation, word form, tense, and articles. The teacher will probably refer this writer to a special grammar class or to a writing lab. Without a continuous tally, these problems might have gone unnoticed.

Applying the PROFILE throughout a course as a teaching and learning aid, the instructor has automatically taught to the "test." Testing situations usually demand clarity, organization of ideas and information, and some kind of time constraints. By analyzing a model for the principles of good writing, then analyzing each component area, students are able to develop their own writing. The progress made will be at the student's own rate of development. Organization may be mastered quickly, but vocabulary and language use may progress slowly throughout the course. Using the PROFILE and Progress Tally sheet regularly will enable both the student and the instructor to see what areas need further practice and what areas have been mastered. If students have mastered the components of the PROFILE, they should be ready for the "test." They should be ready to "stand the test" of using their English successfully and effectively in a competitive, academic world.

---

*The revision process for a paper, using the PROFILE, is presented in Section 7.3.

Sample I-A

Directions: Write a short essay (one or two pages) that describes an important person from your country. You may write about any person you know about. He or she may be a person from the history of your country or someone who is living now; someone in government or politics or someone in science, literature, or art; the person may be anyone you want to tell about. You should spend a few minutes thinking about what you will write. This will help you organize your thoughts. Use an extra page to write notes or an outline about your subjects; then write your essay.

Who was AMIR ABDELKADER? If you want to khnow

~~Idiom~~ him It will be very simple. Come back to the history of Algeria and remove these hisotory's pages and you can find this great and brave man— He was a great patriot against the French colonialists — He wanted to

wf beat them, and he wanted that the ALGERIA will be

wc free, ever free. His is stucked in our brain in every

art Algerian brain, we cannot forget him and the history

art cannot. He was a little bit old when he declare the war against the frenchs. when he was young he was

art a student, he has studied in Egypt and he has used

R-O this writtey for his country—He has wrote many things

t

wc about Algeria in order to make all the citizen working together, unified. Every body khow what is the Ideas

wo of the colonialists), separate and create a war between the citezens, because this one is berbere, that one is Arabe etc—, but they were not successful — He has used and given his blood for his country all this life—he was not alone and was not last— Many and Many

prep of others came after him and have given to ALGERIA her free dom and liberty —

200

ESL COMPOSITION PROFILE

STUDENT _Sample IA_   DATE   TOPIC _Definition: identification_

	SCORE	LEVEL	CRITERIA	COMMENTS
CONTENT	22	30-27	**EXCELLENT TO VERY GOOD:** knowledgeable • substantive • thorough development of thesis • relevant to assigned topic	
		26-22	**GOOD TO AVERAGE:** some knowledge of subject • adequate range • limited development of thesis • mostly relevant to topic, but lacks detail	
		21-17	**FAIR TO POOR:** limited knowledge of subject • little substance • inadequate development of topic	
		16-13	**VERY POOR:** does not show knowledge of subject • non-substantive • not pertinent • OR not enough to evaluate	
ORGANIZATION	10	20-18	**EXCELLENT TO VERY GOOD:** fluent expression • ideas clearly stated/supported • succinct • well-organized • logical sequencing • cohesive	_effective opening statement_
		17-14	**GOOD TO AVERAGE:** somewhat choppy • loosely organized but main ideas stand out • limited support • logical but incomplete sequencing	
		13-10	**FAIR TO POOR:** non-fluent • ideas confused or disconnected • lacks logical sequencing and development	
		9-7	**VERY POOR:** does not communicate • no organization • OR not enough to evaluate	
VOCABULARY	13	20-18	**EXCELLENT TO VERY GOOD:** sophisticated range • effective word/idiom choice and usage • word form mastery • appropriate register	_Some sophisticated word use — good effort_
		17-14	**GOOD TO AVERAGE:** adequate range • occasional errors of word/idiom form, choice, usage _but meaning not obscured_	
		13-10	**FAIR TO POOR:** limited range • frequent errors of word/idiom form, choice, usage • _meaning confused or obscured_	
		9-7	**VERY POOR:** essentially translation • little knowledge of English vocabulary, idioms, word form • OR not enough to evaluate	
LANGUAGE USE	17	25-22	**EXCELLENT TO VERY GOOD:** effective complex constructions • few errors of agreement, tense, number, word order/function, articles, pronouns, prepositions	
		21-18	**GOOD TO AVERAGE:** effective but simple constructions • minor problems in complex constructions • several errors of agreement, tense, number, word order/function, articles, pronouns, prepositions _but meaning seldom obscured_	
		17-11	**FAIR TO POOR:** major problems in simple/complex constructions • frequent errors of negation, agreement, tense, number, word order/function, articles, pronouns, prepositions and/or fragments, run-ons, deletions • _meaning confused or obscured_	
		10-5	**VERY POOR:** virtually no mastery of sentence construction rules • dominated by errors • does not communicate • OR not enough to evaluate	
MECHANICS	3	5	**EXCELLENT TO VERY GOOD:** demonstrates mastery of conventions • few errors of spelling, punctuation, capitalization, paragraphing	
		4	**GOOD TO AVERAGE:** occasional errors of spelling, punctuation, capitalization, paragraphing _but meaning not obscured_	
		3	**FAIR TO POOR:** frequent errors of spelling, punctuation, capitalization, paragraphing • poor handwriting • _meaning confused or obscured_	
		2	**VERY POOR:** no mastery of conventions • dominated by errors of spelling, punctuation, capitalization, paragraphing • handwriting illegible • OR not enough to evaluate	

TOTAL SCORE   READER   COMMENTS _It is obvious that you have a strong feeling about this man, and therefore, much to say about him. Try to reorganize the ideas about him in chronological order from past to present._

65

"Women's liberation"

1 — How was the women's life in many years ago
   a) their customs
   b) Their activities

2 — Their evolution
3 — their life nowadays
   a) their rights
   b) How they can participate for the development
   of their Country.
   c) The results and the success of their participation

———

wo what was do you think the woman many years ago?
She was with the man just like animals, no
difference between them. They have the same
way of life, same lodgings — They choose a wild life.
They hunt together, live without clothes. For them
Summer and winter are the same — But year by year
day by day many things are changed, and become
better and better. The women begans to ameliorate herself.
she learns how to dresse, how to be and what to do —
t she continues to make a great progress until nowadays.
wc where she begans to be among the all. thinks to
the women's liberation this humain being has now
the same rights, her rights like any other humain
wf beings. She can be an agriculture, a teacher

a doctor--- She can do every thing that man can do - she participates gracefully and successfully for the production. She can be a white or blue colour - The Universities and schools are full now by them. Where ever you go you see those inseperable human beings, man an women, happy, loving and working together -

?, wc FINSH

wc

203

ESL COMPOSITION PROFILE

STUDENT _Sample I B_   DATE   TOPIC _Women's liberation — process_

	SCORE	LEVEL	CRITERIA	COMMENTS
CONTENT	21	30-27	**EXCELLENT TO VERY GOOD:** knowledgeable • substantive • thorough development of thesis • relevant to assigned topic	_Interesting topic! look at point 3c in your outline — Can you expand it?_
		26-22	**GOOD TO AVERAGE:** some knowledge of subject • adequate range • limited development of thesis • <u>mostly relevant to topic, but lacks detail</u>	
		21-17	**FAIR TO POOR:** limited knowledge of subject • little substance • inadequate development of topic	
		16-13	**VERY POOR:** does not show knowledge of subject • non-substantive • not pertinent • OR not enough to evaluate	
ORGANIZATION	15	20-18	**EXCELLENT TO VERY GOOD:** fluent expression • ideas clearly stated/supported • succinct • well-organized • logical sequencing • cohesive	_Some repetitions, general statements. Could you add one more time period? This would make the paper more complete._
		17-14	**GOOD TO AVERAGE:** <u>somewhat choppy</u> • loosely organized but main ideas stand out • <u>limited support</u> • <u>logical</u> but incomplete sequencing	
		13-10	**FAIR TO POOR:** non-fluent • ideas confused or disconnected • lacks logical sequencing and development	
		9-7	**VERY POOR:** does not communicate • no organization • OR not enough to evaluate	
VOCABULARY	15	20-18	**EXCELLENT TO VERY GOOD:** sophisticated range • effective word/idiom choice and usage • word form mastery • appropriate register	
		17-14	**GOOD TO AVERAGE:** adequate range • <u>occasional errors of word/idiom form</u>, choice, usage _but meaning not obscured_	
		13-10	**FAIR TO POOR:** limited range • frequent errors of word/idiom form, choice, usage • _meaning confused or obscured_	
		9-7	**VERY POOR:** essentially translation • little knowledge of English vocabulary, idioms, word form • OR not enough to evaluate	
LANGUAGE USE	15	25-22	**EXCELLENT TO VERY GOOD:** effective complex constructions • few errors of agreement, tense, number, word order/function, articles, pronouns, prepositions	
		21-18	**GOOD TO AVERAGE:** effective but simple constructions • minor problems in complex constructions • several errors of agreement, tense, number, word order/function, articles, pronouns, prepositions _but meaning seldom obscured_	
		17-11	**FAIR TO POOR:** <u>major problems in simple/complex constructions</u> • frequent errors of negation, <u>agreement, tense</u>, number, <u>word order</u>/function, articles, pronouns, prepositions and/or fragments, run-ons, deletions • _meaning confused or obscured_	
		10-5	**VERY POOR:** virtually no mastery of sentence construction rules • dominated by errors • does not communicate • OR not enough to evaluate	
MECHANICS	3	5	**EXCELLENT TO VERY GOOD:** demonstrates mastery of conventions • few errors of spelling, punctuation, capitalization, paragraphing	
		4	**GOOD TO AVERAGE:** occasional errors of spelling, punctuation, capitalization, paragraphing _but meaning not obscured_	
		3	**FAIR TO POOR:** frequent errors of spelling, punctuation, capitalization, <u>paragraphing</u> • poor handwriting • _meaning confused or obscured_	
		2	**VERY POOR:** no mastery of conventions • dominated by errors of spelling, punctuation, capitalization, paragraphing • handwriting illegible • OR not enough to evaluate	

TOTAL SCORE   READER   COMMENTS   _Your paper contains many ideas that are worth developing. Each different idea needs to be developed as its own paragraph — some information is general — work on giving each idea specific development._

69

"Constitution"

"The Outline"

1- Generality
2 - American Constitution
   a) how
   b) my opinion
3 - Algerian constitution
   a) comparaison betwen the two constitutions, American and Algerian
   b) The results

p

art

    Every country in the world has its own constitution, and every constitution has minor differences depending on the culture. Let us take two countries, Algeria and United States and compare their systems, we'll find that they don't adopt to the same philosophy. Algeria adopts the Communist ideology, and America accepts the capitalist ideology. Every one wants his nation to be strong.

    After the American colonies declared their independance from great Britain, the American government (looked forward for) one system which __can__ satisfy all the different points of view of the American society and unite the nation. Their experience under the colonist played a great part in their choice and gave them the ability to decree successful rules. __Capitalisation__ was approved by almost everybody and the constitution was accepted by all!

idiom t

wf

illogical connection

shifting tense

    The Americans __feared__ a strong central government which is divided in 3 branches, the legislative, the executive and the judicial. Some of the important powers __are__ kept by the national government and all the rest are kept by the states. All these powers are overlapped in certain ways so that no branch has the upper hand. The powers of one branch are limited by the powers of the others. No one has unlimited authority and can act and do whatever he wishes.

¶ Even the president, the head of the executive branch‸ has no power to do things without the concent of the Congress. Any suggestion he makes must be reviewed by the legislative branch and vice-versa - In

other word every branch has checks on the other.

sp   There is also an important ammendment in the American constitution‸ "The Bill of Rights" - The "bill of rights" guarantees the rights of individual

art in ‸persuit of happiness. Really, I find that American people are the only ones who have their rights and their liberties respected to a certain extent.

Our Constitution is really very different from yours. We have one political party, the socialist party which controls the country. The president of the state is the head of the army. The government is composed of

agr 18 ministers who controls and satisfy the needs of the nation. They are very close together and all of them work for the good of Algerian society.

del   Algeria got ‸independance from France in 1952 ⁎ The country under the French was very backward and

wf the new revolution army government was unstable because there were outsiders backed by the colonists who were working hard to overthrow it ⁎

t, sp So Algeria remains under Marshall law until lately in 1977, the socialist party, adopted a constitution "ADOUSTOUR" which guarantees the liberties of Algeria - The health care and educational faculties are now all provided by the government and offered to everyone. Maybe "ADOUSTOUR" is

206

getting to first base!

wf
wf   Both Constitutions look forward to satisfy the needs of individuals to _persuit_ happiness within the capabilities of the society. The American government is far ahead since it is 200 years old and has a great deal of experience and ~~has a great~~
// p relatively educated society, while Algeria has exercised liberty for less than a quarter of a century, and with its limited resources, works hard to satisfy the needs of the Algerian individual —

This is very well written. Most of the errors are in punctuation and structure.

207

ESL COMPOSITION PROFILE

STUDENT _Sample IC_   DATE _____   TOPIC _Constitution Comparison_

	SCORE	LEVEL	CRITERIA	COMMENTS
CONTENT	28	30-27	**EXCELLENT TO VERY GOOD:** knowledgeable • substantive • <u>thorough development of thesis</u> • relevant to assigned topic	_clear comparisons —_
		26-22	**GOOD TO AVERAGE:** some knowledge of subject • adequate range • limited development of thesis • mostly relevant to topic, but lacks detail	_thorough treatment —_
		21-17	**FAIR TO POOR:** limited knowledge of subject • little substance • inadequate development of topic	_fine use of specific_
		16-13	**VERY POOR:** does not show knowledge of subject • non-substantive • not pertinent • OR not enough to evaluate	_detail._
ORGANIZATION	20	20-18	**EXCELLENT TO VERY GOOD:** fluent expression • <u>ideas clearly stated/supported</u> • succinct • <u>well-organized</u> • <u>logical sequencing</u> • <u>cohesive</u>	_Organization!_
		17-14	**GOOD TO AVERAGE:** somewhat choppy • loosely organized but main ideas stand out • limited support • logical but incomplete sequencing	
		13-10	**FAIR TO POOR:** non-fluent • ideas confused or disconnected • lacks logical sequencing and development	
		9-7	**VERY POOR:** does not communicate • no organization • OR not enough to evaluate	
VOCABULARY	17	20-18	**EXCELLENT TO VERY GOOD:** sophisticated range • effective word/idiom choice and usage • word form mastery • appropriate register	
		17-14	**GOOD TO AVERAGE:** adequate range • <u>occasional errors of word/idiom form</u>, choice, usage _but meaning not obscured_	
		13-10	**FAIR TO POOR:** limited range • frequent errors of word/idiom form, choice, usage • _meaning confused or obscured_	
		9-7	**VERY POOR:** essentially translation • little knowledge of English vocabulary, idioms, word form • OR not enough to evaluate	
LANGUAGE USE	21	25-22	**EXCELLENT TO VERY GOOD:** effective complex constructions • few errors of agreement, tense, number, word order/function, articles, pronouns, prepositions	
		21-18	**GOOD TO AVERAGE:** effective but simple constructions • minor problems in complex constructions • several errors of <u>agreement</u>, <u>tense</u>, number, word order/function, articles, pronouns, prepositions _but meaning seldom obscured_	
		17-11	**FAIR TO POOR:** major problems in simple/complex constructions • frequent errors of negation, agreement, tense, number, word order/function, articles, pronouns, prepositions and/or fragments, run-ons, deletions • _meaning confused or obscured_	
		10-5	**VERY POOR:** virtually no mastery of sentence construction rules • dominated by errors • does not communicate • OR not enough to evaluate	
MECHANICS	4	5	**EXCELLENT TO VERY GOOD:** demonstrates mastery of conventions • few errors of spelling, punctuation, capitalization, paragraphing	
		4	**GOOD TO AVERAGE:** occasional errors of <u>spelling</u>, punctuation, capitalization, paragraphing _but meaning not obscured_	
		3	**FAIR TO POOR:** frequent errors of spelling, punctuation, capitalization, paragraphing • poor handwriting • _meaning confused or obscured_	
		2	**VERY POOR:** no mastery of conventions • dominated by errors of spelling, punctuation, capitalization, paragraphing • handwriting illegible • OR not enough to evaluate	

TOTAL SCORE   READER   COMMENTS _Fine paper! Smooth transition between_

90

discussion of the United States and Algeria. The paper has some word form problems — let's work on those next.

PROGRESS TALLY FOR ESL COMPOSITION PROFILE

STUDENT   _Sample I_

CONTENT

PAPER	SUBSTANTIVE	DEVELOPMENT OF THESIS	RELEVANT TO TOPIC
I A		Limited	ok – but general
I B		— choppy —	
I C	+	improved	good

ORGANIZATION

PAPER	FLUENT	CLEAR	SUCCINCT	ORGANIZED	LOGICAL	COHESIVE
A	effective opening			loose		
B	poor —					
C	+	shows marked improvement —				

VOCABULARY

PAPER	RANGE	W/I CHOICE	W/I FORM	W/I USE	REGISTER
A		—	—	some sophisticated word choices	
B	· low	—	—	—	low
C	✓+	✓	— (however, improved)		✓+

LANGUAGE USE

PAPER	CX CON	NEG	AGR	T	#	WO/F	ART	PRO	PREP	FRAG	R-O	DEL
A				—	—		—		—		—	
B				—			—				—	
C	✓	✓	—	—	—	✓	—	✓	✓	✓	✓	✓

MECHANICS

PAPER	SPELLING	PUNCTUATION	CAPITALIZATION	PARAGRAPHING	HANDWRITING
A	—	—	—	—	
B		—		—	
C	—	—	✓	improved	✓

How will you most affect your own country
When you return.

My country, Taiwan (Republic of China), has
wf — Sustantly suffered from the rapid economic growthing
art — for ^ past twenty years. Taking ^ transportation system,
for example, the used transportation network can
wf — no longer meets the increasing transportation demands.

In view of the situation stated above, the government
art — and the people of ^ Republic of China have devoted
themselves to the "Ten Major Projects", which will be
regarded as an initial step to solve all of
wf — problems caused by rapid growthing.

Among the "Ten Major projects", six of them are
sp — transportation projects, including Hiqways, Railroad,
airport, harbors, and railway electrification. All these
wo — projects need people of my major, namely, transportation
urgently

R-O

engineering, and as I said before, it's only an
initial step to solve the problems. So, after my graduation
I planned to go back to Taiwan (and devote my
knowledge and technologies, which will be "New" over
there, to my own country.

210

ESL COMPOSITION PROFILE

STUDENT _Sample II a_   DATE   TOPIC _Country return — cause effect_

	SCORE	LEVEL	CRITERIA	COMMENTS
CONTENT	20	30-27	**EXCELLENT TO VERY GOOD:** knowledgeable • substantive • thorough development of thesis • relevant to assigned topic	_I know that you can tell me a great deal about the transportation project — why not talk about it in the next paper?_
		26-22	**GOOD TO AVERAGE:** some knowledge of subject • adequate range • limited development of thesis • mostly relevant to topic, but lacks detail	
		21-17	**FAIR TO POOR:** limited knowledge of subject • little substance • inadequate development of topic	
		16-13	**VERY POOR:** does not show knowledge of subject • non-substantive • not pertinent • OR not enough to evaluate	
ORGANIZATION	15	20-18	**EXCELLENT TO VERY GOOD:** fluent expression • ideas clearly stated/supported • succinct • well-organized • logical sequencing • cohesive	
		17-14	**GOOD TO AVERAGE:** somewhat choppy • loosely organized but main ideas stand out • limited support • logical but incomplete sequencing	
		13-10	**FAIR TO POOR:** non-fluent • ideas confused or disconnected • lacks logical sequencing and development	
		9-7	**VERY POOR:** does not communicate • no organization • OR not enough to evaluate	
VOCABULARY	15	20-18	**EXCELLENT TO VERY GOOD:** sophisticated range • effective word/idiom choice and usage • word form mastery • appropriate register	
		17-14	**GOOD TO AVERAGE:** adequate range • occasional errors of word/idiom form, choice, usage _but meaning not obscured_	
		13-10	**FAIR TO POOR:** limited range • frequent errors of word/idiom form, choice, usage • _meaning confused or obscured_	
		9-7	**VERY POOR:** essentially translation • little knowledge of English vocabulary, idioms, word form • OR not enough to evaluate	
LANGUAGE USE	17	25-22	**EXCELLENT TO VERY GOOD:** effective complex constructions • few errors of agreement, tense, number, word order/function, articles, pronouns, prepositions	
		21-18	**GOOD TO AVERAGE:** effective but simple constructions • minor problems in complex constructions • several errors of agreement, tense, number, word order/function, articles, pronouns, prepositions _but meaning seldom obscured_	
		17-11	**FAIR TO POOR:** major problems in simple/complex constructions • frequent errors of negation, agreement, tense, number, word order/function, articles, pronouns, prepositions and/or fragments, run-ons, deletions • _meaning confused or obscured_	
		10-5	**VERY POOR:** virtually no mastery of sentence construction rules • dominated by errors • does not communicate • OR not enough to evaluate	
MECHANICS	3	5	**EXCELLENT TO VERY GOOD:** demonstrates mastery of conventions • few errors of spelling, punctuation, capitalization, paragraphing	
		4	**GOOD TO AVERAGE:** occasional errors of spelling, punctuation, capitalization, paragraphing _but meaning not obscured_	
		3	**FAIR TO POOR:** frequent errors of spelling, punctuation, capitalization, paragraphing • poor handwriting • _meaning confused or obscured_	
		2	**VERY POOR:** no mastery of conventions • dominated by errors of spelling, punctuation, capitalization, paragraphing • handwriting illegible • OR not enough to evaluate	

TOTAL SCORE   READER   COMMENTS

70

Deciding To Get Married

There are a lot of reasons for people to get married. Among all these, two major factors should be considered carefully before making the final decision.

One of them is, of course, _love_. If one ~~don't~~ doesn't ~~really~~ know, although it is hard to define literally, what love really means. Then, just forget it. For people can't get married until they love each other.

dangling clause

del
wc
art
sp

Another important factor should be thought of is the practical _case_, bread. Any family should be based on^sufficient financial foundation. Otherwise, they will face the cruel world befor_ long.

R-O

At last, I want to emphasize again that love and bread are the two legs of the family _, no one could afford to lose any of them, or one will fall down and ~~be hurten badly hurt too~~ get hurt seriously.

ESL COMPOSITION PROFILE

STUDENT *Sample II b* DATE TOPIC *Marriage —argument*

	SCORE	LEVEL	CRITERIA	COMMENTS
CONTENT	19	30-27	**EXCELLENT TO VERY GOOD:** knowledgeable • substantive • thorough development of thesis • relevant to assigned topic	*Topic sentences are suitable, need to be supported with more detail. For what reasons do people marry? Are they the same in each country?*
		26-22	**GOOD TO AVERAGE:** some knowledge of subject • adequate range • limited development of thesis • mostly relevant to topic, but lacks detail	
		21-17	**FAIR TO POOR:** limited knowledge of subject • little substance • inadequate development of topic	
		16-13	**VERY POOR:** does not show knowledge of subject • non-substantive • not pertinent • OR not enough to evaluate	
ORGANIZATION	14	20-18	**EXCELLENT TO VERY GOOD:** fluent expression • ideas clearly stated/supported • succinct • well-organized • logical sequencing • cohesive	
		17-14	**GOOD TO AVERAGE:** somewhat choppy • loosely organized but main ideas stand out • limited support • logical but incomplete sequencing	
		13-10	**FAIR TO POOR:** non-fluent • ideas confused or disconnected • lacks logical sequencing and development	
		9-7	**VERY POOR:** does not communicate • no organization • OR not enough to evaluate	
VOCABULARY	16	20-18	**EXCELLENT TO VERY GOOD:** sophisticated range • effective word/idiom choice and usage • word form mastery • appropriate register	*Shift from formal to informal is a bit abrupt.*
		17-14	**GOOD TO AVERAGE:** adequate range • occasional errors of word/idiom form, choice, usage *but meaning not obscured*	
		13-10	**FAIR TO POOR:** limited range • frequent errors of word/idiom form, choice, usage • *meaning confused or obscured*	
		9-7	**VERY POOR:** essentially translation • little knowledge of English vocabulary, idioms, word form • OR not enough to evaluate	
LANGUAGE USE	16	25-22	**EXCELLENT TO VERY GOOD:** effective complex constructions • few errors of agreement, tense, number, word order/function, articles, pronouns, prepositions	*Review use of compound sentences, introductory dependent clauses, use of modifiers.*
		21-18	**GOOD TO AVERAGE:** effective but simple constructions • minor problems in complex constructions • several errors of agreement, tense, number, word order/function, articles, pronouns, prepositions *but meaning seldom obscured*	
		17-11	**FAIR TO POOR:** major problems in simple/complex constructions • frequent errors of negation, agreement, tense, number, word order/function, articles, pronouns, prepositions and/or fragments, run-ons, deletions • *meaning confused or obscured*	
		10-5	**VERY POOR:** virtually no mastery of sentence construction rules • dominated by errors • does not communicate • OR not enough to evaluate	
MECHANICS	4	5	**EXCELLENT TO VERY GOOD:** demonstrates mastery of conventions • few errors of spelling, punctuation, capitalization, paragraphing	*Review —use of comma and semi-colon.*
		4	**GOOD TO AVERAGE:** occasional errors of spelling, punctuation, capitalization, paragraphing *but meaning not obscured*	
		3	**FAIR TO POOR:** frequent errors of spelling, punctuation, capitalization, paragraphing • poor handwriting • *meaning confused or obscured*	
		2	**VERY POOR:** no mastery of conventions • dominated by errors of spelling, punctuation, capitalization, paragraphing • handwriting illegible • OR not enough to evaluate	

TOTAL SCORE   READER   COMMENTS *Good analogy in the conclusion. Topic could be developed more completely —provide detailed illustrations —can you compare attitudes toward marriage in different countries, at different ages?*

69

continued

213

Suggestions:

Needs to work on:

① *specific content — provide illustrations, examples, comparisons to prove major points. Begin by clearly stating your topic sentences — then prove them.*

② *look at word form: are you using the word correctly? — adj., adv., noun, verb, etc.? Choose words carefully to provide more precise meaning. Work on using a thesaurus and dictionary together to solve these problems.*

③ *language use — review use of compound sentences, introductory dependent clauses, use of modifiers, avoiding fragments and tense agreement.*

④ *Punctuation — study: use of comma, semi-colon*

BETTER TRANSPORTATION FOR YOUR CITY!

The daily movement of people and goods in urban areas has become one of the most complex and difficult problems. Experience has demonstrated that piecemeal efforts are not the answer. Only decisive action, comprehensive transportation planning, can stem the rising tide of traffic congestion, confusion, and accidents threatening the economic and social health of our communities. A successive comprehensive transportation planning process cannot result from single-purpose studies. It is a rather complicated system, nevertheless there exists a common basic approach which can be applied to all forms of transportation planning, whether planning for a city, or planning for a specific new transport facility, such as a new airport, road or rail improvement scheme. In all cases the process may be divided into three distinct but orderly phases: a survey, analysis and model building phase; a forcasting phase; and an evaluation phase.

214

At the survey, analysis and model building stage, two
important questions must be answered. First, what is the existing
travel demand, and secondly, how is this demand satisfied on the
existing transport facilities? The data collected in the surveys
contains the information on existing travel demand and pattern.
Analysis of this mass of data provides an understanding of the
relationship between travel pattern and the urban environment.
This understanding enables models to be built of these relationships which can then be used in the forcasting phase.

The forecasting stage uses the relationships in the analysis
and model building stage to make estimates of the future travel
demand and pattern. As such, it requires information on the
population, the existing transport facilities, economic conditions
and the land use pattern. According to the forecasting data of
travel demand and pattern for the design year, the suitable
policies and arrangements of transport facilities or networks can
be selected.

The final step, namely the evaluation stage, is actually a
feedback step. It assesses the results of the two previous
phases to see whether they satisfied the pre-determined social,
economic, environmental and operational objectives. If it is not,
the different assumptions will be made in the model building
stage to run the program(process) until the evaluation satisfied.

Following this process of transportation planning, the city
should be able to develop a better transportation system which
will enable people and goods to travel safely and economically.
In addition, the journeys will also be comfortable and convenient.

Well done! Shows marked improvement.

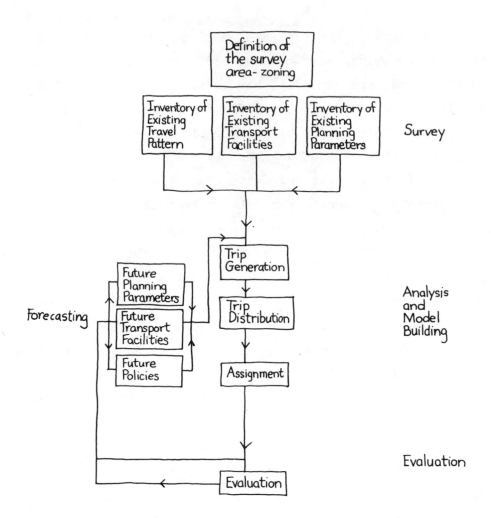

FLOW CHART OF TRANSPORTATION PLANNING PROCESS

ESL COMPOSITION PROFILE

STUDENT _Sample II C_   DATE   TOPIC _Transportation — argument — process_

	SCORE	LEVEL	CRITERIA	COMMENTS
CONTENT	27	30-27	**EXCELLENT TO VERY GOOD:** knowledgeable • substantive • thorough development of thesis • relevant to assigned topic	_Including specific data sources would strengthen your position —_
		26-22	**GOOD TO AVERAGE:** some knowledge of subject • adequate range • limited development of thesis • mostly relevant to topic, but lacks detail	
		21-17	**FAIR TO POOR:** limited knowledge of subject • little substance • inadequate development of topic	
		16-13	**VERY POOR:** does not show knowledge of subject • non-substantive • not pertinent • OR not enough to evaluate	
ORGANIZATION	20	20-18	**EXCELLENT TO VERY GOOD:** fluent expression • ideas clearly stated/supported • succinct • well-organized • logical sequencing • cohesive	_Well done!_
		17-14	**GOOD TO AVERAGE:** somewhat choppy • loosely organized but main ideas stand out • limited support • logical but incomplete sequencing	
		13-10	**FAIR TO POOR:** non-fluent • ideas confused or disconnected • lacks logical sequencing and development	
		9-7	**VERY POOR:** does not communicate • no organization • OR not enough to evaluate	
VOCABULARY	18	20-18	**EXCELLENT TO VERY GOOD:** sophisticated range • effective word/idiom choice and usage • word form mastery • appropriate register	
		17-14	**GOOD TO AVERAGE:** adequate range • occasional errors of word/idiom form, choice, usage _but meaning not obscured_	
		13-10	**FAIR TO POOR:** limited range • frequent errors of word/idiom form, choice, usage • _meaning confused or obscured_	
		9-7	**VERY POOR:** essentially translation • little knowledge of English vocabulary, idioms, word form • OR not enough to evaluate	
LANGUAGE USE	22	25-22	**EXCELLENT TO VERY GOOD:** effective complex constructions • few errors of agreement, tense, number, word order/function, articles, pronouns, prepositions	
		21-18	**GOOD TO AVERAGE:** effective but simple constructions • minor problems in complex constructions • several errors of agreement, tense, number, word order/function, articles, pronouns, prepositions _but meaning seldom obscured_	
		17-11	**FAIR TO POOR:** major problems in simple/complex constructions • frequent errors of negation, agreement, tense, number, word order/function, articles, pronouns, prepositions and/or fragments, run-ons, deletions • _meaning confused or obscured_	
		10-5	**VERY POOR:** virtually no mastery of sentence construction rules • dominated by errors • does not communicate • OR not enough to evaluate	
MECHANICS	5	5	**EXCELLENT TO VERY GOOD:** demonstrates mastery of conventions • few errors of spelling, punctuation, capitalization, paragraphing	
		4	**GOOD TO AVERAGE:** occasional errors of spelling, punctuation, capitalization, paragraphing _but meaning not obscured_	
		3	**FAIR TO POOR:** frequent errors of spelling, punctuation, capitalization, paragraphing • poor handwriting • _meaning confused or obscured_	
		2	**VERY POOR:** no mastery of conventions • dominated by errors of spelling, punctuation, capitalization, paragraphing • handwriting illegible • OR not enough to evaluate	

TOTAL SCORE   READER   COMMENTS   _This paper is well conceived and well written. Give your readers some additional specific data — it's an interesting topic!_

92

PROGRESS TALLY FOR ESL COMPOSITION PROFILE

STUDENT   _Sample II_

CONTENT

	PAPER	SUBSTANTIVE	DEVELOPMENT OF THESIS	RELEVANT TO TOPIC
(i-c)	IIA	no	little or no development	
(o-c)	IIB	—	weak	?
(o-c)	IIC	+	+	+

ORGANIZATION

PAPER	FLUENT	CLEAR	SUCCINCT	ORGANIZED	LOGICAL	COHESIVE	
A	—	red		introduction weak			
B	ok					→	R
C	+					→	

VOCABULARY

PAPER	RANGE	W/I CHOICE	W/I FORM	W/I USE	REGISTER
A		—	—	—	
B		—	—		
C	ok				→

LANGUAGE USE

PAPER	CX CON	NEG	AGR	T	#	WO/F	ART	PRO	PREP	FRAG	R-O	DEL
A	✓						—				—	
B	✓			—		—	—				—	
C	✓						ok Improved	—			ok Improved	

MECHANICS

PAPER	SPELLING	PUNCTUATION	CAPITALIZATION	PARAGRAPHING	HANDWRITING
A		—			
B	—	—			
C	✓	—	✓	✓	✓

CHAPTER EIGHT

IMPLEMENTING WRITING ACTIVITIES

Every individual has an individual learning style and a different rate of learning. Activities in the classroom should take these different modalities into consideration.

Mary Finocchiaro

Throughout this text we have presented writing as a creative process; we have discussed various cycles of that process from invention to shaping; we have examined the principles upon which form and structure are based; and we have offered the PROFILE and its criteria as a workable method for learning and applying those principles, for evaluating papers, and for establishing a writing program.

While a particular classroom situation, the makeup of a class, and a teacher's own imagination will largely determine how he or she will implement these ideas, in this chapter we offer some practical and effective suggestions for stimulating writing, teaching principles, and using the PROFILE for analysis, evaluation, and shaping in writing activities.

Throughout and at the end of each assignment or study unit, teachers should ask their students to write, revise, and rewrite—sentences, paragraphs, whole compositions. With each writing exercise, focus attention on the descriptors and the criteria of the PROFILE which apply to the particular assignment.*

---

*Although these assignments have been developed for intermediate to advanced level students, you can easily select from them or adapt them for use at beginning levels using the PROFILE forms B and C located in Appendix B.

8.1 Finding out where to begin

Before teachers jump into assignments, they first need to *find out where the students are in their writing development and begin there*, where the students are. Diagnose students' abilities and needs by taking a *writing history* for each; that is, obtain information about students' past writing experience. For example, we usually begin each new class with personal introductions and by asking students to provide the following information for us on an index card (see the box at right).

Further diagnosis of students' abilities can be made by taking a *writing sample* and evaluating it with the PROFILE to determine specific rhetorical, linguistic, and mechanical needs (see Chapter 6).

1. What writing experiences have you had previously?
   in your native language?
   in English?

2. How often have you written?

3. What kinds of writing have you done?
   letters   reports
   exams   other?
   publications

4. Who did you write for and why?

5. Did you enjoy or dislike writing? Why?

We have also found it extremely helpful to introduce students, early in the semester, to the writing criteria they will be using. Therefore, we use a series of assignments which introduce the PRO-FILE and its criteria to the students. See the description of how we introduce the PROFILE to the class in Chapter 7.

8.2 How to avoid teaching technique or form as an end in itself

Presenting all forms and techniques, and how they can most effectively develop a piece of writing, early in the semester prevents basing all succeeding assignments on a specific technique and allows students themselves to develop an intuition about what will work for a specific purpose. They must, however, know the techniques so that they can draw on them when they need to. Further, students will discover that purpose, as the focus for writing, will often, in fact almost always, determine the form of the piece. In addition, they will also find that the forms overlap each other and several will be used together to develop a piece of writing. If a student or students are having trouble grasping the use of one or another of the techniques, an assignment can be made which will help them practice that particular form.

8.3 About assignments

What to assign is sometimes a problem for an experienced teacher and often a problem for a new teacher. The suggestions included in this chapter are some of the kinds of assignments that have worked for us. We think that, as often as possible, students should be encouraged to write about subjects in which they are interested or have a concern or a conflict. It is not necessary that all of the students' papers be written about the same subject. In fact, it is usually more interesting for a teacher to read about a variety of things when evaluating and coaching student-writers. And, after all, writers are not competing with each other but rather are working for development of their own expression and communicative ability.

Teachers can present and encourage the use of several or specific heuristics in order to guide that development and help students find their own interests. For instance, a student can work through all these heuristics in developing one paper: listing, brain patterns (sometimes two or more), working outlines, and questions (see Chapter 4).

It may be useful, however, at the beginning of a period of peer evaluation to assign single subjects to a class to demonstrate what to look for in a piece of writing and to illustrate the varied approaches which can be taken with the same topic. Exciting and stimulating discussions often occur when students from a number of different cultures discuss their differing points of view concerning a particular topic. Another valid reason for assigning the same subject to a whole class is for purposes of testing. In either case, the assignment should be made very clear and should involve the solution to a problem, the taking of a position on an issue, or the student's perception of an event or issue so that students will become interested and involved in the writing task.

Further, teachers should provide opportunities for students to read and review the writing of others—to see how other writers write and to give them practice in analyzing writers' purpose, audience, form used for accomplishing a purpose, and how closely writing criteria were followed.

Encourage students to draw on their own experiences as often as possible, and when making specific assignments for discussion or writing, attempt to use universals. Below are some suggested topics which might be helpful in getting a class started.

220

ASSIGNMENTS

Suggested topics for discussion and composition:

- Foreign Travel
- Foods in a New Environment
- Sports
- Comparison of Family Customs
- Loneliness
- Nuclear Energy
- The United Nations
- Power of the Press
- Qualities of a Good Leader
- World Food Supply
- The Olympics
- Cultural Differences
- The Local Transportation System

Or something more general which can be taken in any direction the student wants to go:

- Law
- Time
- Money
- Love
- Power
- Environment
- Friendship

In making writing assignments, it is important that teachers analyze what students need to accomplish with each writing task and frame the assignment carefully and clearly to assure that that need is met. If students need practice, for instance, with specific rhetorical forms or transitions, the assignment can be designed so that those forms or structures automatically evolve. For example,

Assignment:

You are an international student at XYZ University. Your country distributes a handbook to students who go abroad to study. You have been asked to write an article about the registration procedures at the university you are attending. Discuss how and what a student must do to complete registration most efficiently. Spell out the steps that should be taken from beginning to end. Be sure to include any potential problems and how you would advise another student to handle them.

To complete this assignment, students would need to write using the rules and guidelines of process explanation, as well as the transitional words and phrases which make it flow smoothly. Further, students would be writing from experiences they have actually had, as well as writing for a specific purpose and audience.

Perhaps more important than anything else, is the introduction of *invention heuristics*, the idea of *audience awareness* and *establishing a purpose* (see Chapter 4). The following assignments are suggestions for using a combination of what we have discussed to this point.

8.4 Invention assignments

8.4.1 Invent a subject

Assignment:

Engage students in a brainstorming session about a subject of general interest (power, population, etc.). Encourage students to jot down notes about all points of the discussion, both main ideas and specific facts and examples; then apply one of the other heuristics from the list in Chapter 4 to develop their ideas. Next ask students to arrange those ideas in a diagram or outline form (see examples in Chapter 5) in order to begin the development of a paper. Then they should check it with the Organization criteria of the PROFILE.

Assignment:

Ask students to write a journal about whatever they want to record each day of the week. They may want to write about how they feel, relate information about their countries or customs (such as holidays), or talk about what they have observed in this country. They submit the journals once each week to the teacher, who reads but never grades them (except for occasional marks for corrections) and then returns them. The most important thing is for the teacher to respond to the *content* of the journal, to say things like, "I got your message, I understand."

Assignment:

At the beginning of each class period, ask students to write for 10 minutes on a "given" subject, e.g., "I believe . . . ," "The solution to the local water pollution problem is . . . ," or a response to a newspaper editorial.

Assignment:

Ask students to view a subject from different perspectives. Use a series of three pictures in which the content is the same but the focus is different. For instance, an important building, a country scene, or a group of people can be viewed (1) from the air or from a distance, (2) from a closer distance so that features are distinguishable, (3) with the focus *on one part* of the composite picture. Students can write about all three views or choose one perspective from which to write. Students should then share and compare their perspectives with those of the rest of the class.

Assignment:

Draw a picture on the blackboard and ask students to write their reactions to it. Then they should compare notes with each other.

Assignment:

Pair students for introductions. Ask them to interview each other to find out interesting facts about the other and to jot down enough information so that they can introduce their partners to the class. Analyze what kinds of questions were required to gain information. (This works best with small groups.)

Students seem to learn to write better in an atmosphere of warmth and approval. Thus, rapport with the students might be established by offering the question of the day.

Assignment: Question of the Day.

Go around the room, asking each student to respond with one sentence. (If the student can't think of anything, pass him or her by but give an opportunity to respond at the end.)

You might ask such questions as:

1. What is your favorite color and why?

2. What would you do if you could be king of the world for one hour?

3. If you had a choice, where would you be now?

4. What books have you read lately that have had an influence on you?

8.4.2 Identify audience/develop audience awareness

Assignment: Picturing

Bring a number of pictures to class—scenery, family scenes, animals, etc. Number each picture for identification. Ask each member of the class to select a picture and describe it in a paragraph. Then hand the description, without the picture, to another member of the class. Ask the students with the description to draw the picture. Now compare the student drawing with the original picture.

Assignment: Drawing for communication (this assignment takes about 30 minutes).

Preparation:
Prepare two sets of index cards. Cover the cards in Set 1 with meaningless scribbles. Prepare enough so that half of the class will receive a different scribble. On Set 2, draw simple recognizable objects in some kind of order. Prepare enough so that the other half of the class will receive a different card.

Example of Set 1

Example of Set 2

INTRODUCTION:

Discuss the following questions with your class:

1. What is communication?

2. How do we communicate? Discuss several different types of communication. Discuss the strengths and problems with each type of communication mentioned.

2. What are the things that we need to consider when we communicate by writing?

EXERCISE:

Divide the class into pairs of students, sitting back to back. Instruct them that they are not to look at the partner, touch the partner, or look at anything the partner is doing. Designate one member of each pair as the instruction giver and one as the recorder.

INSTRUCTION GIVER:

1. Give each instruction giver one card from Set 1.

2. Ask the instruction giver to describe the picture on the card so that the partner can draw it.

3. Ask the instruction giver not to look at what the partner is drawing.

RECORDER:

1. Give each recorder a blank index card and a pencil.

2. Ask the recorder not to speak at all—no questions, no asking for clarification or repetition.

3. Ask the recorder not to look at the card the partner is describing.

Give them 5 to 10 minutes for this part of the exercise. When they finish this part, they may compare the drawing with the card from Set 1. Now have the partners switch sides. The instruction giver now describes a card from Set 2. Follow the set of instructions for Set 2.

CONCLUSION:

Discuss the following questions in class:

1. Which set of cards was easier to work with? Why?

2. Was it easier to give instructions or to receive instructions? Why?

3. How does this exercise relate to writing? (Ask several students to explain this.)

4. Did anything about this exercise surprise you? What?

5. Ask your students to complete the following sentence: Communication is . . . . Writers should discover that communication means defining and describing specifically and accurately, relating the unfamiliar to the familiar and explaining "how to" do a particular task.

Assignment: Describe My Last Party

Write a paragraph describing the last party that you went to. Write the paragraph five different times to any five of the people listed below:

1. Your best friend

2. Your girl/boy friend (or wife/husband)

3. Your little sister (brother)

4. Your mother

5. One of your high school teachers

6. Your religious leader

7. Your roommate (who missed the party)

8. A friend whom you are trying to talk into giving a party

9. Your father

10. A stranger

Assignment: Know Your Audience!

The president of your college or university has called you to ask you to introduce an important person from your country to the student body in a special meeting on international relations. This important person (Secretary of Education, a member of the government of your country, or a diplomat) is not a stranger to you. This person has visited your family on occasion; so you have some information that is personal as well as official. Write a 5-minute introduction to this person.

Consider:

What will the student body want to know about this person?

Is there some personal story with which you could begin your speech so that the students can identify with this person?

What are the outstanding characteristics of this important person? List achievements, qualifications, and background.

Assignment: See how your audience changes!

Write a short letter to each of the following people:

The president of your college or university—tell the president about the most difficult problem international students have on your campus.

The family of your roommate who has invited you home for the Christmas vacation—explain to them some customs of your country which will enable them to know you better.

Your best friend in America—write about the best thing that has happened to you since you have been in the United States.

Consider:

Did your writing change as you changed audience?

Think of some reasons why writing might change as the audience changes.

Which letter was easiest to write?

Which letter was most difficult to write?

Assignment: Persuade your audience!

Write a debate. Work in triads, with one student taking the *pro* position, one the *con* position, and the third the role of the judge. After each person writes up a position, they exchange positions and the judge evaluates each. Then the pro and con writers prepare successive rounds of written rebuttals. (This exercise could be somewhat time-consuming, but it is excellent practice for advanced students in analyzing audience, persuasion techniques, evaluation, and revision.)

8.4.3 Establishing a purpose

Assignment:

Gather several pieces of writing, either current or classic or both, and have students determine and discuss:

Who wrote each piece

Why it was written

To whom it was written

Whether it communicated successfully and why

(A teacher could use "Of Studies" or "Food" in Chapter 5.)

Assignment:

Ask students to bring to class articles of interest to them. Make dittos or xeroxed copies for the class

so the *purpose, audience,* and *communicative success* of each can be discussed. Students will gain new perspectives about how others react to what interested them.

Assignment:

From one of the 10-minute writings that students have done at the beginning of class, ask each student to find the main idea in that piece of writing and use it as a subject for a new piece of writing. Repeat this procedure again and then ask students to write a tentative thesis statement based on what they have created.

8.5 Shaping assignments

8.5.1 To focus on organization and content

Assignment:

Using information culled from the previous assignment, have the students create a diagram, developing a thesis statement. When the diagram is completed, ask them to write a sentence outline including (1) a thesis statement, (2) three topic sentences, and (3) a conclusion. Check the *Organization* criteria of the PROFILE. Does the outline meet the criteria?

Assignment:

Using the diagram, then the sentence outline, have students develop supporting points such as facts, examples, and incidents for each topic sentence. Encourage them to include at least three specific points for each topic sentence if they can.

Assignment:

Using a heuristic for discovering audience (Chapter 4), ask students to write a description of the audience they expect to read their papers.

Assignment:

Now have students write an introductory paragraph with that audience in mind. Ask them to use a specific technique to gain reader interest and include their thesis statement in the paragraph.

Assignment:

Have students write three paragraphs which will make up the body of the paper, developing the topic sentences and supporting ideas from their outlines. They should then check each paragraph with each component of the PROFILE and the criteria one at a time.

Have your students write a concluding paragraph and then follow the same procedures as above for checking this paragraph with the PROFILE.

8.5.2 To focus on revision: analysis

Assignment:

Have students proofread the completed paper, revise it to include transitional words appropriate to the subject, and check the revision for accuracy of word form and vocabulary appropriate to their audiences.

Assignment:

Put a completed essay on a transparency and ask the class to read it together and discuss what they thought was successful in the paper. What did they understand from it? How do they think it could be improved? Ask them to evaluate it with a PROFILE to determine what should be *revised* in it.

Assignment:

Again using an overhead projector, show the class how a completed paper developed from the original heuristic, through the rough note stage, the outline stage, the first draft, to the final revision. Compare it with a paper which was written with little or no preparation.

8.5.3 To focus on form and organization

Assignment:

Using the rhetorical patterns in Chapter 5, have students analyze various pieces of writing: editorials, magazine articles, textbooks, etc., to determine how the author of each developed that piece of writing.

Assignment:

Ask the members of the class to read each other's completed papers and discuss what they understood or did not understand. If the reader misinterpreted the writer's point, the writer should explain what was meant and rewrite accordingly. Ask students to use the invention and organization processes mentioned earlier to organize the material they have developed from a different point of view, using specific methods of development, such as:

1. Classification: Give students three general terms such as sports, plants, music. Ask them to create specific categories for each term which will serve to define and distinguish each term more completely. Finally, have students choose one of the terms and diagram and outline it.

2. Comparison/Contrast: Take similar objects such as seashells, fruits, or tools to class; ask your class to distinguish similarities and differences and then diagram, outline, and write. Have students determine whether the opposing or alternating method will be more successful.

VARIATION:

Bring two different kinds of the same appliance, a conventional electric popcorn maker/an air popcorn maker, pop-up toaster/oven toaster, coffee pot/coffee maker. Again demonstrate the use of both. Ask the students to compare/contrast the process.

Assignment:

3. Process: Provide some background information and perform an actual process such as making a pot of coffee for your students. Ask them to take notes as the process is performed, then write what they have observed. In a class discussion of the paragraphs, determine whether all important steps are included and whether they are in the proper or logical order. (Serve the coffee and some cakes to the class while they write. They will love it!)

VARIATION:

The students might enjoy working out a *process* for making a banana split. Let each student be responsible for bringing one of the ingredients, utensils, etc., and construct banana splits for the class.

4. Cause/Effect: Set up a classroom drama which illustrates the cause-effect principle— a film or a role-play situation. Ask students to observe and write about the situation, using transitional words appropriate to the method.

5. Argument: Use a subject, such as nuclear disarmament, that lends itself to discussion by all members of the class. You might choose a recent news article for this assignment and ask students to agree or disagree with it. Have students develop oral arguments for both positions and stage a mini-debate in the classroom. Then ask them to write papers presenting their position, (1) making sure that they can support their position with concrete and logical facts or examples, and (2) taking into account their opponent's views.

VARIATION:

Have students themselves determine the subject for debate. The teacher lists on the board the suggestions the students make as to what they think are the most vital and important issues. Some suggestions will overlap; therefore, the teacher can help the class group related issues and determine which one issue is of interest to most of the class. Students then defend orally and in writing one position or the other in regard to the issue they have identified.

8.5.4 To focus on logical ordering

Assignment: Spatial order:

Group students into pairs. Ask each member of the pair to describe some place in the building (this works best if the building is large) to the partner. Ask the partner to leave the classroom to find that place.

When the partners return, they must make some comment about the place to their partner to prove that they have been to the place. (In describing the place, do not use the name of the place. For example, do not say the third floor men's restroom. Instead, send the partner to the left wing of the

227

building, third floor, fourth door on east side of hall. The person finding the room will respond that it was the men's room.)

Assignment: Chronological order, order of importance:

To help students learn the English direct-line method of organization, have students list all ideas related to a subject in a series of sentences. They then "cut and paste," or rearrange parts of their own sentences (or teacher-made materials) to achieve a better ordering of information. The scrambled list of ideas that follows was compiled by a student during the invention process for a paper on the "Textile Industry in Hong Kong." The second listing shows how he was able to order these ideas into a logical grouping, creating the basis for an acceptable paper.

1. In the knitting sector, exports of fabrics registered a sharp increase of 100 percent in 1972.

2. At the end of 1975, Hong Kong replaced Italy as the world's leading exporter of clothing.

3. There are three types of industrial training.

4. The direction of Hong Kong's export trade is influenced by economic conditions and commercial policies in principal markets.

5. There are two major colleges: Hong Kong Technical College and Morrison Hill Technical Institute.

6. The spinning mills, operating some 925,000 spindles, are among the most modern in the world.

7. The textile industry not only dominates Hong Kong's economy, but is also a significant factor in international trade in textiles.

8. Another 25,000 study in prevocational schools.

9. Hong Kong continues to participate in the Cotton Textiles Arrangement (CTA), which aims not only at increasing export possibilities, but also at avoiding disruptive conditions in import markets.

10. In sum, there seems little reason to apprehend great difficulty for Hong Kong in maintaining the exports on which it now lives though the task of developing multi-industry requires great progress.

11. The weaving sector, with 25,000 looms, produces fabrics of various fibers and blends.

12. Under CTA Hong Kong has entered into a number of agreements with governments of developed countries.

13. Firm-subordinate technical schools provide the specific training in certain fields.

14. The manufacture of clothing continues to be the largest sector of the textile industry, with over 200,000 workers, and producing a wide variety of high-quality items.

15. In spite of the restrictions in export on the textile industries, Hong Kong's export of clothing is steadily increasing.

This is the diagram that developed from the student's random list.

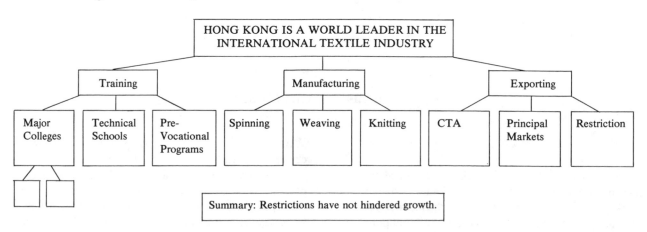

228

The second list shows the writer's success in ordering the material into a logical grouping which became the outline for an effective paper.

Introduction

    1. At the end of 1975, Hong Kong replaced Italy as the world's leading exporter of clothing.

    2. The textile industry not only dominates Hong Kong's economy but is also a significant factor in international trade in textiles.

I. The manufacture of clothing continued to be the largest sector of the textile industry, with over 3,000 establishments employing over 200,000 workers, and producing a wide variety of high-quality items.

    A. The weaving sector, with 25,000 looms, produces fabrics of various fibers and blends.

    B. The spinning mills, operating some 925,000 spindles, are among the most modern in the world.

    C. In the knitting sector, exports of fabrics registered a sharp increase of 100 percent in 1972.

II. There are three types of industrial training.

    A. There are two major colleges.

        1. Hong Kong Technical College

        2. Morrison Hill Technical Institute

    B. Firm-subordinate technical schools provide the specific training in certain fields.

    C. Another 25,000 study in prevocational programs.

III. Hong Kong continues to participate in the Cotton Textiles Arrangement (CTA), which aims not only at increasing export possibilities but also at avoiding disruptive conditions in import markets.

    A. Under CTA, Hong Kong has entered into a number of agreements with governments of developed countries.

    B. The direction of Hong Kong's export trade is influenced by economic conditions and commercial policies in principal markets.

    C. In spite of the restrictions in export on the textile industries, Hong Kong's clothing export is steadily increasing.

Conclusion

In sum, there seems little reason to apprehend great difficulty for Hong Kong in maintaining the exports by which it now lives, though the task of developing multi-industry requires great progress.

8.5.5 To focus on word use and word choice

Assignment:

Use the following information to write a paragraph using structures and words of comparison and words of contrast.

The orange, the lemon, and the lime.

The orange, lemon, and lime are all citrus fruits.

The orange is orange, the lemon is yellow, and the lime is green.

The orange is sweet, the lemon is sour, and the lime is sour.

Size rank: (1) orange, (2) lemon, (3) lime.

Aromatic citrus oils are found in the rind of all three.

When cut open, all three shown an open core, or axis.

Orange segments are separated from each other near the axis; those of lime and lemon are not.

The rag (in which the juicy fruit is contained) separates easily from the juicy vesicles (the little bags of juice) in the lemon and orange, but not in the lime.

The orange and the lemon have moderately thick albedos (the white part of the rind); the lime's albedo is almost nonexistent.

The lemon and the orange have a pebbled (rough) skin; that of the lime is smoother.

Rank of number of segments: (1) orange, (2) lemon, (3) lime.

The orange is used for fruit juice and as fresh fruit. The lemon and the lime are used to make drinks with water; they are also used for cooking and in salads; they are not eaten as fresh fruit.

Production rank: (1) orange, (2) lemon, (3) lime.

Assignment:

Have your students use different styles of language or word choices in order to write the same paragraph on a given subject to four audiences:

1. Family or friends

2. General audience—classmates

3. Technical audience

4. Major professor

Measure these paragraphs against the *Vocabulary* component and its criteria.

Assignment:

After you have scored three or four compositions, notice what areas of vocabulary or language use are weak for most students. Present a unit on each of these during respective class periods.

For article problems: (1) Use a cloze-type exercise with articles deleted asking the students to insert the proper articles.

The best results often are achieved in improving grammar errors when students correct their own errors. Use students' own written work for this whenever it is possible. Take sentences from each student's paper for the class to revise.

For preposition problems: (2) Use cloze-type paragraphs with prepositions deleted asking students to insert the correct prepositions.

For verb tense problems: (3) Ask students to write paragraphs describing what they did yesterday (past tense), what they have been accustomed to for many years (perfect tenses), and what they hope to be doing this time next year, etc. (4) Ask students to examine paragraphs for contextual clues to tense, followed by a cloze-type exercise in which students insert correct verb tense.

For subject-verb agreement problems: (5) Ask students to write a paragraph in the first person. Now ask them to rewrite the paragraph in third person making sure subjects and verbs agree; e.g., ask students to write their opinions about a given subject. Then ask them to state the opinions of another person about that same subject.

For sentence structure problems: (6) Give students a paragraph written in simple sentences. Now ask them to rewrite the paragraph using compound, then complex sentences, and finally a variety of all three. (7) Use sentence combining exercises and build on kernel sentences. Measure each paragraph against the *Vocabulary* and *Language use* components criteria.

Assignment:

Distribute sample compositions and PRO-FILEs to each member of the class. Ask them to score the papers and discuss the results of their scores with each other and with you. Discuss one component at a time, pointing out strengths and weaknesses of the sample papers. Have students:

1. Score a good example.

2. Score a poor example.

3. Score an average example.

4. Again score a good example to emphasize the principles of good writing.

Assignment:

Ask students to exchange and read papers that they themselves have written. They should follow the scoring procedure described in Chapter 6.

Assignment:

When students have completed the next writing assignment, ask them to score their own papers using the same procedure before submitting them for an instructor evaluation. This process shows what the students are (are not) recognizing.

Assignments such as these and the multitude of others that all teachers create to focus on the principles of writing help students achieve their goal, writing that is communicative and informative. Students who are actively engaged in the writing process will create pieces of writing that are more than the sum of their individual parts. They will create pieces of writing that reflect their ideas, beliefs, understandings, and feelings. By understanding the writing process through actively engaging in it, students can approach writing as an exciting adventure. They can write firm in the conviction that whatever is worth saying can be said clearly and interestingly. They can strive to write pieces which embody this description:

To my mind the Cretan countryside resembled good prose, carefully ordered, sober, free from superfluous ornament, powerful and restrained. It expressed all that was necessary with the greatest economy. It had no artifice about it. But between the severe lines one could discern an unexpected sensitiveness and tenderness.
—Kazantzakis

APPENDIXES

APPENDIX A

DEVELOPING AN EFFECTIVE
WRITING PROGRAM

The PROFILE was originally developed because of our need for an accurate and objective way to evaluate and place students in the appropriate classes within the university and within the intensive English program. During the time when we were attempting to develop a writing program and now when we acquaint new instructors with the existing standards of our department, the PROFILE has proved invaluable.

Because the writing abilities of ESL students are highly variable and because program curricula must be flexible, it is not always easy for departments to establish writing standards for a program. The PROFILE provides an objective and specific evaluation which helps identify standards for writing programs. As such, the PROFILE eliminates much of the guesswork. There are at least four important considerations in developing an effective writing program. These include—

1. Determining writing standards

2. Placing students in appropriate ESL courses

3. Making initial diagnosis of students' writing strengths and weaknesses

4. Determining curricula and course structure

STANDARDS AND PLACEMENT

Correct placement of students is essential to the success of any program and to classroom instruction. To accomplish accurate placement either through past experience or by grading sample papers, it will be helpful to clearly define the standards for each composition level in a particular program. What level of writing is or is not acceptable for admission to classes, and further, what score will correspond to different writing levels may be determined with

Table A, on page 236, a criterion-referenced interpretive guide guide, based on PROFILE evaluations. It suggests possible standards, correlated with mastery levels, which could be used for placement.

The table below can guide teachers or administrators in placing ESL students into writing courses appropriate to their levels of proficiency. The "score range" and "skill levels" of the table are based on the analysis of compositions evaluated with the PROFILE and are intended only as suggestions for placing students. Writers with scores 75 to 80 and above usually enter regular English classes. Those below 75 to 80 usually enter intensive English programs. See *Testing ESL Composition,* page 75, for a discussion of how a PROFILE writing score correlates with those of the Michigan Battery and the TOEFL.

INTERPRETIVE GUIDE FOR PLACEMENT INTO
ESL OVERALL SKILL LEVELS

PROFILE SCORE RANGE	ESL WRITING SKILL LEVEL	
100–92	High Advanced	
91–83	Advanced	Advanced
82–74	Low Advanced	(University)
73–65	High Intermediate	
64–56	Intermediate	Intermediate
55–47	Low Intermediate	(Intensive)
46–38	High Beginning	
37–below	Beginning	Beginning

After appropriate standards have been determined for the program, accurate placement of students into writing classes can be determined by the proficiency levels of the students. One way to do this is to administer a 30-minute writing exam, which is then scored with the PROFILE. This

TABLE A
CRITERION-REFERENCED INTERPRETATIVE GUIDE*

Mastery Level	Writing Characteristics/Criteria	Illustrative Profiles	
90%	Writer communicates effectively. Ideas are expressed clearly and fluently, with an obvious sequence to their development in support of the central theme. Vocabulary, sentences, and mechanics work effectively to convey the intended ideas and shades of meaning.	Organization	18
		Content	27
		Vocabulary	18
		Language use	22
		Mechanics	5
		Total	90
75%	Writer achieves minimal communication. Main ideas are apparent but are not carefully organized to develop the central theme; supporting details are incomplete. Incomplete mastery of some of the criteria for vocabulary, language use, and mechanics limit the writer's effectiveness although the flow of ideas is not seriously impeded.	Organization	15
		Content	24
		Vocabulary	15
		Language use	19
		Mechanics	4
		Total	77
50%	Writer communicates only partially. On the whole, ideas are barely discernible and there is little if any elaboration in support of the central theme. Lack of mastery of most of the criteria for vocabulary, language use, and mechanics severely restricts the flow of ideas.	Organization	11
		Content	19
		Vocabulary	11
		Language use	14
		Mechanics	3
		Total	58
25%	Writer achieves almost no communication. Ideas are mostly unclear, confused, and nonfluent. Though the writer may have knowledge of the topic, it fails to show because of nonmastery of the criteria for vocabulary, language use, and mechanics.	Organization	8
		Content	14
		Vocabulary	8
		Language use	7
		Mechanics	2
		Total	39

*See *Testing ESL Composition*, pp. 64–66, for a more complete discussion of Tables A and B.

procedure is presented in full in *Testing ESL Composition*.

In placing students in an ESL program, based on the number of students who have been admitted, program directors can determine the number of classes that need to be offered at each level. Because of the range of language proficiency among our ESL students, we have often found it is best to group students with close scores, forming relatively homogeneous classes, rather than to simply divide students into equal-numbered groups, thereby creating classes which may contain students with widely divergent scores and abilities. For example, if the program is an intensive one with, say, three levels for composition (beginning, intermediate, and advanced) and is placing 52 students whose scores range from 34 to 75, the scores might be listed in order to try to find the most logical writing proficiency levels. In the following example, the most logical divisions seem to fall between the

scores of 41 and 50, where there is a 9-point difference, and between the scores of 61 and 65, where this is a 4-point difference.

Several solutions to class division are then possible. If only three class sections can be staffed, these divisions can be left as they are even though the number of students in the three classes is not equal. Unless the program includes highly individualized instruction, it is probably more efficient and effective to present material to a large homogeneous class of students who are working at or near the same level of writing competence than to a group of students who vary considerably in writing proficiency. By dividing classes simply for the sake of distributing equal numbers of students among them, an instructor could end up with students whose scores differ by up to 17 points. However, at this point an instructor can also examine the PROFILEs which show scores of 65 or 66 to determine whether these writers have problems similar to those of the

ESL CLASS DIVISION					
Beginning ESL Class		Intermediate ESL Class		Advanced ESL CLass	
Profile Score	No. Students	Profile Scores	No. Students	Profile Scores	No. Students
34	3	50	2	65	2
36	1	52	1	66	3
37	5	53	4	67	4
38	1	57	2	68	3
39	1	59	1	69	3
40	3	61	2	70	3
41	2			71	2
				72	4
16 students		12 students		24 students	

writers in the Intermediate level and place them accordingly. If more than three classes are possible, a more ideal solution for both students and instructors would be to divide the Advanced class into two sections; and since 16 students is a large number for a beginning-level class, they too, could be divided into two groups.

DIAGNOSIS

Because the *total* PROFILE scores from composition placement exams do not illustrate the specific areas of each student's strengths or weaknesses, it is important to look at the PROFILE component scores to diagnose students' writing problems. Therefore, when instructors receive class rolls, they need to review the placement exams and the PROFILEs for each student. (If no exam has been administered, teachers should have students write a 30-minute sample and then score it with the PROFILE.) By studying each PROFILE, the teacher is able to pinpoint specific learning needs, based on the problem areas revealed by the PROFILE, by asking questions such as these:

1. How well organized are the papers?

2. What is the content level?

3. At what level should teaching begin—sentence construction? paragraph development? full composition?

4. Is the *Language use* section weak for all or most of the compositions?

5. Is lab time available to address grammar needs?

6. How much individualized instruction and lab work should be planned if the PROFILEs reveal many different kinds of problems?

7. Are spelling and handwriting aids necessary?

8. Are students graduates or undergraduates?

9. What methods of composition should be used with them?

Answers to these questions and others which teachers may identify will provide guidelines for the course structure and curriculum being planned for a given class.

CURRICULA AND COURSE STRUCTURE

In most ESL programs the diversity of student learning needs which result from differences in native language backgrounds, academic major, and overall writing proficiency makes it difficult to offer a writing course in which the content is comparatively fixed each term. The abilities and language needs of classes change from semester to semester based on the particular group of students coming into a program. Therefore, the course structure must be flexible enough to meet the individual needs of each student. A group composed mostly of Chinese students will often have different language needs from a group of Spanish-speaking students, and the considerations will be different yet when a class is a truly heterogeneous class, composed of many nationalities. For example, Chinese students often know English grammar rules by heart, but they may still have difficulty using these syntactic rules to generate successful sentences and paragraphs. Since the Chinese language has no direct equivalent, for example, to the English article, this may be an area that requires special attention. On the other hand, students whose native language is Arabic may need special instruction in handwriting and spelling since the writing systems for English and Arabic differ greatly. Spanish-speaking students frequently have difficulty with English punctuation and also need practice in converting word order from translation patterns to idiomatic English patterns, and so on.

Presented with such a variety of teaching challenges, teachers can use the PROFILE to identify these needs and develop course structure and curriculum. The PROFILE can signal when to design materials for whole classes, or when to individualize in the event that a class is composed of many proficiency levels or nationalities. Furthermore, if the program is large enough, students can be grouped according to their fields of academic interest as well as their PROFILE scores. For instance, in a class for engineers or agronomists writing assignments can be structured to address specific areas of interest and need in these particular groups. With such special-purpose classes, students will be able to analyze and discuss each other's papers in terms of suitability of specific content and vocabulary as well as writing technique.

Drawing together all this information about the capabilities of the class enables a teacher to choose the most appropriate texts and materials for them. Table B, based on the norms and interpretations established in Table 7.9 in *Testing ESL Composition,* p. 66, coordinates suggested curricula with writing ability levels. The curricula suggest the writing skills students must acquire before they can compete successfully in most regular university classes. As indicated in Table 7.9, a score of 75 or above indicates that a student can probably complete writing requirements in regular subject matter courses with little difficulty. Furthermore, Table B illustrates placement and curricula recommendations for students who require further ESL writing instruction.

TABLE B
COORDINATION OF ESL WRITING ABILITY AND CURRICULA

Score Range	Proficiency Evaluation	ESL Curricula Recommendations*	
		Undergraduates	Graduates
74–64	*FAIR WRITING ABILITY* Will probably experience great difficulty completing writing requirements in subject matter courses. Unable to compete fairly with native writers of English. Look at PROFILE to identify areas of strength and weakness.	Should be placed in a course which includes review of thesis statement, topic sentences, introductions, and conclusions; all methods of exposition and argument in fully developed compositions. Some review of sentence structure.	Should be placed in a course which includes all methods of exposition and argument in fully developed compositions; technical reports; research paper; special interest material. Some review of sentence structure.
63–49	*POOR WRITING ABILITY* Not prepared for college-level writing requirements. May also be weak in other language skills (e.g., reading, listening, speaking).	Should be placed in a course which includes review of paragraph development and methods; topic sentences, introductions and conclusions; structure of five-paragraph theme; thesis statement; present definition and classification methods. May require another course.	Should be placed in a course which includes review of paragraph development, full composition using methods of exposition and argument; review of other basic principles as necessary. May require another course.
48–34	*VERY POOR WRITING ABILITY* Has virtually no writing competence. Will not be able to complete writing course requirements by self. Other language skills will probably also be weak.	Should be placed in a course which includes sentence combining and structure; topic sentences; paragraph development using fact, example, or incident; presentation of methods of description, chronological order, comparison/contrast. Probably will require further composition study.	Should be placed in a course which includes sentence structure; presentation of paragraph development using expository methods; progression to full development of a paper. Probably will require further composition study.

*Grammar rules as needed at each level.

238

FORMS

Heuristics reference list

Specific heuristics associated with each "way of knowing" and at least one comprehensive reference source follow:

INTERNAL DISCOVERY TECHNIQUES
Brain pattern (Buzan 1976)
Looping (Cowan and Cowan 1980)
Free association (Burhans 1966; Altshuler 1970; Irmscher 1972)
Interior monologue (Winterowd, 1975b)
Journal (Irmscher 1972; Winterowd 1975b)
Existential sentences/analogy (Burhans 1966; Rougier et al. 1970)
Meditation (Rougier et al. 1970)
Personal Letter (Winterowd 1975b)
Autobiography (Winterowd 1975b)
Blockbusting (Adams 1979)

EXTERNAL DISCOVERY TECHNIQUES
Classical topics (Corbett 1971; Cowan and Cowan 1980)
The Pentad (Burke; Winterowd 1975b; Irmscher 1972)
Tagmemic approach (Young et al. 1970; Winterowd 1975b)
Twenty questions (Berke 1976)
Topic questions (Larson 1968; Adelstein and Pival 1976)
Discourse model (adapted from Roman Jakobson's model by Winterowd 1975b)
Problem solving (Larson 1972)
Synectics (Gordon 1961)

ESL COMPOSITION PROFILE

TOPIC		STUDENT	DATE
COMPONENTS	**RANGE**	**DESCRIPTION**	
CONTENT	30–27	*EXCELLENT TO VERY GOOD:* well-reasoned thesis • related ideas • specific development (personal experience—illustration—examples—facts—opinions) • good use of description/comparison-contrast	
	26–22	*GOOD:* adequate reasoning • thesis partly developed • occasionally unrelated ideas	
	21–17	*FAIR TO POOR:* poor reasoning • unnecessary information • very little development	
	16–13	*VERY POOR:* irrelevant • no development • (or) not enough to evaluate	
ORGANIZATION	20–18	*EXCELLENT TO VERY GOOD:* effective thesis • strong topic sentences • introductory and concluding sentences/paragraphs • use of transitions • organized	
	17–14	*GOOD:* clear topic sentences • no concluding sentences or paragraph • weak transitions • incomplete sequencing/organization	
	13–10	*FAIR TO POOR:* no topic sentence • lacks transitions • little or no sequencing/organization	
	9–7	*VERY POOR:* does not communicate one idea • no evidence of organization • (or) not enough to evaluate	
VOCABULARY	20–18	*EXCELLENT TO VERY GOOD:* correct use of idioms/word forms (prefixes—suffixes—roots—compounds) in context • effective word choice • word meaning precise	
	17–14	*GOOD:* mostly effective and correct idioms/word forms/word choice in context • meaning clear	
	13–10	*FAIR TO POOR:* frequent errors in idioms/word forms/word choice • some translation • meaning confused	
	9–7	*VERY POOR:* little knowledge of English vocabulary • mostly translation • (or) not enough to evaluate	
LANGUAGE USE	25–22	*EXCELLENT TO VERY GOOD:* sentence variety • correct verb tenses • few errors in subject-verb agreement, number, word order/use, articles, pronouns, prepositions	
	21–18	*GOOD:* effective but simple constructions • mostly correct verb tenses • several errors in subject-verb agreement, number, word order/use, articles, pronouns, prepositions, but meaning clear	
	17–11	*FAIR TO POOR:* ineffective simple constructions • frequent errors in verb tense, subject-verb agreement, number, word order/use, articles, pronouns, prepositions	
	10–5	*VERY POOR:* limited mastery of sentence rules • many errors in verb tense, subject-verb agreement, number, word order/use, articles, pronouns, prepositions	
MECHANICS	5	*EXCELLENT TO VERY GOOD:* few errors in spelling, punctuation, capitalization, paragraphing	
	4	*GOOD:* occasional errors in spelling, punctuation, capitalization, paragraphing	
	3	*FAIR TO POOR:* frequent errors in spelling, punctuation, capitalization, paragraphing • handwriting unclear	
	2	*VERY POOR:* dominated by errors in spelling, punctuation, capitalization, paragraphing • illegible handwriting	
TOTAL SCORE	**READER**	**COMMENTS**	

ESL COMPOSITION PROFILE

TOPIC		STUDENT		DATE

COMPONENTS	RANGE	DESCRIPTION
CONTENT	30–27	*EXCELLENT TO VERY GOOD:* one idea expressed • specific development (personal experience—examples—illustration) • good use of description
	26–22	*GOOD:* one idea expressed, but some unnecessary information • some specific development
	21–17	*FAIR TO POOR:* nonspecific statement • incomplete development of topic
	16–13	*VERY POOR:* not related to topic • no development
ORGANIZATION	20–18	*EXCELLENT TO VERY GOOD:* strong topic sentence • use of connecting words within paragraph • logical order (time—space—importance)
	17–14	*GOOD:* adequate topic sentence • weak connecting word(s) • logical but incomplete order
	13–10	*FAIR TO POOR:* no topic sentence • lacks connecting words • illogical order
	9–7	*VERY POOR:* no main idea expressed • no organization • (or) not enough written to evaluate
VOCABULARY	20–18	*EXCELLENT TO VERY GOOD:* correct idioms/word forms (prefixes—suffixes) in context • meaning clear
	17–14	*GOOD:* mostly correct idioms/word forms in context • meaning not hidden
	13–10	*FAIR TO POOR:* often incorrect idioms/word forms in context • meaning unclear • mostly translation
	9–7	*VERY POOR:* not enough to evaluate
LANGUAGE USE	25–22	*EXCELLENT TO VERY GOOD:* complete sentences • correct verb tense/word order/number/articles
	21–18	*GOOD:* mostly complete sentences • several errors in verb tense (past—present—future)/word order/number (singular—plural—count—noncount)/articles (a—an—the)
	17–11	*FAIR TO POOR:* few complete sentences • frequent errors in verb tense (past—present—future)/word order/number (singular—plural—count—noncount)/articles (a—an—the)
	10–5	*VERY POOR:* unable to use sentence rules • many sentence errors: verb tense (past—present—future)/word order/number (singular—plural—count—noncount)/articles (a—an— the)
MECHANICS	5	*EXCELLENT TO VERY GOOD:* few errors of spelling, capital letters, commas, periods, question marks • first sentence indented
	4	*GOOD:* occasional errors in spelling, capital letters, commas, periods, question marks
	3	*FAIR TO POOR:* frequent errors in spelling, capital letters, commas, periods, question marks • difficult to read
	2	*VERY POOR:* many errors in spelling, capital letters, commas, periods, question marks • unreadable
TOTAL SCORE	READER	COMMENTS

PROGRESS TALLY FOR ESL COMPOSITION PROFILE

STUDENT _____

CONTENT

PAPER	SUBSTANTIVE	DEVELOPMENT OF THESIS	RELEVANT TO TOPIC

ORGANIZATION

PAPER	FLUENT	CLEAR	SUCCINCT	ORGANIZED	LOGICAL	COHESIVE

VOCABULARY

PAPER	RANGE	W/I CHOICE	W/I FORM	W/I USE	REGISTER

LANGUAGE USE

PAPER	CX CON	NEG	AGR	T	#	WO/F	ART	PRO	PREP	FRAG	R-O	DEL

MECHANICS

PAPER	SPELLING	PUNCTUATION	CAPITALIZATION	PARAGRAPHING	HANDWRITING

Key to Correction Symbols

Refer to this key each time your teachers return written work to you. Study each mistake carefully and try to decide on the necessary correction. As a rule, you should write out completely the sentence or paragraph with the mistake corrected. If you cannot decide how to correct the mistake even after understanding the correction symbol, be sure to discuss it with your teacher.

SYMBOL	MEANING: HOW TO CORRECT YOUR MISTAKE
agr	*Agreement problem:* make the circled words agree (i.e., subject-verb, pronoun-antecedent, etc.)
art	*Add* an article or *change* the article which you have used
cap	Use a *capital letter*
no cap	Use a *small letter*
?	*Not clear:* either your handwriting is not clear or your meaning is not clear—what are you trying to say?
$\wedge$, del	*Something omitted:* add the indicated word or phrase in this position
frag	*Sentence fragment:* add something to make the fragment a complete sentence (i.e., you probably left out the verb, or did not have the complete verb, or left out the subject or the object, etc.)
$\longrightarrow$	*Indent:* leave several spaces at the beginning of your line of writing
$\smile$	*Join* these two parts together; do not leave a space between them
neg	*Negation:* you have used an incorrect form of the negative. Change it to the correct form
N.I.	*Not idiomatic:* use a more idiomatic word, phrase, or expression
ns	*Nonstandard usage:* use a more formal form or expression (i.e., you may have used something which is acceptable in informal, conversational English, but which is not acceptable in careful written English)
#, n	*Number problem:* change to singular or plural as necessary
Ree	Omit this: you have used an unnecessary word or punctuation mark
¶	Begin a *new paragraph*
No ¶	*No* new paragraph: *continue this sentence in the previous paragraph*
//	*Parallelism:* make the items parallel [the same form, tense, or construction as the other(s)]
(pos)	*Position:* words or phrases are in the wrong place; move them to the position indicated by this mark
prep	*Preposition:* use a preposition or use a *different* preposition
pro	*Pronoun:* use subjective or objective form as necessary
p	Punctuation: *either* change *to the correct punctuation or leave out* the punctuation you used
red	*Redundant:* you have repeated your ideas unnecessarily; change the sentence completely or leave out the unnecessary word or part
RO	*Run-on sentence:* you have joined two clauses or sentences together incorrectly: either separate them into two sentences or add the necessary word or punctuation to join them as one

sp	*Spelling problem:* check your dictionary if necessary
t	*Verb tense:* you have used the wrong verb tense; change it to convey the correct meaning
wc, wu	*Word choice:* the word you have used is not correct in this context; use a different word
wf	*Word form:* change the word(s) to a different form (i.e., you may have used a verb instead of a noun, or an adjective instead of an adverb, etc. Check your dictionary if you are not sure of the correct form)
wo	*Word order:* rearrange the order of the words in the sentence; perhaps the phrase should be placed before the verb or after the prepositional phrase

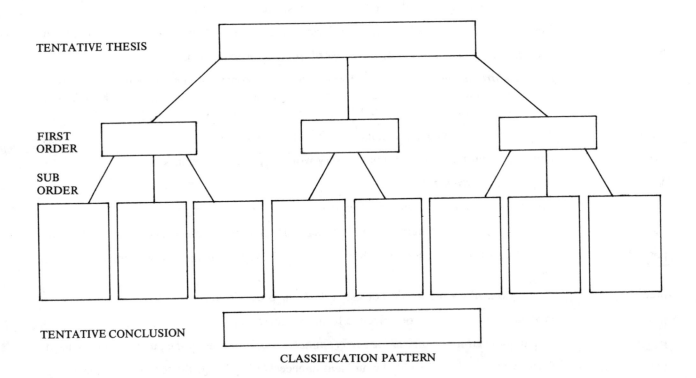

TENTATIVE THESIS

FIRST ORDER

SUB ORDER

TENTATIVE CONCLUSION

CLASSIFICATION PATTERN

_____ is _____ .

That is, _____ .

(It) is like _____ .

For example, _____

_____ .

It contains qualities of _____ and/or

characteristics of _____

_____ .

It is not _____ ;

nor is it like _____ .

It is caused by _____

or originated from _____ .

As a result (of it) _____ .

Therefore, _____ .

DEFINITION PATTERN

TENTATIVE
THESIS

Importance _____

First, _____

Do not _____

Second, _____

After _____

Next, _____

Then, _____

Finally, _____

TENTATIVE
CONCLUSION

PROCESS PATTERN

246

_____ is similar to _____ in terms of:

Physical characteristics:

	A	B
Size	_____	_____
Type	_____	_____
Speed	_____	_____
Weight	_____	_____
Color	_____	_____

Behavioral characteristics:

	A	B
Social habits	_____	_____
Temperament	_____	_____
Eating habits	_____	_____
Other	_____	_____

Functional characteristics:

	A	B
Use	_____	_____
Design	_____	_____
Performance	_____	_____
Other	_____	_____

_____ is different from _____ in terms of:

Physical characteristics:

A	B
_____	_____
_____	_____
_____	_____
_____	_____

Behavioral characteristics:

A	B
_____	_____
_____	_____
_____	_____

Functional characteristics:

_____	_____
_____	_____
_____	_____
_____	_____

COMPARISON-CONTRAST PATTERN
Combined point-by-point and overall

EFFECT	REASONS (CAUSES)

EFFECT   _REASONS (CAUSES)_

_____ because of   1. _____ .

             cause: _____   (effect)

                       _____   (effect)

               2. _____ .

             cause: _____   (effect)

                       _____   (effect)

               3. _____ .

             cause: _____   (effect)

                       _____   (effect)

               4. _____ .

             cause: _____   (effect)

                       _____   (effect)

CAUSE   _RESULTS (EFFECTS)_

What are the _effects of_ _____ on:

           individuals: _____?   cause

           a country: _____?   cause

      a region of the world: _____?   cause

            other: _____?   cause

What are the effects of _____ _in terms of:_

     physical environment: _____?   cause

    emotional environment: _____?   cause

CAUSE-EFFECT PATTERN

SAMPLE PAPERS

Shaker: Rough notes

During the early dynasties, the Egyptian Fortresse, were rectangular. They (~~~~) had ~~a~~ two or more perpendicular roads ~~~~~ and a circumferencial ~~road~~ one running along the ~~(~~~)~~ inner side of the wall.

Although the Fortresses were built later on with different shapes, they followed the same design criteria. ~~principle &.~~ Uronarti, with :5 triangular plan and the L-shaped Semna are excellent examples -

the scribes', and the artisans' dwellings. A social stratification was clearly expressed in the dwelling size and location. The higher the rank of the dweller, the larger the dwelling size and the *(nearer)* ~~nearest~~ to the Pharaoh's palace (it was.)

dangling modifier

One or more huge temples were centrally located in the town. Each temple was normally dedicated to a special god; either Re the sun god of Heliopolis and Memphis, Amon the ram-headed god of Thebes, Osiris the Nile god, Khous the moon god, or any other god they adored. Being the "house of god", the temple was built with stone and surrounded by a wall to separate the god statue in the sanctuary from the natural world. This wall acted as a moral ~~baffle~~ between the divine and the profane world.

wc? buffer?

As the Egyptians believed in a second physical life after death, they considered the Necropolis, or the "City of the Dead"(?) as important as the Royal Town, if not more. Zoser Complex at Sakkara and Giza Pyramids are the most ancient and the most significant Necropolises. ~~(is)~~

p
NI

The penetration within the "City of the Dead" was restricted on certain officials. A masonry wall was surrounding the tombs. It The causeways formed the major circulation artery during the ~~funeral~~ funeral ceremonies. It was consisting of a long axial path bordered by two rows of sphinx or ram statues. Cheops causeway was about 2000± feet long and 60 feet wide.

wc (pass) on

The Pharaoh's tomb was as rich and as big as his

palace. The tomb, or the "house of eternity", contained besides the statues of the buried person, his mummy and the mummy of his beloved animals, his preferred jewelry and his furniture.

The Necropolis was built with unperishable material such as stone, while all other settlements including the Royal Town were built with sun-dried mud bricks.

Although mystery was the dominating objective in the tomb design aiming at preserving its precious contents from thefts, yet monumentality was the major expression to illustrate how important the buried person was. Though Cheops Pyramid (B.C. 2570) is the highest stone construction in the world (481 feet high), the Pharaoh's chamber remained undiscovered for about forty-four centuries. All the tombs were located around the Pharaoh's tomb in the same hierarchy of their dwellings' location in the Royal Town.

⊗ The geographic position of the Necropolis was symbolically selected. It was located on the western bank of the river Nile where the sun sets; as death was thought of as a temporary 'sunset'. On the other hand, all other 'living' settlements were constructed on the eastern bank — the sunrise side. The only exception was the Fortress. Its site location was chosen according to strategic (conditions) considerations rather than symbolic ones.

The Fortress was a defensive frontier settlement of a smaller size than the Royal Town and the Necropolis. It...

SOCIAL LAWS OF TURKEY

A society seems to be ruled by laws put down by the State, but social laws which are not written are very important too. Social laws determine human relations, the way of life, and the social values in a society. The social laws of Turkey can be classified as those determined by culture, economic structure, and geographic location.

Social laws determined by culture are formed of traditions coming from historic background and religion. Since Turks have had many wars in history, today Turkey has a nationalistic society. To be a member of army is respected highly. When young people go for their military service, it is a custom to celebrate the event in the neighborhood. Like nationalism, hospitality is another social law coming from history. In ancient times Turks were a nomadic society, and the rule to help a traveler turned into a tradition of respect for visitors. Another social law coming from history is respect for old people. In the family, in any group or meeting, or in any social event, elderly people are always respected by the younger ones. Religion is the other important element of social laws determined by culture. More than 99% of the population are Muslims in Turkey. Therefore on Islamic religious holidays, it is customary that people visit each other, give presents to children, and help the poor.

Economic development is the second determinant of social laws in Turkey, as well as in any other society. Turkey is a developing country. When compared to highly industrialized countries, she has more characteristics of an agricultural society. Therefore, social laws in Turkey are affected by this agricultural structure. In rural areas families are larger; father is dominant in the family; people are more dependent on each other; and there are close relations between relatives and neighbours. When compared to the less developed countries, Turkey has more characteristics of an industrial society. In urban areas families are getting smaller; a high proportion of women are working; education is highly important; and there is competition in every aspect of life.

Social laws of Turkey are also affected by the location and geographic characteristics. Turkey is in the warm climate belt of the world. Therefore, there are no social rules and traditions based on lack rain and water as in a desert climate, or on characteristics of a jungle as in a tropical climate, or on hunting white bears as in the North Pole. But the country, within limits, shows a variety of climates and land structure. In the east, it is mountainous and cold where people are not tolerant in their relationships; however, in the west, where it is warmer, people have more liberal relationships. For example a new type of behavior or a new idea finds acceptance in the society more easily in the west than in the east. In the south, on the Mediterranean coast people are warm-hearted and like outdoor entertainment. There are very close relationships between friends or neighbours, persons get angry or happy very quickly, they speak loud, and love to sing and dance. On the northern coast — Black Sea coast— because of the lack of land suitable for farming, fishing has become a way of life, and this affects almost all social activities and relations. For example wedding dates, like many other social events, are are arranged according to fishing seasons. Thus food, clothing, festivals, entertainment, wedding ceremonies, folklore, and other social aspects show some differences from region to region.

Social laws are very important for an individual in Turkey, as well as in any other countries. Individuals are supposed to conform to these rules of the society. These rules change slowly overtime since they are determined by culture, economic structure, and geographic location.

Maria

Composition 123 –

Why women should not serve in the military forces in their countries

I object ^to the existence of military forces in a nation, therefore, I am opposed to the participation of ~~the~~ women in the military forces on the basis of no human participation in whatever system or organization which lead to ~~the~~ war.

There are biological and social values of the women related with life and nutruvement, naturally opposed to the destructive characteristic of ~~the~~ war.

Some people like to think about military forces without explicit understanding upon which military really leads. ^the Military is the organization of a phisical force to give security and power to a nation. All the great nations are organized on a military basis and have striven to increase their preparation so as to be stronger than others. Nations which felt themselves weaker made alliances so as to be able to crush others.

source?

The military force gives security to the nation. What ^does this security means? For the nations security is some-times aim of domination, aim of vindicate some offence by force or simply aim of gain some recognized or underlying interest. But that is not for the masses of people, who don't need this security; this security is always (invoqued) never demonstrated.

uf

?

All the problems solved by military force can be solved by another means. Because ^it is more easy to use the reason of the force instead the ^the force of the reason, the nations are engaged in a perilous career that can reach in the complete destruction of ~~the~~ human life in the earth.

Military forces are for war. And war means people killed by another people. As was emphasized in "Which way to peace", by Bertrand Russell (2), the primary object of the war is to lacerate human flesh, to break bones, to inflict torture, to paralize, and to kill. Every army in the field of battle is out for maiming and homicide... This is war.

History learn us that men, rather than women, were making wars. But the devastating conceqquences of the war were being paid for all the people: men, women, and children. Are women either by nature or by socialization less prone to war than men?

The majority of biologist and anthropologist seems to believe that by nature women are phisically less adapted to the war; in a equality plan men are more strongest to be adapted to the adverse conditions in the battle field.

But there are some other aspects in the nature of the women that are opposed to the violence. Since women gave and nurtured life, they, naturally could never oppose men with destructive force. Women work and build and suffer for the future. Human life is and should be sacred for them, and individual character infinitely precious and desirable. The woman doesn't want militarism because she look for diversity, adaptability, freedom and peace.

will As pointing Helena M Swanwick (3), one of the founders of the England's peace commitee, women cannot ever compete with men in a world based in the use of the force) because women are created to nourish life and to give love.

The French theologian, Poullain de la Barre, wrote in 1675, that

"One reason why women are assigned an inferior role in society is because they would not wish to earn honor and glory by killing or being killed for some unknown foreigner deemed an enemy merely because he is called such" (1).

Various psychologists declare that women's interest

256

College Composition and Communication (May 1976), 171–179.

_____. "Selected Bibliography of Research and Writing about the Teaching of Composition, 1977," *College Composition and Communication* (May 1979a), 181–193.

_____. "Language Studies and Composing Processes," *Linguistics, Stylistics, and the Teaching of Composition,* ed. Donald McQuade (University of Akron: Department of English, 1979b), 182–189.

_____. "Discovery through Questioning: A Plan for Teaching Rhetorical Invention," *College English,* 30 (November 1980), 126–134.

Lauer, Janice M. "Toward a Metatheory of Heuristic Procedures," *College Composition and Communication,* 30 (October 1979), 268–269.

Lees, Elaine O. "Evaluating Student Writing," *College Composition and Communication,* 30 (December 1979), 370–374.

Long, Michael H. "Teacher Feedback on Learner Error: Mapping Cognitions," *On TESOL '77, Teaching and Learning English as a Second Language: Trends in Research and Practice,* ed. H. Douglas Brown, Carlos Alfredo Yorio, and Ruth H. Crymes (Washington, D.C.: TESOL, 1977), 278–294.

Lopate, Phillip. "Helping Young Children Start to Write," in *Research on Composing: Points of Departure,* ed. Charles R. Cooper and Lee Odell (Urbana, Ill.: National Council of Teachers of English, 1978), 135–149.

Maimon, Elaine P. "Talking to Strangers," *College Composition and Communication,* 30, no. 4 (December 1979), 364–369.

Mandel, Barret J. "The Writer Writing Is Not at Home," *College Composition and Communication,* 31 (December 1980), 370–377.

Maslow, Abraham H. *Toward a Psychology of Being,* 2d ed. (New York: D. Van Nostrand Co., 1968).

McDonald, E. U., Jr. "The Revising Process and the Marking of Student Papers," *College Composition and Communication,* 29 (May 1978), 167–170.

McQuade, Donald, ed. *Linguistics, Stylistics, and the Teaching of Composition. Studies in Contemporary Language no. 2* (Ohio: University of Akron, 1979).

Murray, Donald. *A Writer Teaches Writing: A Practical Method of Teaching Composition* (Boston: Houghton Mifflin Company, 1968).

_____. "Teaching Writing as a Process Not Product," *Rhetoric and Composition,* ed. Richard L. Graves (New York: Hayden Book Co., 1976), 79–82.

_____. "Internal Revision: A Process of Discovery," *Research on Composing: Points of Departure,* ed. Charles R. Cooper and Lee Odell (Urbana, Ill.: National Council of Teachers of English, 1978a), 85–103.

_____. "Write before Writing," *College Composition and Communication,* 29 (December 1978b), 375–381.

Nelson, Kathryn McDonald. "A New Look at the Teaching of Writing," *The College Board Review,* no. 107 (spring 1978).

Neman, Beth. *Teaching Students to Write* (Columbus: Charles E. Merrell Publishing Co., 1980).

Nicholl, James R. "The In-Class Journal," *College Composition and Communication,* 30 (October 1979), 305–307.

Noreen, Robert G. "Placement Procedures for Freshman Composition: A Survey," *College Composition and Communication* (May 1977), 141–144.

Norris, William E. "Advanced Reading: Goals, Technical Process," *TESOL Quarterly,* 4 (1970), 17–35.

Odell, Lee. "Teachers of Composition and Needed Research in Discourse Theory," *College Composition and Communication,* 30 (February 1979), 39–45.

_____. "The Process of Writing and the Process of Learning," *College Composition and Communication,* 31 (February 1980), 42–50.

Ohman, Richard. "In Lieu of a New Rhetoric," *College English* (October 1964), 19–26.

Oller, J. W. "Discrete-Point Tests versus Tests of Integrative Skills," ed. J. W. Oller and J. C. Richards, *Focus on the Learner* (Rowley, Mass.: Newbury House Publishers, Inc., 1973).

_____. "Pragmatics and Language Testing," ed. B. Spolsky, Center for Applied Linguistics *Advances in Language Testing Series: 2, Approaches to Language Testing* (Arlington, Va.: Center for Applied Linguistics, 1978), 39–57.

_____. *Language Tests at School: A Pragmatic Approach* (London: Longmans, 1979).

Orwell, George. "The Politics of the English Language," *Language Awareness,* ed. Paul A. Eschhols, Alfred F. Rosa, and Virginia P. Clark (New York: St. Martin's Press, 1974), 22–34.

Perl, Sondra, and Arthur Egendorf. "The Process of Creative Discovery: Theory, Research, and Implications for Teaching," *Linguistics, Stylistics, and the Teaching of Compositions,* ed. Donald McQuade (University of Akron: Department of English, 1979), 118–134.

_____. "Understanding Composition," *College Composition and Communication,* 31 (December 1980), 363–369.

Petty, Walter T. "The Writing of Young Children," *Research on Composing: Points of Departure,* ed. Charles R. Cooper and Lee Odell (Urbana, Ill.: National Council of Teachers of English, 1978), 73–83.

Pianko, Sharon. "Reflection: A Critical Component of the Composing Process," *College Composition and Communication,* 30 (1979), 275–278.

Pike, Kenneth. "Beyond the Sentence," *College Composition and Communication,* 15, no. 3 (October 1964), 129–135.

Prator, Clifford H. "In Search of a Method," *Readings in English as a Second Language,* ed. Kenneth Croft

(Cambridge: Winthrop Publishers, Inc., 1980), 13–25.

Raimes, Ann. *Language in Education: Theory and Practice* (Arlington, Va.: Center for Applied Linguistics, 1979).

_____ . "Composition: Controlled for Teacher, Free for the Student," *Readings in English as a Second Language,* ed. Kenneth Croft (Cambridge: Winthrop Publishers, Inc., 1980), 386–398.

Rainsbury, Robert C. "Deep Structure," *Journal of English as a Second Language,* III, no. 2 (fall 1968).

Rohman, D. Gordon. "Prewriting: The Stage of Discovery in the Writing Process," *College Composition and Communication,* 16 (May 1965), 106–112.

Root, Christine. "Practical Considerations in Teaching Speakers of Other Languages," *English Composition,* NAFSA Newsletter (May 1980), 201–202.

Rose, Mike. "Rigid Rules, Inflexible Plans and the Stifling of Language: A Cognitivist's Analysis of Writer's Block," *College Composition and Communication,* 31 (December 1980), 387–400.

_____ . "Sophisticated, Ineffective Books—The Dismantling of Process in Composition Texts," *College Composition and Communication,* 32 (February 1981), 65–71.

Rothman, Donald. "What Students Don't Realize," *College Composition and Communication,* 29 (May 1978), 196–197.

Rougier, Harry, and E. Krage Stockum. *Getting Started—A Preface to Writing* (New York: W .W. Norton & Company, Inc., 1970).

Russell, Peter. *The Brain Book* (New York: E. P. Dutton Publishers, 1979).

Schor, Sandra. "Style through Control: The Pleasures of the Beginning Writer," *Linguistics, Stylistics and the Teaching of Composition,* ed. Donald McQuade (University of Akron: Department of English, 1979), 72–79.

Schultz, John. "Story Workshop," *Research on Composing: Points of Departure,* ed. Charles R. Cooper and Lee Odell (Urbana, Ill.: National Council for Teachers of English, 1978), 151–187.

Schumann, John H. "Affective Factors and the Problems of Age in Second Language Acquisition," *Readings on English as a Second Language,* ed. Kenneth Croft (Cambridge: Winthrop Publishers, Inc., 1980), 222–247.

Shahn, Ben. *The Shape of Content* (Cambridge: Harvard University Press, 1957).

Shaughnessy, Mina P. *Errors and Expectations—A Guide for the Teacher of Basic Writing* (New York: Oxford University Press, 1977).

Silber, Patricia. "Teaching Written English as a Second Language," *College Composition and Communication,* 30 (October 1979), 296–300.

Smith, Frank. "Demonstrations, Engagement and Sensitivity: A Revised Approach to Language Learning." *Language Arts* (January 1981a).

_____ . *Writing and the Writer* (New York: Holt, Rinehart and Winston, 1981b).

Sommers, Nancy. "Counterstatement," *College Composition and Communication,* 29 (May 1978), 209–211.

_____ . "The Needs for Theory in Composition Research," *College Composition and Communication,* 30 (February 1979), 46–94.

_____ . "Revision Strategies of Student Writers and Experienced Adult Writers," College Composition *and Communication,* 31 (December 1980), 378–388.

Spear, Karen I. "Psychotherapy and Composition: Effective Teaching beyond Methodology," *College Composition and Communication,* 29 (December 1978), 372–374.

Stallard, Charles. "Composing: A Cognitive Process Theory," *College Composition and Communication,* 27 (May 1976), 181–184.

Stalter, William. "A Sense of Structure," *College Composition and Communication,* 29 (December 1978), 342–345.

Stengal, E. "On Learning a New Language," *International Journal of Psychoanalysis,* 20 (1939), 471–479.

Stern, H. H. "Directions in Language Teaching Theory and Research," *Applied Linguistics Problem and Solution,* ed. J. Quistquard, H. Schwarz, and H. Spong-Hansen (Heidelberg: Julius Groos, 1974).

_____ . "What Can We Learn from the Good Language Learner?" *Readings on English as a Second Language,* ed. Kenneth Croft (Cambridge: Winthrop Publishers, Inc., 1980), 54–71.

Stewart, Donald G. "Composition Textbooks and the Assault on Tradition," *College Composition and Communication,* 29 (May 1979), 171–176.

Strunk, William, and E. B. White. *The Elements of Style* (New York: The Macmillian Company, 1972).

Taylor, Barry P. "Teaching Composition Skills to Low-Level ESL Students," *Readings on English as a Second Language,* ed. Kenneth Croft (Cambridge: Winthrop Publishers, Inc., 1980), 367–385.

_____ . "Content and Written Form: A Two-Way Street," *TESOL Quarterly,* 15 (March 1981), 5–13.

Thompson, George J. "Revision: Nine Ways to Achieve a Disinterested Perspective," *College Composition and Communication,* 29 (May 1978), 200–202.

Tomiyana, Machiko. "Grammatical Errors Communication Breakdown," *TESOL Quarterly,* 14, no. 1 (March 1980), 71–79.

Vitanza, Victor J. "A Tagmemic Heuristic for the Whole Composition," *College Composition and Communication,* 30 (October 1979), 270–273.

Vygotsky, L. S. *Thought and Language,* ed. and trans. Eugenia Hanfmann and Gertrude Vakar (New York: John Wiley & Sons, Inc., 1962).

Weiner, Eva S., and Larry E. Smith. "Language Development through Writing," *Cross Currents,* ed.

Gerry Ryan, Howard Sietou, and Nobuhito Seto, 7, no. 2 (1980), 9–15.

Weiss, Robert H., and John P. Field. "No, Not Case Grammar: The Case Approach to Writing for Foreign Students," *TECFORS,* 1, no. 6 (November 1978), 3–5.

_____ and Michael Peich. "Faculty Attitude Change in a Cross-Disciplinary Writing Workshop," *College Composition and Communication,* 31 (February 1980), 33–41.

Widdowson, H. G. *Teaching Language as Communication* (Oxford: Oxford University Press, 1978).

Winterowd, W. Ross. *Rhetoric: A Synthesis* (New York: Holt, Rinehart and Winston, 1968).

_____ . *Contemporary Rhetoric: A Conceptual Background with Readings* (New York: Harcourt Brace Jovanovich, Inc., 1975a).

_____ . *The Contemporary Writer: A Practical Rhetoric* (New York: Harcourt Brace Jovanovich, Inc., 1975b).

_____ . "Brain, Rhetoric, and Style," *Linguistics, Stylistics and the Teaching of Composition,* ed.

Donald McQuade (Akron: Department of English, 1979), 151–181.

Witte, Stephen P., and Lester Faigley. "Coherence, Cohesion, and Writing Quality," *College Composition and Communication,* 31 (December 1980), 189–203.

Young, Richard E. "Paradigms and Problems: Needed Research in Rhetorical Invention," *Research on Composing: Points of Departure,* ed. Charles R. Cooper and Lee Odell (Urbana, Ill.: National Council of Teachers of English, 1978), 29–47.

_____ , A. L. Becker, and K. L. Pike. *Rhetoric: Discovery and Change* (New York: Harcourt, Brace and World, Inc., 1970).

Zamel, Vivian. "Teaching Composition in the ESL Classroom: What We Can Learn from Research in the Teaching of English," *TESOL Quarterly,* 10, no. 1 (March 1976), 67–76.

_____ . "Re-evaluating Sentence-Combining Practice," *TESOL Quarterly,* 14, no. 1 (March 1980), 81–90.